ELEMENTARY EDUCATION

An Anthology of Trends and Issues

Edited by

J. Michael Palardy

UNIVERSITY
PRESS OF
AMERICA

LANHAM • NEW YORK • LONDON

Copyright © 1983 by

University Press of America,™ Inc.

4720 Boston Way
Lanham, MD 20706

3 Henrietta Street
London WC2E 8LU England

Library of Congress Cataloging in Publication Data
Main entry under title:

Elementary education.

    1. Elementary school teaching–Addresses, essays,
lectures. 2. Education, Elementary–Curricula –
Addresses, essays, lectures. 3. Cognition in children–
Addresses, essays, lectures. 4. Behavior modification–
Addresses, essays, lectures. 5. Classroom management–
Addresses, essays, lectures. I. Palardy, J. Michael.
LB1569.E43   1983   372   83–3637
ISBN 0–8191–3113–X
ISBN 0–8191–3114–8 (pbk.)

All University Press of America books are produced on acid-free
paper which exceeds the minimum standards set by the National
Historical Publications and Records Commission.

dedicated to

TOMMY, MICHAEL, TERRI, and MARY ELLEN

PREFACE

This anthology is intended principally for prospective and practicing elementary teachers. It is intended also for others interested in focusing on the key trends and issues affecting elementary education today.

The range of trends and issues is reflected in the book's six parts. Part 1 deals with the goals and objectives of education; Part 2 with strategies for promoting students' cognitive and affective development; Part 3 with techniques of teaching and testing; Part 4 with suggestions for motivating students and managing their behavior; Part 5 with ways of organizing students for instruction; and Part 6 with ideas and developments related to such current topics as mainstreaming, merit pay, tuition tax credits, and teacher evaluation.

Articles for each part were selected on the basis of three criteria. First, they were deemed particularly capable of provoking thought and discussion at varying conceptual levels. Second, they were viewed as being highly related to the curricular and instructional concerns of elementary educators. And, third, they were seen as representing a variety of current viewpoints.

To the writers and publishers who kindly granted permission to reprint their materials the editor extends his sincere thanks, and to the readers of these materials he wishes the best of success.

J.M.P.

CONTENTS

Part 1: THE GOALS AND OBJECTIVES OF EDUCATION   1

"Three Radical Proposals for Strengthening
Education"   2
   Robert L. Ebel

"What the Future Demands of Education"   14
   Arthur W. Combs

"The Troubled Years: An Interpretive
Analysis of Public Schooling Since 1950"   27
   Tommy M. Tomlinson

"In Pursuit of Confident Education"   40
   Mary Anne Raywid

"Quality and Equality in American Education"   55
   James S. Coleman

Part 2: PROMOTING STUDENTS' COGNITIVE AND AFFEC-
   TIVE DEVELOPMENT   71

"General Principles of Learning and Motivation"   72
   Nancy A. Carlson

"A Learning Styles Primer"   80
   Rita Dunn

"Piaget: Implications for Teaching and
Learning"   91
   Patricia Kimberly Webb

"Learning Disabilities: Futile Attempts at
a Simplistic Definition"   101
   Roger Reger

"Every Student a Success: Improving Self-
Image to Increase Learning Potential"   107
   Lloyd P. Campbell

"Can Schools Teach Kids Values?"   110
    Amitai Etzioni

Part 3: TECHNIQUES OF TEACHING AND TESTING   121

"Competency Testing: A Social and His-
torical Perspective"   122
    Vito Perrone

"Minimum Competency Testing: A Propon-
ent's View"   134
    Jacob G. Beard

"Peer Tutoring as a Strategy for Individualizing Instruction"   143
    Ann Candler, Gary Blackburn, and
    Virginia Sowell

"Improving Learning Strategies with
Computer-Based Education"   149
    Robert M. Caldwell

"Successful Teaching Strategies for the
Inner-City Child"   154
    Jere Brophy

"What about Homework?"   164
    Elizabeth E. Yeary

"Promoting Excellence through Mastery
Learning"   169
    James H. Block

"In Defense of Grade Inflation"   187
    Ralph J. Kane

"Student Nonpromotion and Teacher Attitude"   189
    Maurice Miller, Catherine C. Frazier,
    and D. Dean Richey

Part 4: MOTIVATING STUDENTS AND MANAGING THEIR
         BEHAVIOR   195

"What Can Schools Do about Violence?"   196
    Francis A. J. Ianni and Elizabeth
    Reuss-Ianni

viii

"Competency-Based Approach to Discipline –
It's Assertive"   206
    Lee Canter

"Strategies in Classroom Management"   212
    Robert L. Shrigley

"Discipline: Four Approaches"   223
    J. Michael Palardy and James E. Mudrey

"Motivation Maxims: Why They Fail to
Motivate"   236
    Len Froyen and Charles Dedrick

"Milestones in Motivation"   247
    Marlow Ediger

Part 5: ORGANIZING STUDENTS FOR INSTRUCTION   251

"Invest Early for Later Dividends"   252
    Irving Lazar

"Why Our Open Classrooms Fail"   258
    Kenneth T. Henson

"Developmental Characteristics of Middle
Schoolers and Middle School Organization"   265
    Hershel D. Thornburg

"The Makings of the Middle School: 21
Key Ingredients"   275
    William Tim Brown

"Alternatives for the Eighties: A Second
Decade of Development"   280
    Robert D. Barr

"Ability Grouping: Separate and Unequal?"   294
    Bill Waltman

"Questions Teachers Ask about Team Teaching"   299
    William L. Rutherford

Part 6: KEEPING CURRENT   303

"Effective Schools: Accumulating Research
Findings"   304
    Michael Cohen

"Johnny and Mary _Are_ Reading Better"   313
    Wayne Martin

"How to Evaluate Thee, Teacher -
Let Me Count the Ways"   319
    Donald L. Haefele

"The De-Professionalization of Teachers"   333
    Thomas R. McDaniel

"Merit Pay - Yes! Vouchers - No!"   345
    Jack Frymier

"Teacher Salaries: Past, Present, Future"   351
    Allan Ornstein

"Tuition Tax Credits"   360
    Virginia Sparling

"Interpretations, Misconceptions, and
Responsibilities Relating to Public Law
94-142"   368
    Natalie C. Barraga

Part 1

THE GOALS AND OBJECTIVES
OF EDUCATION

THREE RADICAL PROPOSALS
FOR STRENGTHENING EDUCATION

Robert L. Ebel

Public education in the U.S. is in trouble. Many schools evince low pupil achievement and poor environments for learning. There are widespread expressions of public discontent.

Not all competent observers agree that the need to strengthen public education is urgent. Some feel that our schools have done and continue to do a remarkably good job. The critics, they say, have unrealistic expectations and a tendency to exaggerate alleged defects and shortcomings. The main problem of education, in their view, is one of public relations, of telling the true story, of selling education to the people.

Perhaps defenders of the status quo in education are right, but a large number of well-informed citizens -- including many educators -- do not think so. These people, and I am one of them, believe that reforms are overdue and need to be promoted vigorously. I believe that the key to strengthening U.S. education in the Eighties is comprehensive monitoring of pupil achievement in learning. That monitoring will involve extensive use of tests.

Three Radical Proposals

In support and amplification of this thesis, I shall present and defend three radical proposals. The proposals are radical in two senses of the term. First, they propose a considerable departure from usual school practice. Second, they are directed at the root of our current problems in education. Although

Reprinted from PHI DELTA KAPPAN, 63 (6): 375-378 (February 1982) by permission of author and publisher.

the proposals are radical, they are nonetheless rational. They embody values that Horace Mann, William James, Matthew Arnold, James B. Conant, and John Gardner advocated and would support. The proposals are also feasible. And I have no doubt that, if they were to be adopted, they would be effective. Here they are:

1. No instructional program should be undertaken or continued in the absence of evidence of its effectiveness in producing learning.

2. Each school system should publish annually the results of systematic public assessments of pupil achievements in learning.

3. Each teacher should submit evidence periodically of the learning achievements of pupils in the teacher's classes.

Let us consider each of these proposals in turn.

Evidence of Effectiveness

The first proposal calls for evidence that an educational program is effective in producing learning. At first thought it may seem surprising that such a proposal even needs to be mentioned, to say nothing of mentioning it as a "radical" proposal. Should not the worth of any instructional program be judged by the results it achieves? Yet evidence of program results is the exception, not the rule. Educators advocate new methods of instruction on the ground that they <u>ought</u> to work better, without a shred of evidence that they <u>do</u> <u>in</u> <u>fact</u> work better.

Humanistic education is a case in point. Arthur W. Combs has argued that humanism creates the right kind of a learning environment for children. But there is no evidence whatsoever that children learn more, or learn it better, or learn more appropriate things when they are educated humanistically than when they are educated under other philosophies.

What is true of humanistic education is also true of many other schemes and proposals designed to improve education. Almost always the emphasis is on the attractiveness of the process. Seldom is the potential user provided with data on the quality of the product. The prevailing assumption is that if the <u>process</u> looks good, the <u>product</u> will also be good. This is a dangerous assumption. Education dollars should not be spent to buy promises.

3

Availability of Evidence

If evidence on the effectiveness of an instructional program can be obtained, it should be provided. But can it be? Are not some outcomes of instruction subtle and intangible? Are not some unforeseen? Are not some too complex to be assessed by usual means? Are not some apparent only after years of experience and maturity? To this host of questions there is a host of answers. No important outcome of instruction is intangible. To be important, it must make an observable difference in behavior. If it does, it cannot be intangible. If it does, it is measurable, because all that measurement requires, fundamentally, is the observation of differences.

Some outcomes of the instructional process are indeed unforeseen. Obviously they cannot be used to judge the effectiveness of a program before they have been seen. Afterward they pose no problem. Any complex outcome that has been defined clearly enough to be taught effectively can be tested effectively. Finally, any instruction that has long-term consequences also has short-term consequences. Our concerns as program evaluators are necessarily limited to the immediate results.

Thus it appears that evidence of the effectiveness of an educational program can be obtained. None of the common excuses for not obtaining it holds water. Indeed, if they did -- if the effectiveness of an educational program could not be determined -- education would be reduced to an idle guessing game that no one could ever win. Teachers cannot say they know what they are trying to do if they cannot tell when they have done it. Claims for the effectiveness of an instructional program that cannot be substantiated ought not to be believed.

The Purpose of Schooling

Let us turn our attention to the suggestion that instructional programs should be effective in producing learning. Again, it may seem surprising that this suggestion would need defending. Schools are for learning. That is why they are built and maintained at public expense. That is why parents send their children to attend them. That is why parents often sacrifice to keep their children in college.

4

True, schools have been used for other purposes. They have been used as custodial institutions to keep nonstudents off the streets or out of the job market. They have been used as adjustment centers to help disaffected young people come to terms with life. They have been used to provide recreational facilities. In recent years, they have been used as instruments in programs of social reconstruction. As George Boaz put it, "Education is for learning things, and teaching is the teaching of what you learn. All else comes by the way if it comes at all."

Earlier in this century there were influential educators who thought otherwise. John Dewey was one of them. He said education was the process of living, not preparation for future living. He said teachers should spend little energy making children learn certain things. I think he was wrong on both counts. Of course education is part of the process of living, but to say that schooling is not preparation for future living is nonsense. The life of every educated adult is evidence to the contrary. Of course teachers cannot "make" children learn, but they should spend a great deal of energy helping children to learn. The antilearning stance of the Progressive Education Association probably accounts for its unpopularity with the public and its relatively short life span among professionals. Most of us, and most of the public we serve, have no difficulty in accepting the proposition that schools are for learning.

What Should Be Learned?

Pupils learn many things in school. They learn about themselves. They learn about getting along with others. They learn physical skills. In good schools they learn moral responsibility. But the main thing they are expected to learn is useful verbal knowledge. The special excellence of human beings, distinct among all the creatures in the world, is their ability to produce and to use verbal knowledge. It is the foundation for effective behavior, for wisdom, for moral judgment

What is meant by knowledge in this context can be clarified by a few words on its relation to information, to understanding, and to ability. Knowledge is built from information through thinking. Knowledge is the structure of relationships among items of

5

information. Awareness of that structure, or of a particular part of it, is what we call understanding. Seeing the relation of this to that, of moon to tides, of thunder to lightning, of frustration to aggression enables us to understand these things. Finally, a mental ability is nothing more nor less than knowledge of how to do something.

Affective Objectives

Acquisition of useful verbal knowledge is a cognitive objective. What of the affective objectives? The word _affect_ as a noun refers to such things as attitudes, feelings, interests, and values. That affective dispositions are important to a person's success and happiness is beyond question. So is the fact that cognitive instruction usually has affective consequences -- sometimes planned but often quite casual and incidental; sometimes favorable to learning, sometimes unfavorable.

But there are things related to affective outcomes of instruction that may be open to question. Is it appropriate for teachers to prescribe the affective objectives their pupils ought to attain? That is, should teachers decide what feelings, attitudes, interests, and values pupils ought to have and then "teach" pupils to have them? Should affective outcomes be made objectives of direct instruction, or should they be considered by-products of good teaching in a good learning environment? If direct instruction toward an affective objective is attempted, will it not be essentially cognitive, resulting in knowledge _about_ affect? Can systematic instruction ever be other than cognitive? Pondering such questions as these, most teachers may conclude that they should continue to emphasize cognitive instruction. Surely they should be sensitive to the affective dispositions and responses of their pupils, but they should use this sensitivity primarily to achieve cognitive objectives. They should make only limited and discreet efforts to reshape pupils' affective dispositions by any means that are not primarily cognitive.

Thus far we have suggested that the value of an instructional program should be judged by its effectiveness in producing learning, that evidence of such effectiveness can be provided, and that what ought to be learned is mainly cognitive. Let us proceed to the second radical proposal. School systems should systematically assess students' achievement and publish the results.

School Testing Programs

To run a school without systematic audits of pupil achievement makes no more sense than to run a business without keeping track of income and expenses, of profits and losses. Not to do so in either case is almost to guarantee that the enterprise will fail. To audit pupil achievement is to add powerful motivation to teacher and pupil efforts. Learning is often hard work. So is teaching. Recognition and rewards, in both cases, are likely to call forth greater effort. A good society shows that it values the achievements of its members. Systematic public assessment of student achievement in learning makes possible the recognition of the successes of both the students and their teachers. Then the public -- employers, selection committees, administrators, taxpayers, voters -- can be counted on to provide the rewards.

Testing to Motivate Learning

There are many examples of successful use of systematic public assessments to increase pupil achievements in learning. Beginning in 1929 a major university in a midwestern state provided objective tests in each of the major subjects of study in high schools. On a designated day toward the end of the school year these tests were given to pupils in every participating high school in the state. The students who scored highest were invited to district contests in which they took new, somewhat more difficult tests in their subjects of competence. The winners of the district contests were invited to a state contest where other, still more difficult tests were administered. Those who scored highest on the state tests were awarded university scholarships.

A principal whose school had sent several students to the state contest the first year was determined to do as well or better the next year. When school opened in the fall, he arranged to drop in after school on teachers whose pupils had been tested the previous spring. To the algebra teacher he might have said, "Miss Olson, I see that six of your pupils went on to the district contest and two reached the state. That's good. I'm proud of them and of you. I hope you can keep it up this year. If there is anything I can do to help, just let me know." To the physics teacher he might have said, "Mr. Miller, we didn't get a single pupil into the district contest last year. Have you any idea why? Is there anything I can do to help you get it turned around this year?" The teachers got the point that someone was watching and that somebody cared -- indeed a whole lot of somebodies in the school and the community. It worked. As long as the academic contests continued, this school was consistently a leader in pupil achievement.

Clearly, we are capable of assessing pupils' achievement, but few schools or colleges have committed themselves to comprehensive public assessment of their students. Note the emphasis on public assessment. To be public, an assessment must be: 1) based on a syllabus expressing expert consensus on the content to be sampled by the test; 2) obtained from a test whose questions, whose correct answers, and whose scoring rules are written and available for public inspection after the test has been used; and 3) followed by a report and statistical analysis of students' scores on the test.

Most current assessments of student achievement in U.S. schools and colleges are not public in these ways. They are, instead, intensely private, highly subjective, uniquely individualistic, and unsystematic. Except in the hands of a few outstanding teachers and professors who are firmly committed to excellence in learning, the typical methods of assessment offer little resistance to the manifold temptations and pressures to lower standards of achievement. Legislation in the states to mandate the establishment and operation of effective local assessment programs would strengthen education greatly in the 1980s. Promising steps in this direction have already been taken in several states.

Excuses for Not Testing

Of course there will be objections -- excuses for not testing -- centering mainly on supposed shortcomings of the tests. Opponents will say that the tests are too narrow in scope, too focused on cognitive learning. But cognitive learning is what schools are

8

expected, in the main, to produce. Opponents will say that tests do not reflect the enormous complexity of what goes on in schools. Of course they do not, but neither do they need to. Their job is to measure how well the primary mission of the school has been achieved. Those who believe that cognitive tests ignore important objectives of education have a problem. They must be able to show how we can produce dependable evidence of the extent of pupil attainment of those objectives. If they cannot, they ought to stop claiming that those objectives are important. If the behavior of a person who has attained more of a given objective is not perceptibly different from the behavior of one who has attained less, how can the objective be said to be important? But if different degrees of attainment make observable differences in behavior, then evidence of the extent of attainment can be produced.

Some will argue that teachers will teach to the tests. Indeed they will, and they should. The content of most standardized tests represents consensus by expert teachers on what pupils ought to be learning in a given subject at a given grade level. Teaching pupils to deal with the <u>kinds</u> of questions that appear on a test is likely to be good teaching. But we should treat as a pedagogical swindler any teacher who deals with the <u>particular</u> questions on a particular test as a catechism, whose answers are to be memorized by the pupils.

Some will say that available tests do not match what is taught in particular schools. When that is the case, the local curriculum is probably at fault. Why should any school fail to teach what committees of expert teachers believe all pupils ought to learn? Others will say that the tests are biased against cultural minorities. But if the test includes only tasks that all young people should be able to handle, it is not biased against any of them. The low scores that minority children may make can be attributed more to inadequate education than to test bias.

Some will argue that tests should be used to help teachers improve their teaching instead of to assess their pupils' learning. This suggestion smacks of a ploy to avoid accountability. To engage in formative testing to facilitate learning does not require that we abandon summative testing to measure what has been learned. Formative testing is sometimes advocated as

9

a way of helping teachers to make better instructional decisions. There is little evidence that it actually helps very much. Test scores and item responses may give teachers some guidance in deciding what to teach; they will be of very little help in deciding how to teach it. And, if we abandon summative testing, we shall never find out how helpful the formative testing has been.

Some opponents will claim that tests ought to be criterion referenced, reporting what a pupil has learned, not how his or her knowledge compares with that of other pupils. Obviously, both kinds of information are useful and necessary. It is much easier to provide accurate information about the relative achievements of people than about the absolute amounts of subject matter they have learned, however. Abandoning assessment of comparative achievement would serve no good purpose.

Other objections to the use of tests to measure pupil achievement in learning have been made and will continue to be made. But no alternative that is demonstrably better has been developed. Since evidence of the effectiveness of instructional programs is essential if education is to be strengthened, the use of tests is likely to continue. The sooner all schools begin systematic public assessments of pupil achievements in learning, the more rapid this strengthening is likely to be.

Evidence from Teachers

My third radical proposal is that all teachers should submit evidence periodically of the learning achievements of pupils in their classes. When the learning of an individual pupil falters, it can be -- and often is -- the fault of the pupil. When the learning of a whole class falters, it can be -- and often is -- the fault of the teacher. Surely evaluations of teacher effectiveness should take account of pupils' backgrounds for and interest in learning. Surely many teachers today do not have sufficient control over the conditions that influence learning to be held entirely responsible for the results. But just as surely it would be absurd to claim that pupil achievements are unrelated to teacher effectiveness. Professionally trained teachers can be given (and in good schools they are given) considerable control over the strategies and tactics of instruction and over the classroom environment for learning. Under these conditions, teachers can quite properly be held responsible for the general level of their pupils' learning achievement.

Despite recent efforts to systematize or to mechanize the processes of instruction, teaching remains an art. Effective teachers -- those whose pupils are most successful in learning -- have a repertoire of strategies and tactics of instruction. They select from this repertoire the ones that work best for them and are most effective with the pupils they are teaching. There is no best method of instruction for all teachers in all subjects with all pupils. Research that attempts to discover whether one method of instruction is superior to another is unlikely to be decisive or widely generalizable. The crucial question is more specific and particular: Which methods of instruction in the hands of this teacher will produce the greatest amount of learning with these pupils? The best research on teaching is likely to be action research by individual teachers in the field.

There are several reasons why teachers themselves should provide the evidence of their effectiveness. This responsibility is consistent with the teacher's status as a professional and with the teacher's role as a largely independent manager of the instructional process. Teachers ordinarily are not, and should not be, subject to detailed direction of their classroom activities.

If the teachers themselves have the opportunity to choose what evidence of teaching effectiveness to provide, how to collect it, and how to present it, they will have more flexibility in fitting the assessment to the instruction. They will have better opportunities to point out special strengths and to explain apparent weaknesses. Finally, because they themselves are in charge of the assessment process, they are likely to find assessment much more acceptable.

Of course, assessment data will have to be presented to and reviewed by the instructional supervisor. Such presentations will provide the occasions for those periodic reviews of a teacher's performance that are essential to the management of an effective educational institution. Among the questions that might be discussed are these:

How adequate is the evidence of pupil learning?

How appropriate are the teacher's instructional goals?

How effective are the teacher's instructional methods?

What could the school do to help the teacher maintain a better environment for learning in the classroom?

Too often in contemporary schools, the administrators are so busy administering that they neglect their important responsibilities as supervisors of instruction. Meetings with each teacher to review the teacher's assessment of pupil learnings would provide the occasions and the incentives for instructional supervision. The administrator may know no more about good teaching than the teacher does, but the administrator does have authority and resources. The results of a discussion of instructional goals, outcomes, and problems are almost certain to be mutually beneficial. Such instructional supervision is also more likely to move the school along the road to educational excellence.

Conclusions

The proposals I have presented in these pages are derived from three fundamental convictions: that educators ought to be definite and clear about what they are trying to do; that what they ought to be trying to do, in the main, is to facilitate the cognitive development of their pupils; and that they ought to provide credible evidence of how well they have succeeded in doing that job. These convictions and the proposals growing out of them are so reasonable, it seems to me, and so conducive to excellence in education that they ought not to be controversial. On the other hand, they are so much at variance with current practice in many schools that I suspect they will be controversial.

Some will argue that the proposals reflect a simplistic notion of the complex objectives of contemporary schools. But the proposals include all of the schools' objectives that involve pupil learning. What legitimate objectives are there that do not involve pupil learning? And is there not virtue in simplicity.

12

Shakespeare has referred to "simple truth miscalled simplicity." To call the objectives of education complex may be a way of excusing our failure to attain many of them. As George Berkeley said of philosophers, "We first raise a dust and then complain that we cannot see."

Strong opposition to proposals such as these is not likely to come from citizens, from parents, or even from the pupils themselves. High school pupils are beginning to complain that they are not being made to work hard enough to get a good education. Nor is strong opposition likely to come from the many skilled teachers who continue to foster abundant learning, sometimes in difficult circumstances. No, the opposition is likely to arise from those who have come to terms with mediocrity, whose educational ideals and enthusiasms have burned out, whose pursuit of excellence has slowed to a saunter, who are anxious to avoid an audit.

Parents, taxpayers, and the legislators who represent them are interested in results. If they cannot persuade the public schools to justify public support by providing reliable, quantitative evidence of pupils' achievements in learning, they are likely to turn to nonpublic schools -- as many inner-city parents have already done. A public institution that refuses to respond to public demands is unlikely to survive.

U.S. public education does need strengthening. The first step toward that strengthening is not more federal aid, or more state aid, or higher local millages. The necessary first step is more comprehensive and systematic assessment of pupils' learning achievements.

WHAT THE FUTURE DEMANDS OF EDUCATION

Arthur W. Combs

Futurist Alvin Toffler begins his book LEARNING FOR TOMORROW (New York: Vintage Books, 1974) with these sentences: "All education springs from some image of the future. If the image of the future held by a society is grossly inaccurate, its educational system will betray its youth."

Preparation for the future has always been a primary objective for education. Until recently the future to be prepared for was generally stable and predictable. As a consequence, curricula designed for youth could concentrate on the learning of precisely defined skills and the acquisition of subject matter. But this is no longer adequate. Futurists tell us we are living in the midst of a profound revolution that most people are not even aware exists. The futures they paint for us are not wild dreams or science fiction. They are hard realities already upon us, and they cannot be prepared for in traditional fashion.

Some images of the future can only be dimly perceived at present. Others are absolutely certain and demand new directions for educational thought and practice. They call for changes now. In this article I should like to name just four of the certainties about the future we now confront and suggest what these seem to me to require of education.

Certainty 1: The Information Explosion

Almost everyone is aware of how much more there is to be learned today than just a few years ago. One hears frequent reference to the "information explosion." But few of us really comprehend the extent of

Reprinted from PHI DELTA KAPPAN, 62 (5): 369-372 (January 1981), by permission of author and publisher.

the increase in available information. Here are a few statistics provided by futurists: Ninety percent of all the scientists who have ever lived are alive today. Technical information doubles every 10 years. There are 100,000 technical journals available now, and the number doubles every 15 years.

In my own field of study, doctoral students in 1940 were expected to stand examinations in the entire field of psychology. Today, the idea that any one person could have a grasp of the entire field is absurd.

Similar explosions of knowledge have occurred in every other discipline, and futurists tell us this is only the beginning. The explosion will continue at even faster rates in years to come.

Once it was true that a teacher was regarded as one of the smartest people in town. Those days are gone forever. The information explosion has made the concept of the teacher as fountainhead of knowledge ridiculous. Science has provided us with marvelous techniques for the dissemination of information: television, radio, movies, computers, recordings, and many more. These devices are capable of placing vast quantities of information in the hands of almost anyone quickly and efficiently. They have also made the role of the teacher as information provider obsolete. Today's teachers frequently find their students better informed than themselves on many topics. (Not long ago a kindergarten teacher told me with a sense of shock about a little boy in her class who corrected her terminology.)

Certainty 2: Increasing Pace of Change

Even very young persons can count many changes in the nature and function of the world in their lifetimes. Few of us, however, are aware of the full significance of the changes going on about us. Futurists tell us, for example, that the speed of communication, transportation, and computation and the amount of power available to us just since 1945 has increased by figures of 10 to the seventh, eighth, and ninth power over all the rest of human history. The present is changing and the future will continue to change at even more rapid rates. There are some 90,000 different occupations in our society, and the number keeps increasing. Students coming out of high school today may have to change their life work four or five times. The preparation of youth for a world of such rapid change must surely be quite different from that required for a stable, predictable future.

Educational Implications

Here are some educational implications of the information explosion and increasing rapidity of change:

1. We can never again hope to design a curriculum to be required of everyone. A common content is simply no longer a valid goal for education. For many years we were able to plan curricula with the assurance that "these things are essential," but those days are past. Curricula can generally be defined in terms of content, skills, and processes. With respect to content, the quantity of available information is so great, change is so rapid, and the future needs of students are so diverse that it is impossible to be certain that any specific subject matter will be essential to cope with life even in the very near future. With respect to skills, reading, writing, and arithmetic, at least to the level of the very early grades, seem likely to be significant requirements for successful functioning for some time to come. But even these can no longer be regarded as vital for every student. Television and radio have made it possible for many citizens to get along quite adequately in modern society with very little reading. The typewriter and telephone have done the same thing for writing, and calculators are increasingly employed by everyone, even for such simple tasks as balancing a checkbook. Only the process aspects of curriculum meet the criterion "essential" to prepare youth adequately for the world they will inherit.

2. Intelligent persons -- the new goal for education. An educational system unable to predict the knowledge or behaviors demanded by the future will have to concentrate instead on producing persons able to solve problems that cannot presently be foreseen. Tomorrow's citizens must be effective problem solvers, persons able to make good choices, to create solutions on the spot. That is precisely what intelligence is all about. Unable to forecast the future in specific terms, schooling must be directed toward the production of intelligent persons. To achieve that end, education must concentrate on the growth and development

of persons rather than on content and subject matter.

3. <u>Process-oriented education</u>. Effective problem solving is learned by confronting events, defining problems, puzzling with them, experimenting, trying, searching for effective solutions. Problem solving is using your brain and all the resources you can command to search for solutions. It is a creative process not tied to any particular subject. One can solve problems effectively in any area of human endeavor. Who is to say which area of knowledge or experience is superior or even essential as a vehicle for learning effective problem solving? Concentration on processes and the production of intelligent persons has some interesting implications for our current preoccupation with behavioral objectives and competencies. If behaviors or competencies for intelligent behavior could be precisely defined in advance, the behavior would not be intelligent. It would be mechanical.

Problem solving is best learned from confronting real problems, not artificial ones. Applying that criterion to most of our present schools, we can only find them sadly lacking. The problems most students are asked to confront are rarely personal and nearly always artificial. Earl Kelley once said, "We have these marvelous schools, this magnificent curriculum, highly accredited teachers and administrators, and then, damn it all, the parents send us the wrong kids!" Our current schools are far more concerned with the acquisition of subject matter than with effective problem solving. If schools really accept learning the skills of problem solving as a primary goal, it seems to me they must become far more concerned with the problems of the communities in which students live. To do this schools will certainly need to move outside their own walls. Breaking down the barriers between school and community has long been advocated by many of our leading education theorists, but most schools have hardly begun to implement such ideas. If we truly accept the importance of problem solving as a primary goal, involvement of students in the larger community seems essential.

The students' own personal problems seem like a logical place to begin. In problem solving, process takes precedence over subject matter. Moreover, personal problems have the distinct advantage of built-in motivation. A review of research on motivation suggests that students are most likely to be motivated

when problems are real and personally relevant, when
students feel solutions are reasonably within their
capacities, and when results are immediately discerni-
ble. Most current curricula would have great difficulty meeting those criteria.

4. A future of choices requires an emphasis on
values. Our students will be moving into a world of
choices. To maintain stability and to stay on track
toward worthwhile goals will require a framework of
values as a basis for choices. People do not behave
much on the basis of facts. More often they behave
according to their feelings, attitudes, beliefs, values, hopes, aspirations, understandings, and misunderstandings. These internal guidelines determine the
choices people make from among the myriad possibilities at any moment.

Modern perceptual psychologists have helped us
understand that the behaviors we observe are only
symptoms. To deal effectively with human behavior, it
is necessary to make some change in the causes of behavior. These have to do with the inner lives of persons: what they think, believe, perceive, and understand. To this end humanistic educators have called
for greater emphasis in curricula upon student values,
self-concepts, student perceptions of challenge and
threat, feelings of identification, and the like. Some
observers have been horrified by these new roles for
education. They have condemned them as "secular humanism" or rejected them outright as not legitimate
business for education. They have sometimes loudly demanded, "What do you want? Education for intellect or
education for adjustment?" -- as though we had to make
a choice between smart psychotics or well-adjusted
dopes.

Affective, humanistic education is no frill. Emotion is what we experience when events are important
to us. I do not get emotional about your child; I am
quite emotional about my own. Emotion is an indicator
of the degree to which an event seems important to the
person. Significant learning is always accompanied by
some degree of emotion. Thus affective education is a
necessity for meaningful learning. Schools that rule
it out are diminishing their own effectiveness.

5. A future of change demands lifelong education.
Opportunities for learning must be available at any
time in a student's life when problems arise for which

there are no immediate solutions. The idea of an education completed at any given age or within any finite period is obsolete for the world into which we are moving. Education for the future must be lifelong. Actually, we have already made great progress toward attainment of that goal. Such programs as community education, community colleges, adult education programs, and a thousand varieties of programs under public or private auspices bring together people with common needs to solve common problems. In the quarterly offerings of community colleges and adult education programs one can find an extraordinary array of learning opportunities.

There is an intriguing corollary of the movement toward lifelong education. If learning opportunities are going to be available lifelong, there is no longer an important reason for completing any part of education during any particular period. Nor is there need to require mature young people to attend school for any given number of hours to complete any given curriculum. Combine that fact with the observation I have already made that problem solving is not tied to any particular subject, that effective problem solving may best be learned in personal confrontation with real problems, and the way is open for alternative programs in what are now the high school years. Suppose, for example, we were to give young people three alternatives for spending their time until they reach adulthood. One alternative might be to attend a traditional high school or trade school. Another might be to work out some combination of in-school and out-of-school programs that would permit taking advantage of community opportunities to work, learn a trade, or develop special talents. The third alternative might be for students to formulate personal growth plans with the help of school, parent, and community resources. Such plans might be monitored by an expanded school guidance department and then subjected to modification as required. Currently we have thousands of students who feel trapped in schools where they do not want to be. Often these students become serious discipline problems and disrupt opportunities for others. Worse yet, their feelings of being coerced often result in permanent rejection of anything that smacks of education. An education system fully committed to lifelong education need not create such problems for students and faculties.

Certainty 3: The Primacy of Social Problems

Returning to our list of four certain problems of the future, let us look at the new urgency of social problems, or problems of human interdependence. For more than a million years after the first appearance of humans on earth, the primary problem of human beings was to wrest from the environment the food, shelter, clothing, and power required for personal or general welfare. With the developments of science in the past 100 years and industry in the past 70, and with the discovery of atomic power in the last 40 years, all of that has changed, producing an enormous revolution in the fundamental nature of the problems faced by humankind. Science gave us the know-how to solve the problems of food, clothing, and shelter. Industry gave us the technological understanding to produce goods and services in enormous quantities, and the discovery of atomic power has given us unlimited power to make it all work (or destroy us all). It has been said that the discovery of atomic power marked the end of the era of the physical sciences and the beginning of the era of the social sciences.

We live in the most interdependent, cooperative society the world has ever known. Few of us could live more than a few hours totally out of touch with other people. The more complex and technological the world becomes, the more each of us is dependent upon thousands of persons whom we do not know and have never even seen. One need but stand before the well-filled shelves in a typical supermarket and imagine the number of persons required to supply those commodities to become aware of how very much we are dependent on our fellows. We could not even drive if we could not count on other drivers to stay on their side of the road.

We now have the knowledge and the technology to feed, clothe, and house the entire world, only to find ourselves faced with a new problem: how to use this knowledge and technology for the general (i.e., world-wide) welfare. The major problems we face today and the primary problems we shall face in the future have to do with ourselves and other people. Problems of poverty, ecology, pollution, overpopulation, food distribution, use of energy, war and peace, health, aging, crime and violence, terrorism, and human rights are all essentially social. Even the atomic bomb is no problem in itself; it is the people who might use it with whom we must be concerned.

20

Certainty 4: Personal Fulfillment
Increasingly Important

Not only are we thoroughly dependent on others, but all of our technological advances make the world an ever smaller place, in which the power of individuals for good or evil is immensely increased. Technological advances make us so interdependent that a single person at the right place and time can bring chaos by assassinating a leader, skyjacking a plane, holding people hostage, or going berserk in an automobile. Or on a much more destructive level, by pulling the wrong switch in a nuclear plant or setting off an atomic bomb. Interdependence makes terrorism simpler and more dangerous for ever larger numbers of people. More than ever, societies of the future will be dependent upon caring, responsible citizens, willing and able to pull their own weight. Persons who feel frustrated and alienated from society are a danger to everyone. After all, if you do not feel you are a member of the club, there is no reason to pay your dues or look out for the other members. The personal fulfillment of citizens in an interdependent society is a necessary ingredient for its continuing safety and welfare.

Even if personal fulfillment were not so essential for the safety and welfare of future societies, it is destined to become an increasingly important motive for everyone. The more we succeed in providing people with satisfaction of basic needs, the more persons are freed to seek the fulfillment of personal aspirations and goals. Abraham Maslow pointed out that human needs exist in a series of steps from basic needs for food, water, and shelter to safety needs -- security, stability, and freedom from fear -- to belonging and love needs, to needs for affection and esteem, to needs for achievement and personal adequacy. At the top of this hierarchy are needs for self-actualization or fulfillment, to achieve one's full potential. Maslow also pointed out that people cannot advance to the satisfaction of higher-order needs until lower ones are satisfied. One cannot think nice ideas about democracy, for example, on an empty stomach. On the other hand, as people's basic needs are fulfilled, they are at the same time set free to explore at higher levels. From this it follows that the more a society succeeds in providing human beings with goods and services that fulfill basic needs, the more its citizens will seek the fulfillment of higher needs.

Implications for Education

1. <u>Concentration</u> <u>on</u> <u>the</u> <u>human</u> <u>condition</u>. To meet our responsibilities in preparing youth for the future, curriculum planning must concentrate far more attention on the human condition than is currently the case. The social sciences -- psychology, sociology, anthropology, and political science -- were invented to help us understand the nature of human beings and their interactions with each other. These sciences, now almost 100 years old, still do not appear in the curriculum of most school programs except occasionally as elective courses open to high school seniors -- if they have good grades in traditional subject-matter courses. The contributions of the social sciences cannot be reserved as proper subjects only for the elite.

Understanding human beings and their interactions is no frill in preparing for the future. It is an absolute necessity. The understandings available from the social sciences must become an integral part of the growth of all students from nursery school on. Even the youngest children can grasp the fundamental principles of human growth and interaction if given a chance. Take, for example, this principle from modern perceptual humanistic psychology: People behave in accordance with their perception of reality. To explore this idea in kindergarten, one of my students rewrote JACK AND THE BEANSTALK from the point of view of the giant. When you do this, Jack turns out to be a murderer and a thief. Remember? He stole into the giant's castle and ran off with the giant's hen that laid the golden eggs. Then when the giant chased him down the beanstalk, Jack chopped it down and killed the giant. Reading this version to kindergarteners produced spirited discussion of what it means to be honest, what is right and just, and why it is important to care for other people. The same basic principle could be explored with greater maturity by high school students studying the Civil War -- or any of a thousand other topics.

2. <u>The</u> <u>curriculum</u> <u>must</u> <u>become</u> <u>increasingly</u> <u>personal</u> <u>and</u> <u>individual</u>. If the search for personal fulfillment is to become a major part of life in the future, today's schools must accept the challenge and begin serious preparation of youth for such goals. The fulfillment of personal needs is not "self-indulgence" but a necessary step to higher levels of motivation, achievement, and responsible citizenship. One's needs

are always pressing and urgent. They can be set aside or ignored only for very short periods. The fulfillment of personal needs, on the other hand, frees people to work for higher ones. The genius of good teaching lies in helping students to fulfill their personal needs and to discover higher-level needs they never knew existed. To achieve such ends, schools must become increasingly personal and individual.

The search for personal identity and fulfillment is already a major characteristic of today's youth. One can hear it in their songs, "I've Got to Be Me" and "I Did It My Way." It can be observed in the rejection by many young people of the things-oriented world of adults. It can be observed in the tremendous growth of interest in "consciousness expanding" activities, in "self-awareness" movements, and in a hundred varieties of self-improvement programs. Many educators have already recognized the importance of the discovery of identity and personal meaning for students in the middle school and high school years. Despite this recognition, the matter is given little more than lip service in most places, and students continue to complain that schooling has little to do with the world in which they live. Far too many complain that their educational experience is largely irrelevant.

We have paid a great price for our large schools. We need large schools, we told ourselves, to provide a rich curriculum. But individual students get lost in large schools, and personal growth and uniqueness suffer. For 150 years we have been trying to teach students as though they were alike. We have grouped them, tracked them, grade-leveled them, and tried to homogenize and organize them into one kind of group or another for administrative expedience. For at least 50 years since we have begun doing serious educational research we have also been unable to demonstrate that any method of organizing or grouping is truly superior to any other method or to no grouping at all. It is time for us to recognize that human uniqueness is a characteristic of the species and cannot be ignored or set aside. It must be dealt with. The future for which we must prepare young people necessitates personal, individual learning programs.

3. A curriculum for the future must emphasize social interaction and responsibility. The increasingly interrelated society of the future can only operate effectively if citizens can be counted on to

pull their own weight and look out for their fellows.
It follows that schools preparing youth for the future
must place heavy emphasis on responsibility and effective human relationships. Such goals must be prime
considerations for curriculum planning. Too much preoccupation with subject matter can defeat those goals.
Earl Kelley used to say, "Our world can get along a
great deal better with a bad reader than with a bi-
got." We do a lot about reading but very little about
bigotry, responsibility, and effective human relationships.

Responsibility is learned from being given responsibility, never by having it withheld. Responsibility is learned like math or any other subject; by
successful experiences at simple levels followed by
increasingly difficult problems paced to the student's
readiness and capacity. Learning responsibility requires confronting problems, making choices, being involved in decisions, accepting the consequences of
one's actions, learning from mistakes -- not with respect to artificial problems but real ones, relevant
to current experience. Similarly, effective social interaction requires personal involvement with others.
It is learned from personal experience, from opportunities to relate to others in increasingly successful
ways. It requires social contact, opportunities to
learn social skills. It requires the student to experiment, think about, and explore ideas with others.
It is learned from cooperation, rarely from competition.

4. Schools as microcosms. In a world where human
problems and responsible interactions are essential,
schools must themselves become microcosms of such experience. People are scripted by personal experience.
They learn far more permanently from personal experience than from any amount of subject matter. Schools
that hope to prepare youth for an increasingly humane
future must, therefore, themselves operate in ever
more humanistic fashion. Concern for individuals, respect for human dignity and integrity, cooperative effort, respect for human rights, caring for others,
must be established not only as matters for students
to learn about but as guidelines for action and criteria for educational assessment in all aspects of
schooling.

All school personnel must be keenly aware of the
side effects of personal actions, teaching practices,

administrative behavior, even organization of programs. People learn most and best from personal experience. To prepare for a future dependent upon successful human interaction, therefore, calls for
schools that confront students daily with significant
human problems, where students and faculty are con-
tinuously exploring effective interrelationships,
where humanistic goals have high priority, and all
school personnel are actively seeking to model good
human relationships.

5. The need for a humanistic basis for planning.
For several decades most educational planning has been
based upon some form of behavioristic psychology. The
behavioral approach regards learning as a problem in
stimulus and response or, more recently, as behavior
and its consequents (behavior modification). For behaviorists, the control or facilitation of learning is
a matter of conditioning, that is, changing student
behavior by manipulation of stimuli or consequents.
Motivation in such a system is conceived as a problem
in management -- what teachers do in order to get students to do what teachers desire. This approach to
learning served schools well when goals were clear and
simple -- when they could be defined in precise behavioral terms as, for example, in spelling, simple math,
reading, and the learning of other specific skills.

The most current expression of behavioral thinking is to be found in attempts to measure educational
outcomes in terms of highly specific "competencies" or
"behavioral objectives." The movement has captured
great attention because it appears so logical and
businesslike. It seems obvious that if you want to
measure the effectiveness of education you should establish objectives in behavioral terms, set up the machinery to reach those objectives, put the machinery
in operation, and then measure whether, indeed, the
objectives were achieved. Such closed-system thinking
works fine when the future is clearly known and curriculum goals are primarily subject-oriented. It is
hardly adequate for the kind of world futurists are
forecasting.

The future demands effective problem solvers and
citizens willing and able to deal effectively with
themselves and each other in the solution of human
problems. It requires open-system thinking and an emphasis on values, processes, human problems, and the
human condition. Furthermore, an educational system

that hopes to prepare youth adequately for the future must be concerned with student feelings, attitudes, beliefs, understandings, values -- the things that make us human -- as well as with student behavior. Such goals call for a humanistic psychology as a basis for curriculum planning.

Fortunately, such a humanistic psychology is already available. One can find it under such names as self-psychology, perceptual psychology, humanistic psychology, existential psychology, and the like. A major thesis of perceptual-humanistic psychology is that behavior represents only a symptom, whereas an adequate understanding of human beings requires understanding of the causes of behavior that lie in the inner lives of individuals -- in their feelings, attitudes, beliefs, understandings, and values. Few of us would be satisfied going to a doctor who did no more than deal with our symptoms. So, too, an educational system that hopes to prepare youth adequately for the future must base its planning on humanistic approaches to the nature and function of persons.

Humanistic education based on such a psychology is already being adopted in many schools and classrooms. The movement is barely beginning, however, while the future is already upon us. To meet its demands requires new bases for curriculum planning and new approaches to organization and practice now.

THE TROUBLED YEARS:
AN INTERPRETIVE ANALYSIS OF PUBLIC SCHOOLING
SINCE 1950

Tommy M. Tomlinson

When gripped by nostalgia, educators are fond of recalling that until about 1950 the modern history of public schooling was marked by comparative tranquility and public esteem. In memory, arguments were largely parochial and confined to disputes about matters of pedagogical theory. The public, grateful for the services rendered, regarded schools in a light akin to the church: as institutions of integrity, peopled by teachers and principals whose standards of conduct approached the moral level of the clergy, and whose dedication to their task of educating the young held them harmless from occasional complaints of dissatisfied parents or unhappy children. Although socially imposed standards of conduct were strict and pay was meager, teachers were partially consoled by the public's esteem and gratitude and by their own generally unquestioned and unchallenged classroom authority.

An as-yet-unrealized consolation was provided by a public that gave little thought to such things as teacher competence. Teachers were popularly understood to be nurturant and, although some had "pets," largely fair in their judgments. Character and conduct were critical and, even more than subject-matter competence, seemed to determine eligibility to teach. Indeed, in many instances, especially in rural settings, competence was assumed if a teacher's knowledge just exceeded that of the children.

The accepted style of classroom practice was narrow, as was the world of teachers, whose backgrounds and experiences, after all, were expected to reflect the idealized standards of the community. Teachers,

Reprinted from PHI DELTA KAPPAN, 62 (5): 373-376 (Jan. 1981), by permission of author and publisher.

27

especially as they grew older, might now and then be humorously viewed as a little eccentric, but seldom as ineffective. Their job was to expose children to information and to inculcate knowledge. But whatever they taught and however they taught it, they rarely were held responsible for how much a child learned. Teachers were a constant in the education of children.

The responsibility for acquiring knowledge - that is, for achievement - lay with the children. It was their variable ability and motivation that determined how much they learned. If children failed, it was thought to be due either to their inability or their lack of effort; if they excelled, it was due to their intellect and their industry. The one qualifier in this construction held that, regardless of ability, children could, through hard work, "overachieve," or, if they failed to work, "underachieve."

To borrow an industrial analogy, children, as workers, were the "locus of production"; their ability and effort were the "machine" that determined their performance. The quality and quantity of the teachers' input were fixed; they supplied the raw material. The children then treated that material with their ability and effort. The end product, academic achievement, reflected the children's success in manufacturing learning out of the raw material of instruction. Variations in performance merely illustrated different levels of effort and ability among the children.

Things have turned about in recent times. The ability and labor of teachers have replaced the ability and labor of students as the putative determinants of academic production. According to current reports, the student is the constant, and it is the variable ability and motivation of teachers, along with the variable quality of educational resources, that now determine student performance.

Accompanying this shift has been a decline, many educators believe, in the level of student achievement across the U.S. and Canada, coupled with intractable underachievement among many poor and minority children. I intend to argue that the turnabout in responsibility for learning, and the efforts that schools have made to accommodate to this shift, have caused a substantial fraction of the shortfall. But in order to understand the causes and consequences of the shift in responsibility, we must examine the assumptions and consequences of some pedagogical beliefs that guided teachers and schools as, in 1950, they entered the 30 years of trouble.

   Prior assumptions. The belief that pupil achievement varied according to the ability and effort of the child, and that teachers were innocent of causing differences among them, was rationalized by two critical assumptions. First, the most fundamental and most powerful cause of learning was intelligence. Second, the level of a child's effort - that is, work - could enhance or reduce the effects of intelligence.

   Intelligence. Intelligence - or IQ, as it came to be called - was assumed in most quarters to be inborn and relatively fixed. Once determined or discovered, the measure was often treated by teachers and parents as a built-in limit on ability. And because intelligence measures varied from child to child, it was also assumed that everybody had different amounts of it. Some children seemed to have very little and some a great deal, while almost everyone else had an "average" amount. If intelligence were resident and fixed in a child, it followed that its effect on the intellectual performance of the child should be dealt with as a natural phenomenon. Further, since variations in intelligence were determined by nature, variations among children's intellectual achievements, the product of intelligence, were largely beyond control of the teacher.

   Schooling was aimed at educating all children according to their ability. That is, the teachers' concern was to insure that children learned as much as their native endowment would permit. Since IQ was a measure of intellectual power, it was the standard against which to set academic expectations. The teachers' expectations were, perforce, conditioned by their perception of the children's capabilities. They reasoned that a dull child could not keep up with a smart one; slow learners ought not to be burdened with work and expectations beyond their ability. On its face, the concern was fair and humane.

   The concern, however, was forfeit to a competitive reward system in which success assumed the possession and expression of an attribute, intelligence, that was beyond the control of the children. The logic of "rewards for intellect" punished the less able, who in accordance with the system's own assumptions, were not responsible for the quality of their performance. Children quickly learned that merit was determined by achievement; low achievement usually meant poor intelligence, a concept confirmed by the reward system. Few gave much thought to the social and psychic costs of this procedure. Indeed, in this respect intellectual ability was treated like all other abilities, from forensics to sports. Performance was limited by the children's abilities; the school's job was to elicit and shape performances according to the "talent" the children possessed and not to worry much about those who had little of it.

There was no guile in the procedure. After all, other things being equal, winning a place on the varsity sports teams was a measure of athletic talent; the aspirants who failed were not missed or mourned. Only the "failures" held themselves to account, most blaming themselves for their deficiency, some blaming bad luck or ill will. Few challenged this concept of talent or its presumed first determinant, the luck of birth, as a just system of selection and reward.

So it was with academics. Few questioned the justice of a selection process or a system of rewards and punishments designed to uncover and develop talent at the expense of apparent deviance or ineptitude. Neither was much thought given to the notion that academic failure might be more potent in life than athletic incompetence, nor that some children, driven by academic failure, might treat athletics as preparation for life.

Work. But surely I have exaggerated the power of intelligence. It was well known among teachers that IQ was a less than perfect predictor of academic performance. Some high-IQ children were mediocre performers, while some low-IQ children rose to the average. Thus the second critical assumption: Level of effort could alter the performance predicted by a specific child's IQ. Hard work was the great equalizer.

Further, unlike intelligence, the ability to work was possessed by all in equal measure. While everyone had equal potential for work, however, it remained in their discretion to use it - for example, to study - in any amount they chose. The expressed limit of ability could be multiplied or divided by a self-determined level of effort. Thus, within rather broad limits, it was believed that children received the reward they deserved. Of course, compared to the pure gold of intelligence, hard work might carry the taint of over-achievement. Indeed, there was often more honor in being called an underachiever; better to be smart but lazy than dull but hardworking. But no matter, the phenomenon itself was taken as proof that children were largely in control of their own academic destiny. IQ might set an upper limit to performance, but it need not, by any means, prevent industrious children from succeeding in school.

Schooling, then, was premised in part on natural selection and in part on self-determination, but seldom on the competence or effectiveness of teachers or the characteristics of the schools. That is, performance differences among children were treated as natural, partly nature's scheme (ability), partly parent's influence (attitude), and partly the children's behavior (effort). Any concern that children tended to achieve according to their social class was trumped by the belief that hardworking, smart children would surface regardless of the background; cream always rose to the top.

Setting the Stage

With rare exceptions, these assumptions guided the conduct of public schooling and the practice of teaching into the 1960s, when they were abruptly disputed by a sweeping redefinition of merit and eligibility. The movement for civil rights found expression in affirmative action and collective justice. Caught in an exposed position by the forces for equality, the competitive criteria of intellectual merit came to be viewed as hopelessly elitist, probably racist, and certainly destructive to the aspirations of poor children, something to be dismissed as but a myth and a vestige of a corrupt and unfair system of selection.

Black children were to receive a high-quality education and, with irony reserved for the future, it would be precisely the same as for whites. With high-quality schools at last, the latent ability and talent, which had been restrained by arbitrary and unjust laws, would surely burst forth. In the exuberance of the times, who dared reckon with the nature of the schools and their procedural assumptions, much less with the nature of the new class of children and how they might respond to a system of education which, black or white, aimed to sort according to academic talent?

Hidden in the compelling arguments about the destructive effects of segregation were certain undeniable imlications for the educational prospects of poor black children. After generations of exclusion and aggressive neglect, the educational legacy of racism - born of laws that made criminals of blacks who learned to read - saw large numbers of black children fail at the task of competitive schooling. The starved academic aptitude of many black children was little nourished by the mere offer of enriched schooling. This reality was and still is a bitter one, both for blacks who could not abide the idea that they or their children were not prepared to compete and for the lawmakers and reformers who believed education was the solution to poverty and racism.

If the system was elitist, was it also racist? Perhaps, if one twists the logic, but in everyday terms it would not seem so, and therein lies further irony. Prior to de jure desegregation, black schools, especially the elite ones, had treated black children in much the same manner as white schools had treated theirs; the rules of academic competition were closely followed. Like whites, few black educators or parents complained about this aspect of segregated school life. Only the patent differences in quality of resources and instruction were cited as sources of difference in student achievement between black and white children. Exposure to white children might be salutary for social relations, but it was not presumed to be related to academic performance. Equal resources meant equal competition, and that meant equal performance. Disillusionment was at hand, and in due course the inherently unfair merit system of competitive academics was exposed.

Early Disappointments. Initial attempts of the schools to cope with the Brown decision were disastrous. Many schools would not and did not attempt to integrate. Among those that did, even among those that welcomed the change, little thought was given to the suitability for black children, most of whom were poor, of a system that had always been devastating for large numbers of lower-class whites. Educators, having serenely attributed the dull performance of lower-class white children to fate and family, now faced a new class of mostly poor black children whose failure could not be dismissed with the previous contempt or indifference. Nonetheless, the schools, following their long-standing and accepted custom, continued their conception of efficiency and fairness in the assignment of children to ability tracks based on performance and measured intelligence. Accordingly, schools assigned most black children to tracks whose standards were commensurate with the psychometric estimate of the children's likely performance, and the children performed in line with the estimate.

The affront was twofold: It defeated the purpose of desegregation and it implied that black children were intellectually deficient. The practice was declared illegal. Black children and white children were to be integrated in classrooms regardless of evident ability or performance. Otherwise there would be neither integration nor quality education for black children.

Heterogeneous classrooms did not substantially alter the situation from the standpoint of either the comparison process or the performance. From all evidence, the children still distinguished among themselves through their performances, teacher expectations still varied accordingly, everyone still chose to associate only with members of his or her own social or racial group, and black children still occupied the academic low ground.

Explaining Failure. In 30 years very little has changed about minority achievement, except perhaps the emergence of competing ethnic identities. The average achievement of most poor and minority children remains below the average of the remaining competitors, and social class is becoming as powerful for blacks as for whites in predicting academic performance. Indeed, the average performance of all children, marginals and mainstream alike, has apparently declined. Although a variety of explanations and remedies have been offered to vindicate or improve the performance of minority children, the issue of school quality remains salient.

From the Brown decision of 1954 until the mid-60s common sense and the conventional wisdom left little doubt that schools attended by minority children were inferior in quality of instruction and resources to those found in white neighborhoods. In 1965 the report of James Coleman challenged this explanation with research indicating that variation in school resources

33

made little difference in observed academic performance. Student achievement, said the report, was due mostly to student ability (inferred) and background.

Both minority and educational interests rejected the implications of the Coleman Report, insisting that variations in school quality could make a difference in student achievement regardless of ability or class. This position remains dominant today and provides fuel for the current search and research for effective and efficient schools. Despite years of effort and good intentions, the evidence for positive school-produced variation in student achievement is only beginning to accumulate and to inform practice. Until recently, the factors that are related to differences in the quality of schools and that led to more or less student learning have resisted definition, measurement, and the ascription of causality. We have had trouble identifying and proving discrete, school-produced causes of learning.

In addition, most measured differences between putatively more or less effective schools have proved difficult to transfer from time to time or place to place. Many are of uncertain meaning, seldom explain the relationship between school characteristics and student achievement, and are hence of dubious value for policy or practice. Moreover, observed differences in student performance resulting from myriad measures of school quality have been largely confined to elementary schools, and are so modest that they must be considered trivial when compared to the consistently powerful effects of ability and background.

Nevertheless, the search for effective schools continues, especially for those immune to the consequences of social and economic background. Despite early disappointments, we expect in time to have some useful answers. I think that we are now looking in the right places. Although not everyone will enjoy the news, cumulating evidence indicates that certain characteristics of pre-1950 schooling, which in the name of equality were subsequently lightly held or enforced, are inherently necessary for learning, regardless of a child's ability or background.

This conclusion is neither a back-to-basics preamble nor an indictment of the schools. It is, however, the logical consequence of attempts made over the past 30 years to cope with the imperative to teach all children. Because of this imperative, the casual disregard for low achievers, which worked so smoothly before, was no longer an acceptable posture; all children must learn the basics and all should have a diploma for their efforts. The persistent fact that not all children learned the basics or received diplomas was considered a disgrace to the schools and the society. The schools were pressed to discover methods and procedures by which to satisfy the public's demand for equal education for all.

Following the surge of underachieving children and ever-tightening restraints on their own behavior, schools gradually relinquished the necessary conditions for learning. These necessary conditions include teachers willing and able to teach, a curriculum that everyone can learn, order and stability in the learning environment, minimal distraction from the learning process, and children willing and able to learn what they are taught. While it became and remains fashionable to blame teachers and curricula for the shortfall in achievement, it became distinctly unfashionable to cite the remaining conditions. The delicacies of fashion notwithstanding, all of these conditions must obtain at once to establish an effective learning context. When the conditions are optimal, achievement is theoretically limited only by individual differences in the abilities and effort of the children and the teachers. Put differently, under optimal conditions the structure and events that surround and make up the classroom do not distract from learning, and students' and the teacher's own resources, their abilities and efforts, can, for better or worse, be fully expressed.

When one or more of these conditions is sub-optimal, achievement will be reduced. To illustrate: We have spent considerable time and money on improving the quality of teaching and curricula, and, in the lab, the improvements have worked reasonably well. The effect of these efforts, however, has been lost when placed in a context of instability and distraction, a state characterizing many schools, most visibly those in the inner city. Since all the conditions for learning must be present, it is less than surprising to discover a counter-learning impact when equal or more powerful negative conditions exist.

These conditions are the requirements of an effective school; they are reliable and valid at almost any time or place and with most any child. I can think

35

of no exceptions to these rules. Learning is more likely to take place in a tranquil context than in a chaotic one, in a distraction-free context than in one that diverts children's attention to other than the course of instruction, and in a context that provides youngsters with optimal time on task. Because modern schools provide these conditions less often than before, we have indeed strayed from the fundamentals -- not from the curricula or content so much as from the context that learning requires.

Establishing these conditions has never been easy and today it sometimes seems impossible. For example, it is perfectly obvious that distracting or diverting children from the learning task reduces effectively the amount of time and attention -- that is, work -- spent on the task. Indeed, time spent on task (i.e., work) is one of the few consistent, relatively robust differences between schools considered effective and schools considered less effective. Yet this apparently self-evident fact, which need not draw upon "school resources," is transformed into a complex recommendation by the disorder inherent in conflicting governmental policy, the inconsistent positions and demands of a variety of special interests, and a prevailing school and community climate that is inconsistent with and uncongenial to the requirements of learning. Educational practice and research has much to say about how to get the most learning out of students but very little to say about how to reconcile disparate and antagonistic interests.

Less obvious, perhaps, is the effect on learning of some of the more subtle and scarcely tested side effects of reform rhetoric and practice. Consider, for example, the strange fate of standardized tests. All agree that the achievement of minority children is far below an acceptable level. The children's defenders accuse society and teachers of selling the children out, citing reasons ranging from insufficient school resources to negative attitudes about the children's potential. The main evidence buttressing the accusations derives from standardized test scores indicating that, on the average, minority children are failing to keep up. The defenders, at pains to discover reasons for the low scores, accuse accordingly.

But wait. Other defenders of minority children have pressed the case that tests revealing the underachievement - those very same standardized tests - are biased and invalid indicators of either achievement or knowledge and should be abolished. Surely the public, all of it, must be confused by this contretemps. Are the children learning or aren't they? Do parents' demands that test scores improve make sense in view of claims that the scores do not reflect what the schools have taught or how much the children have learned? Parents must also be wondering what will signal relative or absolute change and improvement in the schooling of their youngsters if tests are not to be used. Surely parents will not trust teachers to develop that information, since teachers are viewed as one of the causes of underachievement, and surely the parents' skepticism is advanced by the demands of some teachers that the use of standardized tests -- the evidence of alleged teacher incompetence -- be placed in hiatus or abolished altogether.

Withal, this annoying hypocrisy might find its justification in the omissions born of using average test scores as a gauge of student achievement. On average, most low-income and minority children do fare poorly compared to the rest, but the competition is unfair. But averages are unfair because they screen public consideration of individual differences in achievement. One consequence of this construction is a statistical report that, implicitly and insidiously, supports the mistaken conception that all middle-class or white children are academically outperforming all minority or poor children. Worse, it has nurtured the impressions that minority children do not and cannot excel in academic competition. The impact of these descriptive artifacts on the aspirations of the children themselves is unknown, but it is as unlikely to be salutary as would be the elimination of standardized tests to lift achievement.

So, indeed, there _are_ reasons for the public "crisis in confidence." The maze of arguments, some patently defensive and self-serving, but most just confusing, is taking its toll on everyone. As a corrective, albeit a presumptuous and probably unpopular one, I think we should come to grips with the role of children in learning. The first step in getting there will be the recognition that school resources are _not_ the first or generic cause of learning; the ability and effort of the child is the prime cause, and the task of schools is to enable children to use their abilities and efforts in the most effective and efficient manner. In the last analysis, that translates as undistracted work, and neither schools nor research has discovered methods or resources that obviate this fact. Nonetheless, we continue to resist this essentially positive conclusion. We are becoming both immobilized and irrational, neither able to face the unpleasant but possibly benign truth (which might make us free) nor able to take cheer in the exceptions (which might give us hope).

We should take solace from the emerging evidence: It signifies a situation we can alter. The essential thread of meaning in all that research has disclosed tells us that academically effective schools are <u>merely</u> schools organized on behalf of the consistent and undeviating pursuit of learning. The parties to the enterprise -- principals, teachers, parents, and students -- coalesce on the purpose, justification, and methods of schooling. Their common energies are spent on teaching and learning in a systematic fashion. They are serious about, even dedicated to, the proposition that children can and shall learn in school. No special treatment and no magic, just provision of the essential conditions for learning.

Can all schools follow this model? In theory yes. It is, after all, a straightforward, empirically and historically effective method. In practice, though, not likely. The "model" does require at least tacit collective agreement among the parties to schooling along with firm control of the operation. As it now stands, there is massive disagreement on procedures, control is divided among those interests powerful enough to make themselves heard, and learning and student achievement may simply be falling through the crack of expressive politics.

What does all of this sum up to? I think, in an honorable attempt to be just, that we have neglected certain truths about learning. Thus, as they say, we have thrown out the baby with the bathwater. Those who would attempt to retrieve the discarded child through back-to-basics, competency testing, and the like are the complement of those who would seek salvation by rejecting the evidence. Both have elected singularly narrow, sometimes reactionary, and certainly inefficient remedies born of their confusion as to cause. Clearly, in attempting to get rid of an invidious and unfair system of education-for-selection, we have discarded, along with its trappings, some elements that are crucial to achievement in any setting.

These elements will have to be reinstated. Educating poor children -- or any children, for that matter -- will be difficult in settings that, for example, treat work as a middle-class hang-up and academic ability as an unfair advantage. But even in schools congenial to learning, few children are working to capacity, including many who "work" very hard. For we seldom teach them how to learn and how to improve the efficiency of their own labor. Once again, poor children, who for a variety of reasons are at a disadvantage, and who can least afford to waste either their ability or their time, are the "victims" most at risk in the ebb and flow of reform and reaction.

We must also set about repairing the damage to a system rendered incompetent by the struggle to avoid blame for past injustice and current failure. The struggle, if it continues, will further deepen the ravages of a system that was ostensibly abandoned. The parties to the conflict must think carefully about their priorities, since educating the young does not seem very high on the popular list. Not so high, for example, as insuring that children retain discretion in deciding whether they care to go to school or not, or once there, whether they will concede the worth of learning, if not for themselves, then for those who might otherwise want it.

Given the mutual suspicions and the images that must be protected, I am not altogether convinced that we have the courage or clear sight necessary to fix the situation. It will be a pity if we don't, because in the long run those most deceived by the image are the children themselves. All children can learn under conditions that permit and sustain steady attention to instruction and study. Given the necessary optimum conditions, it is likely that even average teaching -- an inescapable fact of school life -- can penetrate with positive effect simply because the only distraction would be the teachers themselves. In such a setting it might once again be fair to consider children as the locus of production, providing that this time we do not penalize them for doing the best they can.

IN PURSUIT OF CONFIDENT EDUCATION

Mary Anne Raywid

Many educators are too worried about just keeping
schools open to worry about the luxury of doing so
with confidence. But we must also be mindful of the
place that confidence and optimism have in the success
of any endeavor, including education. If we are really
committed to the success of teachers and schools, then
"confident education" is an important goal for the
education community.

Under what conditions can it be realistic to hope
for confident education? Two sorts of answers take
shape in my mind. The first consists of a set of
assumptions about the contemporary educational scene -
a list of awarenesses to be kept in mind in seeking
genuine solutions to educational problems. Any solution that fails to recognize or take note of these
conditions can't offer much promise, at least in my
eyes. Based on these awarenesses, we can then begin
trying to formulate educational solutions that we
might reasonably feel confident about.

I want to begin, then, with a list of nine awarenesses or recognitions that, it seems to me, must un-
dergird any search or realistic hope for confident
education:

1. We must recognize that everybody wants to be
part of the action.

The last decade has done some interesting things
to our expectations. Those of us whose memories go
back that far may recall that just before everything
went sour and we began to worry about limits to growth
and affluence, there was a period marked by sharply
rising expectations. For some groups, part of the new

Reprinted from PRINCIPAL, 60 (2): 8-14 (November
1980), by permission of author and publisher.

expectancy was simply for a piece of the pie -- better jobs, higher salaries, and so on. But others called for a piece of the action. The new expectancies pertained to more advantageous socioeconomic and political arrangements. During the "politics of confrontation" epidemic, a number of demands called very explicitly for participation in the processes of decision making. It was more than just the right decisions that were being sought; it was a share in reaching them. In fact, much of the discussion of "rights" current in those years focused precisely on the right to a share in policy making.

This aspect of our heightened expectations has not diminished. A 1977 curriculum study found people a lot more interested in who will make curricular decisions than in what those decisions will be (1). That is an ironic finding to those of us who have worked so hard on the logical grounds of curriculum making and on building the knowledge base that would render such decisions a matter of precision and expertise. Nevertheless, the major concern was not what would be decided, but who would do the deciding.

We have since witnessed a rash of proposals at both state and local levels that seem to be predicated on exactly the same concern. A number of Proposition 13 sorts of bills have not only been proposals for limiting taxes, they have also been provisions for direct public decision on a range of matters. And one of the major arguments against a federal constitutional convention has addressed just this sort of sentiment, centering on the possibility that, once given the chance, citizens might truly flex their muscles in an extensive redo of our Constitution and our most fundamental procedures for decision making.

2. We must also recognize that those people asserting their right to be part of the action are absolutely correct in believing that, as of now, they are not.

Parents and community have come to have less and less to say about what happens in schools, in part because educational decisions are increasingly made at the federal and state levels. (If the decisions are not explicitly made by judicial and legislative bodies then for all practical purposes they are implicitly made on the basis of the external funds that come with built-in controls and are given or withheld accordingly.) An illustration that occasioned some good times for columnists recently is the federally subsidized lunch program, which banned from all schools receiving the funds any lunch food containing less than 5 percent of the recommended daily allowances of vitamins and minerals. As one columnist put it, the regulation "consigned the jelly bean to outer darkness." (2)

In the last ten years, we have become increasingly aware that a number of minorities have been closed out of the decisions made in and for public schools. Revisionist historians have made us face up to how many of the teachings that we presumed were based on national consensus, or societal universals, seem instead to be more a matter of the domination of the empowered over the relatively powerless. It even turns out that the children of the powerless get taught different messages than do youngsters from middle- or upper-class families. It seems pretty clear, in fact, that schools reward middle-class youngsters for individuality, achievement, and aggressiveness, while rewarding lower-class children for obedience and passivity. (3)

But it is just not society's disadvantaged populations that are ruled out of the action in school decisions -- it is all of us. The growing professionalization of teaching and administration, which means that more and more decisions are relegated to the professional staff, is partly responsible. With the technologizing of education -- construing it as an enterprise to be directed by expert knowledge -- has also come the tendency to see schooling as a realm in which there is one best way to do things: one best curriculum, one best set of methods, one best way to prepare teachers, one best way to organize and administer schools. But if there is one best way, then what happens to parents' prerogatives? For one thing, their choices begin to narrow. Families in my school district get to make exactly two choices during the three years their children are in junior high: whether and which foreign language, and typing or no typing. That is all. All the rest of the decisions are made by the professional staff.

Collective public control of education fares little better, as political scientists have established. "Whatever parents believe about it, control has indeed been lost," was the conclusion of a research team that traced just how it came to be that school control was "wrested from the people." (4) School board members, the team reported, don't even see themselves as representing the school administration to the public. Thus, when parents and other citizens complain that they lack a piece of the action, there is a great deal of evidence that theirs is an accurate perception and not just peevishness or paranoia.

3. As we consider what might bring a turnaround in public sentiment, we must also recognize the scope of what the schools are presently up against.

When public education was undergoing some intense criticism thirty years ago, it could be said with considerable justification that the critics were a small, though noisy, minority who represented a lunatic fringe position in relation to the rest of the public. Despite some hard times at the end of the 1940s and early 50s, however, most citizens remained absolutely convinced that American public education in general was in good shape. (5) Unfortunately, the same cannot be said today. The typical school critics of 1980 are not likely to be isolated ax-grinders, but the people who live on your block -- perhaps even most of them.

School criticism is no longer confined to any single point on the political spectrum, and it is fairly generously distributed. Although the latest Gallup Poll of attitudes toward education was ballyhooed as showing a turn in the public's disenchantment with their schools, hardly more than a third of the American people (35 percent) were willing to grade their schools A or B -- even in a time of grade inflation. Finally, it seems worth reiterating that it is just not antagonists and soreheads who are the critics but those we count our friends. Keep in mind, for instance, that almost a dozen national committees over the last ten years have called for a pretty thorough overhauling of American education. So it is hard to consider the critics as dark and hostile forces "out there."

4. We must acknowledge that much of the criticism does not emanate from ignorance of what is happening in the schools.

All too often, in fact, criticism of the schools seems inspired by a detailed grasp of what is going on. The press has done a rather meticulous job of recounting such bad news as declining test scores, the limited skills and competencies of high school graduates, school violence and vandalism, and more. As Harold Hodgkinson explained in a recent article trying to establish "What's Right with Education," "The press is not necessarily hostile toward education; it's just that we hand them such excellent information on our failures." (6) But given the way such information has been featured by all the media, there seems little justification in assuming that all we need is some really effective PR work.

Thirty years ago, when public sentiment seemed to be strongly in our corner, there was considerable logic in assuming that a better informed public would be a more strongly supportive public. That kind of thinking no longer seems valid. We need to acknowledge that the accurately and extensively informed individual may just as well turn out to be a school critic as a school supporter.

5. We must be fully aware of the extent to which all we do in schools is value laden -- and of the full import of that fact.

Virtually any educational program is simply saturated with values. My students challenged me on this claim not long ago, so I simply went into an elementary school classroom and listed for them some of the things I saw there. One was a sign proclaiming, "Good Food for Good Health: Eat Three Balanced Meals Every Day." Another was a poster admonishing, "Help Others," while another reminded, "Have a Happy Day." A list of names showing various achievements was titled, "Hey, Look What I Did." Each entry on the achievement list reflects and imparts value judgments on what is desirable. I assure you the list contained no entries such as, "John Smith beat up his neighbor yesterday" or, "Evelyn Jones skipped school last Tuesday." Even the very existence of such a list teaches some values about sharing the word of our successes and accepting social rewards for them.

Don't misunderstand me. I liked and shared the values of every one of the things I've mentioned. But they do involve values -- and to eliminate or modify any one of them would also involve values. I see no way to significantly reduce the value component in a classroom without moving in the direction of divorcing education from how life should be lived, which seems a

44

prohibitively high cost.

But we have not been facing up to and handling this value situation very forthrightly. For a couple of decades, we tried to shove it under the rug by assuming that value issues were separable from the rest of an educational program. According to this position, the value questions cluster exclusively around educational aims or goals, which the public can have a voice in, while the means questions are just matters of engineering to be determined by the professionals. That may be true of the assembly line, but as the hidden curriculum should certainly have shown us, it simply isn't so in the classroom.

We have also often deluded ourselves into thinking that the only values built into schooling are firmly grounded either in national agreement or in expert knowledge. But these assumptions appear increasingly dubious. There suddenly seem to be fewer national agreements and a lot more differences in values. And honesty compels us to admit that a lot of what is decided in and by schools is every bit as much a matter of values as of technical knowledge. In fact, more often than not, our technical knowledge as educators doesn't even recommend one alternative more strongly than another -- which is to say that in such matters, educators themselves may be basing their choices on other considerations. Take for instance such questions as whether to spend whatever athletic funds are available on interschool competition for varsity teams or on intramural games for all; or whether the services provided for able students will be primarily enrichment programs or geared instead to acceleration; or whether relationships in the school shall be formal and proper or informal and casual; or whether knowledge taught ought to be weighted on the side of data or the side of concepts. As we all know, there are numerous views on such value-related issues -- among us in the education family as well as outside it -- and there is no body of facts that lends clear and compelling support to any single position.

But if all this is so, doesn't it suggest that a number of the educational questions we answer for the public -- and then impose on them, willing or not -- are really quite properly _theirs_ to answer in some way? By what right do those of us who work in schools find it our prerogative to impose our own choices on large groups that seem increasingly to be objecting to those choices? It is almost as if the duly appointed picnic committee began insisting that we all had to go bowling (though many preferred tennis) -- and that we'd be served nothing but peanut butter sandwiches when we got there!

6. We will also have to recognize that a great many of our difficulties stem from forces and tendencies outside the school, many of them unlikely to let up.

There seems no end in sight to inflation's spiral and hence to our financial woes. Indeed, it might prove self-defeating even to hope for a time when education funds are plentiful and cheerfully given. Over most of the country, declining school populations are an important part of the reality that limits school growth -- and limits the exuberance and optimism that growth seems to breed.

An extensive consumerism seems abroad in the land, a spirit of "I'll do it myself," tied to suspicions of government and business and a not entirely trustful view of leaders in both public and private spheres. Over the last decade, our faith in a number of institutions -- not only the schools -- has plummeted, which suggests that schools are not being scapegoated, but simply taking their lumps along with other institutions. Yet even if it were possible to wave a magic wand and suddenly restore the school's tarnished image, it is unlikely the sparkle could long endure, given today's climate of opinion. The very breadth of the problem suggests something about its likely durability. And if that's so, we will need to adjust our sights for confident education according to how much and what kind of public support we might reasonably expect.

7. The American public is no longer willing to tolerate the "you can't win 'em all" orientation for public schools.

Teachers are extraordinarily hardworking people, but it seems to be part of the ethos of schools and teachers that nothing we do will work with some youngsters -- who are, by implication, hopeless cases. Having lost a few struggles myself (and what teacher has not?), I am highly sympathetic to that view, but I don't think we can maintain it. Several years ago, New Jersey passed a law assuring a thorough and efficient education to every child within the state. Do you realize the implications of such a promise? It doesn't mean that the school must give it a real try, no matter how difficult and unpleasant the case; it means the school must keep trying <u>until it succeeds</u> with that child and with every other youngster. We've legislated the same sentiment into PL 94-142, which, I suspect, will eventually revolutionize all schooling, not just that of the identifiably handicapped. That law promises suitable educational circumstances not just for some or most children, but for every single child in the land.

The onus has most explicitly been placed on teachers. It is a frighteningly formidable obligation, and one that may well require us to reorganize a great deal of our thinking about and our arrangements for education. Public sentiment, as articulated and expressed in PL 94-142, will no longer allow us the luxury of mere statistical success. It will no longer suffice to say, "We succeeded with 75, or 85, or even 95 percent of the children." We are expected and obliged to succeed with them all.

8. <u>We simply must accept that, so far as schools are concerned, the bloom is off the rose.</u>

Having grown up in a family that prized education very highly, I find the current devaluation of it extremely difficult to accept. I am repeatedly struck with amazement that in just one decade, our most hallowed institution went from the top of the list of what we revere to somewhere near the bottom. It was only ten years ago that Ivan Illich sounded the first note about "deschooling society." But today, the chorus of voices offering support of various kinds to the proposal is astounding. The revisionist sociologists and economists claim the schools aren't making good on their promise to be a "social escalator" that allows a poor youngster to improve his socioeconomic status. Joining them are the revisionist historians, who claim that, what's more, the schools never did function that way. Then there are the voucher folks, at least some of whom not only want a private school option but a <u>no</u> school option as well. And then there is the burgeoning home instruction movement -- the parents who are educating their own children themselves, rather than sending them to school at all. Most people are not enlisting in the deschooling movement in any such direct way, but they are among the supporters of minimum

competency requirements for high school graduation, on
the grounds that a high school diploma carries no
prima facie evidence of accomplishment whatsoever.
And they are among those in favor of cutting back on
compulsory education so that it is not required of all
-- or not for so many years.

A number of people are even asking whether the
schools aren't inimical to the welfare of human beings. The evidence suggests that, especially in urban
areas, schools can be quite dangerous places, with
alarming rates of crime and violence. And some are
convinced that even in schools where the students'
physical safety is not in jeopardy, their psychic
well-being is.

Thus, from a variety of concerns and perspectives, the school's desirability as an institution is
being challenged quite fundamentally. Any informed attempt at confident education must recognize and take
cognizance of this disaffection. (I distinguish the
critics who think the schools ought to be doing better
from the deschoolers who are saying that the failures
are in the nature of the case and inevitable -- perhaps even intended. A sizable number of people are of
that persuasion.)

9. Finally, we must recognize that these anti-
school feelings are not restricted to those outside
education. The turned-off include a good many teachers
as well.

We have lately been hearing a good deal about
teacher burnout. It's an interesting phenomenon in
the way it differs so considerably depending on who is
doing the talking. In some discussions, burnout is a
matter of extreme fatigue; in others, of overwhelming
stress and tension; in still others, of a kind of psychic withdrawal or dropping out. And I've even heard
some administrators apply the term to teachers they
judge to be goof-offs barely putting in the time and
effort to keep their jobs. There seems to be one element common to these several understandings, however.
Each condition may be described as a way station along
the route to alienation. And that is what I think is
happening to many teachers. This is in no way to doubt
the feelings of fatigue and tension they report, but
it is to say something about the genesis of those
feelings, and their likely outcome.

We have shown considerable concern about turned-off students and turned-off communities. We have shown much less for turned-off teachers -- which is somewhat ironic, given their key role in school improvement. Teachers have been subject to a horrible battering over the past decade. They have been battered by the economy, as they have been penalized more than many other groups in the inflation squeeze and job insecurities; by the public, in response to the unionization of teaching, among other things; by the media, in their exposure of extensive school failures nationwide; and finally, by school administrators, who have all too frequently responded to the pressures by aligning themselves against the teachers, as "management," and by tightening the reins of control.

It would be interesting to find out how many school administrators have moved from more democratic, trusting administrative patterns (McGregor's Theory Y) to an autocratic "tight ship" orientation (Theory X), in response to the past decade's external pressures. I don't know why we, as educators, could not have predicted teacher turn-off in consequence of that change. One study's finding that in seven of the eight schools examined, teachers didn't seem to care very much about school goals and values, is hardly surprising. And it seems far more than coincidence that within the seven schools, teachers felt they were without power to alter those goals and values to any significant extent. (7)

Urie Bronfenbrenner has called the schools "one of the most potent breeding grounds of alienation in society." (8) It is not surprising that they are functioning this way for teachers as well as for students. But we don't seem to have reached a widespread awareness of that fact, or of its significance, and it is with that final recognition that I think we must begin any search for confident education.

Confident education, it seems to me, has two dimensions. One is concerned with sound and effective education; the other, with the way people feel about their education. So far I have examined the second of these dimensions more extensively than the first. So let me now say a few things about directions in which I think we must move in order to improve education's effectiveness -- and make it less necessary to fall back on that "you can't win 'em all" posture.

For one thing, we must begin to take far more seriously the idea of differentiated educations. The evidence is overwhelming that we simply cannot put all kids through the same hoop -- which is exactly what our "one best system" orientation tries to do. A recent report from the Carnegie Council called for differentiation and multiple educational environments. So far, the main application we have made of this idea has been individualized instruction. I am a bit wary of individualized instruction, on several counts. I am worried that it may prove just one more impossible dream that teachers are somehow expected to carry out. If it's impossible for a high school teacher to prepare and execute seven completely successful lessons a day -- and it seems increasingly evident that that is an impossible assignment -- then how in the world is an elementary teacher going to be able to carry out thirty such plans?

Another problematic feature of individualized instruction is that it has rather quickly settled not into genuinely <u>individualized</u> instruction -- that is, differentiated as to method according to learner needs -- but into <u>solitary</u> self-instruction, which is, of course, not the same thing. If we really believe that people learn differently, it would follow that at least some of them learn best in groups, or out of doors, or in service activities, or even in formal classrooms conducted by teachers. But most individualized instruction makes no allowance for such possibilities. Most typically, it has all youngsters learning in just one environment and via what is essentially a single pedagogical strategy: the solitary pursuit, by self-instruction, of subject matter that is similar from student to student but pursued at different rates of speed.

We need to go back to the drawing boards for more ways to put into practice our knowledge about the differences in human learning. In fact, since what we have found is almost endless variability, what we really need is a mechanism for continuous invention -- for making sure that we continue to provide for variation in learners by providing newly differentiated programs as they are needed. This would constitute a real departure in educational history, which has been marked instead by the tendency to quickly freeze any new proposal into a new "one best system" for everybody.

Actually, I think we have the beginning of such a mechanism for invention in the alternative schools concept. The very notion of differentiated educations, and alternatives among which to choose, stands as a means whereby the system can inform and correct itself. As students are unable to succeed in a given program, they can move to another. There need be no stigma or shame attached. What such a system assumes is not poor learners or poor teachers, but a poor match between the two. And as this sort of experience displays the need for additional differentiation, hence new alternatives, the machinery for creating them is already in place.

Educational research typically proceeds on the assumption that the educational program is the important variable, thus ignoring the attributes of the learner. Alternative education, on the other hand, assumes a relationship between particular learner characteristics and particular educational programs. I am convinced that this is the most promising direction in which to look for substantial educational improvement. It will respond to what every teacher knows intuitively: that you simply cannot impose the same thing successfully on everybody. And it will indicate directions for educational research that can be far more applicable to classrooms, and more helpful to educating, than what we've got now.

And what of the "confidence" aspect of confident education? The challenge is to make our pursuit a community enterprise, keeping in mind the nature of the situation we must transform. More than half of the nine awarenesses listed above add up to a need for two things: involvement and empowerment. The two are not the same, and the difference is important. More than one innovative, well-intentioned educational reform has foundered on confusing them. To offer a vote is not necessarily to obtain genuine psychological involvement and ownership, and it is no guarantee of such involvement. Conversely, to obtain involvement is not necessarily to offer empowerment.

We must rethink the power structure of education. Seventy years ago, there seemed excellent reason to concentrate increased educational power in the hands of professionals, and to centralize that power. Today there seems good reason for trying to disperse the power now held centrally, but efforts to do so have not been highly successful. The decentralization attempts in New York City, which sought in part to dismantle the central administration's tight control over individual schools, never managed to diffuse the authority for decisions related to curriculum, personnel, or budget. And the parent advisory councils mandated by the federal government and some states have not met with much success. "School councils are not... by and large, effective vehicles for citizens to affect educational policies and decisions," one study concludes. (9) And another adds: "Policymakers who intended that the councils provide a means to develop participatory democracy at the grass roots level were disappointed with the results. Parents and citizens who served on the councils 'were even more frustrated.'" (10)

It would seem that the mechanisms for successful empowerment have yet to be devised, but differentiated educations, among which families can choose, may hold the key. Students and their parents need a greater amount of personal educational control than they now have. A democratic society simply must offer its citizens some degree of self-determination on so fundamental a matter as education.

But how can families be assigned their rightful piece of the action without sacrificing the advantages of the professional direction of what is, after all, a complicated and technical process? I certainly don't advocate lesson planning by parental vote -- or the scuttling of lesson plans by parental veto. But I see no reason why we in education cannot articulate different curricular orientations, and different perspectives about how schools should operate, and have students and their families choose among them. Moreover, because we as educators have different value orientations, mirroring differences in the rest of the population, teachers as well as parents ought to be able to select the kind of education they will be involved with. Such choice seems to me, in fact, a minimal ingredient of professional prerogative.

An alternatives system could thus well provide the desired, and desirable, piece of the action for all participants. It offers what strikes me as the most appropriate way to provide for the differences in our values, and the entitlement of all of us to live in accord with our own values.

But empowerment is not all that's needed. An

options system extends choice to those with children in school, but demographic changes are rapidly bringing us to a time when a large preponderance of the adult population will not have children in school. How are we to achieve the involvement of this growing segment of the community? That is something educators have not worked very hard on. Even the public relations programs have presupposed that, ultimately, the school's strongest supporters would be those with children enrolled in the school. That need not be the case. There are other sorts of involvement that may, for some, yield an even stronger sense of psychological ownership. And here, again, alternative education seems to offer the key.

Differentiated programs have yielded a variety of ways community members can have a genuine part in education. Some have involved volunteer programs that bring adults into the classroom in an array of new roles. Others have involved sending youngsters out into the community where they become the students -- and often the assistants and collaborators -- of functioning professionals, government officials, and men and women in business. And still other alternative programs have given youngsters the luxury of performing a service -- of contributing something that matters and genuinely making a difference to some segment of the community. These several modes of seeking community involvement offer almost endless possibilities for giving nonparents, and older parents, a real stake in the schools -- for enabling them to take a psychological ownership that has until recently been the privilege of only a very few. It is not, of course, that alternatives have invented all these arrangements. But they do seem to have supplied the conditions for making them work when they have not always worked before. Involving, and empowering, the community provides the key to confident education.

Notes

1. John Schaffarizick and Gary Sykes, NIE's Role in Curriculum Development: Findings, Policy Options, and Recommendations (Washington: NIE, 8 February 77).
2. James J. Kilpatrick, "Hey, Don't Swipe My Lollipop!" NEWSDAY, 25 July 1979.

3. See, for example, Martin Carnoy, EDUCATION AS CULTURAL IMPERIALISM (New York: David McKay, 1974); and Samuel Bowles and Herbert Gintis, SCHOOLING IN CAPITALIST AMERICA: EDUCATIONAL REFORM AND THE CONTRADICTIONS OF ECONOMIC LIFE (New York: Basic Books, 1976).

4. L. Harmon Ziegler; Harvey J. Tucker; and L.A. Wilson, "How School Control Was Wrested from the People," PHI DELTA KAPPAN 58 (March 1977): 534.

5. "What U.S. Thinks about Its Schools," LIFE, 16 October 1950, p. 11.

6. Harold Hodgkinson, "What's Right with Education," PHI DELTA KAPPAN 61 (November 1979): 159.

7. From the report of a Kettering study conducted by Williams, Wall, Martin, and Berchin, cited in Charlotte Ryan, THE OPEN PARTNERSHIP (New York: McGraw Hill, 1976).

8. Urie Bronfenbrenner, "The Origins of Alienation," SCIENTIFIC AMERICAN 231 (August 1974): 53.

9. Don Davies and others, SHARING THE POWER? quoted in Lois S. Steinberg, "The Changing Role of Parent Groups in Educational Decision Making," in PARTNERS: PARENTS AND SCHOOLS, ed. Ronald S. Brandt (Alexandria: Association for Supervision and Curriculum Development, 1979), p. 50.

10. Steinberg, "Changing Role," p. 50.

QUALITY AND EQUALITY IN AMERICAN EDUCATION: PUBLIC AND CATHOLIC SCHOOLS

James S. Coleman

The report, "Public and Private Schools," of which I was an author, has raised some questions about certain fundamental assumptions and ideals underlying American education (1). In this article, I shall first describe briefly the results that raise these questions. Then, I shall examine in greater detail these fundamental assumptions and ideals, together with changes in our society that have violated the assumptions and made the ideals increasingly unattainable. I shall then indicate the negative consequences that these violations have created for both equality of educational opportunity in U.S. public schools and for the quality of education they offer. Finally, I shall suggest what seems to me the direction that a new set of ideals and assumptions must take if the schools are to serve American children effectively.

A number of the results of "Public and Private Schools" have been subjected to intense reexamination and reanalysis. The report has occasioned a good deal of debate and controversy, as well as a two-day conference at the National Institute of Education and a one-day conference at the National Academy of Sciences, both in late July. Part of the controversy appears to have arisen because of the serious methodological difficulties in eliminating bias due to self-selection into the private sector. Another part appears to have arisen because the report was seen as an attack of the public schools at a time when tuition tax credit legislation was being proposed in Congress.

I shall not discuss the controversy except to say that all the results summarized in the first portion of this article have been challenged by at least one

Reprinted from PHI DELTA KAPPAN, 63 (3): 159-164 (November 1981), by permission of author and publisher.

critic; I would not report them here if these criticisms or our own further analyses had led me to have serious doubts about them. Despite this confidence, the results could be incorrect because of the methodological difficulties involved in answering any cause-and-effect question when exposure to the different treatments (that is, to the various types of schools) is so far from random. Most of my comparisons will be between the Catholic and the public schools. The non-Catholic private schools constitute a much more heterogeneous array of schools; our sample in those schools is considerably smaller (631 sophomores and 551 seniors in 27 schools), and the sample may be biased by the fact that a substantial number of schools refused to participate. For these reasons, any generalizations about the non-Catholic private sector must be tenuous. Fortunately, the principal results of interest are to be found in the Catholic schools.

There are five principal results of our study, two having to do with quality of education provided in both the public and private sectors and three related to equality of education.

First, we found evidence of higher academic achievement in basic cognitive skills (reading comprehension, vocabulary, and mathematics) in Catholic schools than in public schools for students from comparable family backgrounds. The difference is roughly one grade level, which is not a great difference. But, since students in Catholic schools take, on the average, a slightly greater number of academic courses, the difference could well be greater for tests more closely attuned to the high school curriculum. And the higher achievement is attained in the Catholic schools with a lower expenditure per pupil and a slightly higher pupil/teacher ratio than in the public schools.

The second result concerning educational quality must be stated with a little less certainty. We found that aspirations for higher education are higher among students in Catholic schools than among comparable students in public schools, despite the fact that, according to the students' retrospective reports, about the same proportion had planned to attend college when they were in the sixth grade.

The first two results concerning equality in edu-

56

cation are parallel to the first two results; one concerns achievement in cognitive skills and the other,
plans to attend college. For both of these outcomes
of schooling, family background matters less in the
Catholic schools than in the public schools. In both
achievement and aspirations, blacks are closer to
whites, Hispanics are closer to Anglos, and children
from less well-educated parents are closer to those
from better-educated parents in Catholic schools than
in public schools. Moreover, in Catholic schools the
gap narrows between the sophomore and senior years,
while in the public schools the gap in both achievement and aspirations widens.

It is important to note that, unlike the results
related to educational quality, these results related
to equality do not hold generally for the public/pri-
vate comparison. That is, the results concerning
equality are limited to the comparison between public
schools and Catholic schools. Within other segments
of the private sector (e.g., Lutheran schools or Jew-
ish schools) similar results for educational differences might well hold (though these other segments
have too few blacks and Hispanics to allow racial and
ethnic comparisons), but they are not sufficiently
represented in the sample to allow separate examination.

The final result concerning educational equality
is in the area of racial and ethnic integration. Catholic schools have, proportionally, only about half as
many black students as do the public schools (about 6%
compared to about 14%); but internally they are less
segregated. In terms of their effect on the overall
degree of racial integration in U.S. schools, these
two factors work in opposing directions; to a large
extent they cancel each other out. But of interest to
our examination here, which concerns the internal
functioning of the public and Catholic sectors of education, is the less internal segregation of blacks in
the Catholic sector. Part of this is due to the smaller percentage of black students in Catholic schools,
for a general conclusion in the school desegregation
literature is that school systems with smaller proportions of a disadvantaged minority are less segregated
than those with larger proportions. But part seems
due to factors beyond the simple proportions. A similar result is that, even though the Catholic schools
in our sample have slightly higher proportions of Hispanic students than the public schools, they have

slightly less Hispanic/Anglo segregation.

These are the results from our research on public and private schools that raise questions about certain fundamental assumptions of American education. Catholic schools appear to be characterized by <u>both</u> higher quality, on the average, <u>and</u> greater equality than the public schools. How can this be when the public schools are, first, more expensive, which should lead to higher quality, and, second, explicitly designed to increase equality of opportunity? The answer lies, I believe, in the organization of public education in the United States, and that organization in turn is grounded in several fundamental assumptions. It is to these assumptions that I now turn.

Four Basic Ideals and Their Violation

Perhaps the ideal most central to American education is the ideal of the common school, a school attended by all children. The assumption that all social classes should attend the same school contrasted with the two-tiered educational systems in Europe, which reflected their feudal origins. Both in the beginning and at crucial moments of choice (such as the massive explosion of secondary education in the early part of this century), American education followed the pattern of common, or comprehensive, schools, including all students from the community and all courses of study. Only in the largest eastern cities were there differentiated, selective high schools, and even that practice declined over time, with new high schools generally following the pattern of the comprehensive school.

One implication of the common-school ideal has been the deliberate and complete exclusion of religion from the schools. In contrast, many (perhaps most) other countries have some form of support for schools operated by religious groups. In many countries, even including very small ones such as the Netherlands and Israel, there is a state secular school system, as well as publicly supported schools under the control of religious groups. But the melting-pot ideology that shaped American education dictated that there would be a single set of publicly supported schools, and the reaction to European religious intolerance dictated that they be free of religious influence (2).

58

The absence of social class, curriculum, or religious bases for selection of students into different
schools meant that, in American schooling, attendance
at a given school was dictated by location of residence. This method worked well in sparsely settled
areas and in towns and smaller cities, and it was a
principle compatible with a secular democracy. Two
factors have, however, led this mode of school assignment to violate the assumptions of the common school.
One is the movement of the U.S. population to cities
with high population densities, resulting in economically homogeneous residential areas. The other is
the more recent, largely post World War II expansion
of personal transportation, leading to the development
of extensive, economically differentiated suburbs surrounding large cities.

The combined effect of these two changes has been
that in metropolitan areas the assumptions of common
school are no longer met. The residential basis of
school assignment, in an ironic twist, has proved to
be segregative and exclusionary, separating economic
levels just as surely as do the explicitly selective
systems of European countries and separating racial
groups even more completely. The larger the metropolitan area, the more true this is, so that in the
largest metropolitan areas the schools form a set of
layers of economically stratified and racially distinct schools, while in small cities and towns the
schools continue to approximate the economically and
racially heterogeneous mix that was Horace Mann's vision of the common school in America.

In retrospect, only the temporary constraints on
residential movement imposed by economic and technological conditions allowed the common-school ideal to
be realized even for a time. As those constraints continue to decrease, individual choice will play an
increasing role in school attendance (principally
through location of residence), and the common-school
assumption will be increasingly violated. Assignment
to a school in a single publicly supported school system on the basis of residence is no longer a means of
achieving the common-school ideal. And, in fact, the
ideal of the common school may no longer be attainable
through any means short of highly coercive ones.

The courts have attempted to undo the racially
segregative impact of residential choice, reconstitut-
ing the common-school ideal through compulsory busing

of children into different residential areas (3).
These attempts, however, have been largely thwarted by
families who, exercising that same opportunity for
choice of school through residence, move out of the
court's jurisdiction. The unpopularity and imperma-
nence of these court-ordered attempts to reinstitute
the common school suggest that attempts to reimpose by
law the constraints that economics and technology once
placed upon school choice will fail and that, in the
absence of those naturally imposed constraints, the
common-school ideal will give way before an even
stronger ideal -- that of individual liberty.

It is necessary, then, to recognize the failure
of school assignment by residence and to reexamine the
partially conflicting ideals of American education in
order to determine which of those ideals we want to
preserve and which to discard. For example, in high
schools distinguished by variations in curriculum, one
form of which is a type of magnet school and another
form of which is the technical high school, a more
stable racial mix of students is possible than in comprehensive high schools. As another example, Catholic
schools are less racially and economically segregated
than are U.S. public schools; this suggests that, when
a school is defined around and controlled by a religious community, families may tolerate more racial and
economic heterogeneity than they would in a school defined around a residential area and controlled by government officials.

A second ideal of American education has been the
concept of local control. This has meant both control
by the local school board and superintendent and the
responsivenes of the school staff to parents. But
these conditions have changed as well. The local
school board and superintendent now have far less control over educational policy than only 20 years ago.
A large part of the policy-making function has shifted
to the national level; this shift was caused primarily
by the issue of racial discrimination, but it has also
affected the areas of sex discrimination, bilingual
education, and education for the handicapped, among
others. Part of the policy-making power has shifted
to the school staff or their union representatives, as
professionalism and collective bargaining have accompanied the growth in size of school districts and the
breakdown of a sense of community at the local level.

The loss of control by school boards and superintendents has been accompanied by a reduced responsiveness of the school to parents. This too has resulted in part from the breakdown of community at the local level and the increasing professionalization of teachers, both of which have helped to free the teacher from community control. The changes have been accompanied and reinforced by the trend to larger urban agglomerates and larger school districts. And some of the changes introduced to overcome racial segregation, in particular busing to a distant school, have led to greater distances between parent and teacher.

A result of this loss of local control has been that parents are more distant from their children's school, less able to exert influence, less comfortable about the school as an extension of their own child rearing. Public support for public schools, as evidenced in the passage of school tax referenda and school bond issues and in the responses to public opinion polls, has declined since the mid-1960s, probably in part as a result of this loss of local control. Even more recently, in a backlash against the increasingly alien control of the schools, some communities have attempted to counter what they see as moral relativism in the curriculum and have attempted to ban the teaching of evolution.

Technological and ecological changes make it unlikely that local control of education policy can be reconstituted as it has existed in the past, that is, through a local school board controlling a single public school system and representing the consensus of the community. Individuals may regain such local control by moving even farther from large cities (as the 1980 census shows they have been doing), but the educational system as a whole cannot be reconstituted along the old local-control lines. Again, as in the case of the common-school ideal, present conditions (and the likelihood that they will persist) make the ideal unrealizable. One alternative is to resign ourselves to ever-decreasing public support for the public schools as they move further from the ideal. Another, however, is to attempt to find new principles for the organization of American education that will bring back parental support.

A third fundamental assumption of American public schooling, closely connected to local control, has been local financing of education. Some of the same factors that have brought about a loss of local control have shifted an increasing portion of education financing to the state and federal levels. Local taxes currently support only about 40% of expenditures for public schooling; federal support amounts to about 8% or 9% and state support, slightly over half of the total. The shift from local to state (and, to a lesser extent, federal) levels of financing has resulted from the attempt to reduce inequalities of educational expenditures among school districts. Inequalities that were once of little concern come to be deeply felt when local communities are no longer isolated but interdependent and in close proximity. The result has been the attempt in some states, responding to the Serrano decision in California, to effect complete equality in educational expenditures for all students within the state. This becomes difficult to achieve without full statewide financing, which negates the principle of local financing.

Yet the justification for student assignment to the schools within the family's taxation district has been that the parents were paying for the schools in that district. That justification vanishes under a system of statewide taxation. The rationale for assignment by residence, already weakened by the economic and racial differences among students from different locales, is further weakened by the decline in local financing.

A fourth ideal of American public education has been the principle of in loco parentis. In committing their child to a school, parents expect that the school will exercise comparable authority over and responsibility for the child. The principle of in loco parentis was, until the past two decades, assumed not only at the elementary and secondary levels but at the college level as well. However, this assumption vanished as colleges abdicated the responsibility and parents of college students shortened the scope of their authority over their children's behavior from the end of college to the end of high school.

Most parents, however, continue to expect the school to exercise authority over and responsibility for their children through the end of high school. Yet public schools have been less and less successful in acting in loco parentis. In part, this is due to the loss of authority in the society as a whole, manifested in high school by a decreasing willingness of high school-age youths to be subject to anyone's

62

authority in matters of dress and conduct. In part, it is due to the increasing dissensus among parents themselves about the authority of the school to exercise discipline over their children, sometimes leading to legal suits to limit the school's authority. And, in part, it is due to the courts, which, in response to these suits, have expanded the scope of children's civil rights in school, thus effectively limiting the school's authority to something less than that implied by the principle of in loco parentis.

There has been a major shift among some middle-class parents -- a shift that will probably become even more evident as the children of parents now in their thirties move into high school -- toward an early truncation of responsibility for and authority over their adolescent children. This stems in part from two changes -- an increase in longevity and a decrease in number of children -- which, taken together, remove child rearing from the central place it once held for adults. Many modern adults who begin child rearing late and end early are eager to resume the leisure and consumption activities that preceded their child-rearing period; they encourage early autonomy for their young. But the high school often continues to act as if it had parental support for its authority. In some cases it does; in others it does not. The community consensus on which a school's authority depends has vanished.

An additional difficulty is created by the increasing size and bureaucratization of the school. The exercising of authority -- regarded as humane and fair when the teacher knows the student and parents well -- comes to be regarded as inhumane and unfair when it is impersonally administered by a school staff member (teacher or otherwise) who hardly knows the student and seldom sees the parents. Thus there arises in such large, impersonal settings an additional demand for sharply defined limits on authority.

This combination of factors gives public schools less power to exercise the responsibility for and authority over students that are necessary to the school's functioning. The result is a breakdown of discipline in the public schools and, in the extreme, a feeling by some parents that their children are not safe in school. Again, a large portion of the change stems from the lack of consensus that once characterized the parental community about the kind and amount

of authority over their children they wished to dele-
gate to the school -- a lack of consensus exploited by
some students eager to escape authority and responded
to by the courts in limiting the school's authority.
And, once again, this raises questions about what form
of reorganization of American education would restore
the functioning of the school and even whether it is
possible to reinstate the implicit contract between
parent and school that initially allowed the school to
act in loco parentis.

The violation of these four basic assumptions of
American education -- the common school, local control, local financing, and in loco parentis -- along
with our failure to establish a new set of attainable
ideals, has hurt both the quality and the equality of
American education. For this change in society, without a corresponding change in the ideals that shape
its educational policies, reduces the capability of
its schools to achieve quality and equality, which
even in the best of circumstances are uncomfortable
bedfellows.

Next I shall give some indications of how the
pursuit of each of these goals of quality and equality
is impeded by policies guided by the four assumptions
I have examined, beginning first with the goal of
equality.

The organization of U.S. education is assignment
to school by residence, guided by the common-school,
local-control, and local-financing assumptions, despite those elements that violate these assumptions.
In a few locations, school assignment is relieved by
student choice of school or by school choice of student. But, in general, the principle observed in
American education (thus making it different from the
educational systems of many countries) has been that
of a rigid assignment by residence, a practice that
upholds the common-school myth and the local-control
and local-financing myths.

It is commonly assumed that the restriction of
choice through rigid assignment by residence is of
relative benefit to those least well off, from whom
those better off would escape if choice were available. But matters are not always as they seem. Assignment by residence leaves two avenues open to parents: to move their residence, choosing a school by

choice of residence; or to choose to attend a private school. But those avenues are open only to those who are sufficiently affluent to choose a school by choosing residence or to choose a private school. The latter choice may be partially subsidized by a religious community operating the school, or, in rare instances, by scholarships. But these partial exceptions do not hide the central point: that the organization of education through rigid assignment by residence hurts most those without money (and those whose choice is constrained by race or ethnicity), and this increases the inequality of educational opportunity. The reason, of course, is that, because of principles of individual liberty, we are unwilling to close the two avenues of choice: moving residence and choosing a private school. And although economic and technological constraints once kept all but a few from exercising these options, that is no longer true. The constraints are of declining importance; the option of residential change to satisfy educational choice (the less expensive of the two options) is exercised by larger numbers of families. And in that exercise of choice, different economic levels are sorted into different schools by the economic level of the community they can afford.

We must conclude that the restrictions on educational choice in the public sector and the presence of tuition costs in the private sector are restrictions that operate to the relative disadvantage of the least well off. Only when these restrictions were reinforced by the economic and technological constraints that once existed could they be regarded as effective in helping to achieve a "common school." At present, and increasingly in the future, they are working to the disadvantage of the least well off, increasing even more the inequality of educational opportunities.

One of the results of our recent study of public and private schools suggests these processes at work. Among Catholic schools, achievement of students from less-advantaged backgrounds -- blacks, Hispanics, and those whose parents are poorly educated -- is closer to that of students from advantaged backgrounds than is true in the public sector. Family background makes much less difference for achievement in Catholic schools than in public schools. This greater homgeneity of achievement in the Catholic sector (as well as the lesser racial and ethnic segregation of the Catholic sector) suggests that the ideal of the common

65

school is more nearly met in the Catholic schools than in the public schools. This may be because a religious community continues to constitute a functional community to a greater extent than does a residential area, and in such a functional community there will be less stratification by family background, both within a school and between schools.

At the same time, the organization of American education is harmful to quality of education. The absence of consensus, in a community defined by residence, about what kind and amount of authority should be exercised by the school removes the chief means by which the school has brought about achievement among its students. Once there was such consensus, because residential areas were communities that maintained a set of norms reflected in the schools' and the parents' beliefs about what was appropriate for children. The norms varied in different communities, but they were consistent within each community. That is no longer true at the high school level, for the reasons I have described. The result is what some have called a crisis of authority.

In our study of high school sophomores and seniors in both public and private schools, we found not only higher achievement in the Catholic and other private schools for students from comparable backgrounds, but also major differences between the functioning of the public schools and the schools of the private sector. ✓ The principal differences were in the greater academic demands made and the greater disciplinary standards maintained in private schools, even when schools with students from comparable backgrounds were compared. This suggests that achievement increases as the demands, both academic and disciplinary, are greater. The suggestion is confirmed by two comparisons: Among the public schools, those that have academic demands and disciplinary standards at the same level as the average private school have achievement at the level of that in the private sector (all comparisons, of course, involving students from comparable backgrounds). And, among the private schools, those with academic demands and disciplinary standards at the level of the average public school showed achievement levels similar to those of the average public school.

The evidence from these data -- and from other

recent studies -- is that <u>stronger academic demands</u> <u>and disciplinary standards produce better achievement.</u> Yet the public schools are in a poor position to establish and maintain these demands. The loss of authority of the local school board, superintendent, and principal to federal policy and court rulings, the rise of student rights (which has an impact both in shaping a "student-defined" curriculum and in impeding discipline), and, perhaps most fundamental, the breakdown in consensus among parents about the schools' authority over and responsibility for their children - all of these factors put the average public school in an untenable position to bring about achievement.

Many public high schools have adjusted to these changes by reducing their academic demands (through reduction of standards, elimination of competition, grade inflation, and a proliferation of undemanding courses) and by slackening their disciplinary standards (making "truancy" a word of the past and ignoring cutting of classes and the use of drugs or alcohol).

These accommodations may be necessary, or at least they may facilitate keeping the peace, in some schools. But the peace they bring is bought at the price of lower achievement, that is, a reduced quality of education.

One may ask whether such accommodations are inevitable or whether a different organization of education might make them unnecessary. It is to this final question that I now turn.

Abandoning Old Assumptions

The old assumptions that have governed American education all lead to a policy of assignment of students to school by place of residence and to a standard conception of a school. Yet a variety of recent developments, both within the public sector and outside it, suggest that attainment of the twin goals of quality and equality may be incompatible with this. One development is the establishment, first outside the public sector and then in a few places within it as well, of elementary schools governed by different philosophies of education and chosen by parents who subscribe to those philosophies. Montessori schools at the early levels, open education, and basic education are examples. In some communities, this principal of parental choice has been used to maintain more stable racial integration than occurs in schools with fixed pupil assignment and a standard educational philosophy. At the secondary level, magnet schools, with specialized curricula or intensive programs in a given area (e.g., music or performing arts), have been introduced, similarly drawing a clientele who have some consensus on which a demanding and effective program can be built. Alternative schools have flourished with both students and staff who accept the earlier autonomy to which I have referred. This is not to say, of course, that all magnet schools and all alternative schools are successful, for many are not. But if they were products of a well-conceived pluralistic conception of modes of secondary education, with some policy guidelines for viability, success would be easier to achieve.

Outside the public sector, the growth of church-operated schools is probably the most prominent development, reflecting a different desire by parents for a non-standard education. But apart from the religious schools, there is an increasingly wide range of educational philosophies from the traditional preparatory school to the free school and the parent-run cooperative school.

I believe that these developments suggest an abandonment of the principle of assignment by residence and an expansion of the modes of education supported by public funds. Whether this expansion goes so far as to include all or part of what is now the private sector or is instead a reorganization of the public alone is an open question. The old proscriptions against public support of religious education should not be allowed to stand in the way of a serious examination of this question. But the elements of successful reorganization remain, whether it stays within the public sector or encompasses the private: a pluralistic conception of education, based on "communities" defined by interests, values, and educational preferences rather than residence; a commitment of parent and student that can provide the school a lever for extracting from students their best efforts; and the educational choice for all that is now available only to those with money.

Others may not agree with this mode of organizing education. But it is clear that the goals of education in a liberal democracy may not be furthered, and may in fact be impeded, by blind adherence to the ideals and assumptions that once served U.S. education (some of which may be unattainable in modern America) and by the mode of school organization that these ideals and assumptions brought into being. There may be extensive debate over what set of ideals is both desirable and attainable and over what mode of organization can best attain these ideals, but it is a debate that should begin immediately. Within the public sector, the once-standard curriculum is beginning to take a variety of forms, some of which reflect the search for a new mode of organizing schooling. And an increasing (though still small) fraction of youngsters are in private schools, some of which exemplify alternative modes of organizing schooling. These developments can be starting points toward the creation of an educational philosophy to guide the reorganization of American schooling in ways fruitful for the youth who experience it.

---

1. The two other authors are Thomas Hoffer and Sally Kilgore. A first draft of "Public and Private Schools" was completed on 2 September 1980. A revised draft was released by the National Center for Educational Statistics (NCES) on 7 April 1981. A final draft is being submitted to NCES this fall. A revised version of the April 7 draft is being published this fall by Basic Books as ACHIEVEMENT IN HIGH SCHOOL: PUBLIC AND PRIVATE SCHOOLS COMPARED.

2. It has nevertheless been true that in many religiously homogeneous communities, ordinarily Protestant, religious influence did infiltrate the schools. Only since the Supreme Court's ban on prayer in the schools has even nonsectarian religious influence been abolished.

3. The legal rationale for these decisions has been past discriminatory practices by school systems; but, in fact, the remedies have constituted attempts to overcome the effects of residential choice.

Part 2

PROMOTING STUDENTS' COGNITIVE

AND AFFECTIVE DEVELOPMENT

GENERAL PRINCIPLES
OF LEARNING AND MOTIVATION

Nancy A. Carlson

A principle, for the purposes of this article, is
a truth or guiding light enabling us to plan instruction so that as much as possible has been done to insure that the intended learning takes place. These
are viable principles and we should at all times bear
them in mind when planning, delivering and evaluating
instruction.

When planning instruction for a learner who experiences difficulty in academic and social skills,
this is more than just a guiding light, it is absolutely imperative. If there are any "truths" to be
found in the currently overwritten and overemphasized
field of learning disabilities, it is that any program
of instruction that fails to take into consideration
certain principles of learning will be doomed to failure with most handicapped learners. The converse,
sadly enough, is not always true. A program that does
rationally consider all the principles will not always
experience success with all learners; but it is much
more likely to produce intended changes in behavior.
In Las Vegas terms, the odds are with you rather than
against you if you employ these principles.

Many of the following principles are straightforward common sense, and undoubtedly have been heard of
or experienced before. They are presented in light of
what we know about children with learning problems.

Meaningfulness

A student is more likely to be motivated to learn

From TEACHING EXCEPTIONAL CHILDREN 12 (2): 60-62 (Winter 1980). Copyright 1980 by The Council for Exceptional Children. Reprinted with permission.

things that are meaningful to him or her.

1. As concerned teachers, we should try to relate intended learning to the student's experiences. What is known for certain that the learner has experienced? Analogies may help him or her see the relationship if the analogous situation or relationship is very concrete.

2. Relating to each student's interests and values is very helpful. One of the best ways to do this is to allow the student(s) more voice in decisions that affect them; decisions such as:

-- What objectives shall be set?

-- What procedures will best achieve those objectives?

-- At what rate should the material be learned?

-- With what degree of accuracy?

-- How much practice time and how often?

3. Whenever possible, we should try to explain how this particular experience will affect the learner now and in the future. An advance organizer is a useful tool; it is a verbal or written explanation or overview of the material that will follow. Often it contains the rationale for the instructional experience. The use of an advance organizer, if perceived as meaningful to the student(s), will go a long way toward answering a multitude of often unasked questions. (For example, "We are doing this because _____ _____.") If the explanation can be related to nonschool experiences, so much the better.

TIP: Whenever the above blank cannot be filled in, think about eliminating the experience.

Prerequisites

A student is more likely to learn something if he or she has all the prerequisites.

1. Past learning is the most important factor in determining success or failure in learning. (Note: it said "past learning" and not past teaching or past exposure.)

2. To determine the necessary prerequisites, it is often helpful (and sometimes necessary) for the teacher, and occasionally the student, to engage in two operations:

-- Task description. What are the operations one must perform and the decisions one must make to reach the objective? A flowchart may be helpful. Flowcharts can follow the traditional structure or can be constructed using sequenced pictures or drawings for nonreaders.

-- Task analysis. After a task description is complete, it is easier to look at the underlying assumptions, concepts, and skills that a learner must already have mastered in order to successfully accomplish this new task. Information on task analysis and task description is readily available to the interested reader.

3. Test for prerequisites, and by all means let the learner in on it. In order for intended learning to occur, the student should perceive the relationship between what he or she knows and what he or she needs to know. Too often this step is missed, especially if the child has a learning problem. Just a simple "Here's what you can do now -- here's what I would like you to be able to do..." will suffice.

Modeling

A student is more likely to acquire a new behavior if he or she is presented with a model performance to watch and imitate.

1. In modeling, it is critical to label the important aspects of behavior as they are being demonstrated. (Said differently, present a good visual, auditory, and, whenever possible, kinesthetic experience.) For example, "Johnny, let's do this together. First we take the small stick and put it here, then the medium sized stick and put it next to the other two. Small, medium, large. That's ordering by size. Now you do the same thing."

2. Students should see the model receiving rewards for a particular behavior. This is extremely important, but in practice the modeled behavior is often inappropriately or negatively rewarded or even overlooked.

3. The model should be perceived as a person of high status, so as not to be in conflict with the student's values or beliefs. This may explain why cross age teaching succeeds in the elementary school -- fifth graders are perceived as high status by second graders.

4. Modeling applies when teaching either technical or social skills. In fact, it is not always necessary that the teacher model the behavior; it becomes very apparent that another (high status) student could model the desired behavior, receiving praise immediately. "Did you see Sally walking backwards on the balance beam and explaining what she was doing? That's an interesting way to use the beam. Can anyone else do something on the beam?"

Open Communication

A student is more likely to learn if the medium used in the learning situation is structured so that the teacher's messages are open to the learner's inspection.

State all the messages you intend to have students receive and state them in a way that will insure reception. In other words, don't have a "hidden agenda." Following are some tips:

1. State objectives to each student. This tells the student what to attend to during presentations.

2. Point out relationships; give prompts and cues.

3. Avoid talking about something in its absence; avoid abstractions. This is important in the elementary school, and for any learner in the secondary system who is still functioning in a concrete manner.

4. Structure your presentation so that the student can both see and hear.

5. Ask questions to verify. Remember, some students are too embarrassed to ask questions themselves. Asking questions is also an example of modeling. If you ask questions and really listen to the answers, then you are providing an appropriate model. Wouldn't you like the children to ask questions and then listen?

All of this looks like you're giving the learner many different chances for success. After all, you're telling him or her what you want him or her to learn. But isn't that what good teaching is all about? The learner should never have to figure out what the teacher wants -- it should be apparent.

Novelty

A student is more likely to learn if his or her attention is attracted by relatively novel presentations.

Any variation in the format, the mode of presentation, or the groupings in order to make it a more unusual and creative experience will be deeply appreciated. It is also more likely to be learned. Occassionally, too much novelty will produce over-reaction, an inappropriate behavior. Common sense on the teacher's part will avoid this problem.

Active Appropriate Practice

A student is more likely to learn if he or she takes an active part in practice geared to reach an instructional objective.

The range of options when talking about an active role for learners can run from the totally "open" classroom or free schools to a totally structured but still participative role in a more traditional classroom. The key to success is to have the learner involved.

If active is a key word in the above principle, we must also recognize appropriate and practice. Inappropriate or incorrect practice can actually cause incorrect habits to form, thus making further teaching/learning more difficult.

Distributing Practice

A student is more likely to learn if practice is done in short periods over time.

All of us can get tired and bored with any task at some time. No matter how exciting the task, we need to get away from it, even if it's only to be more excited about starting the next time. For children with learning problems, this is an axiom. Many will show signs of boredom and fatigue, or will make too many mistakes. Some will not have the ability to attend for very long no matter what the task. For these children it is better to break up a task into short do-able segments, than to expect the entire task to be finished at one time. <u>Short</u> for some children may be 1 to 3 minutes.

Fading

A student is more likely to learn if instructional prompts are withdrawn gradually.

Instructional prompts, or crutches as some call them, are perfectly appropriate and should be used. During the learning process many children need the help of a finger on a word in a sentence, or a "window" to single out the specific word for oral and silent reading. Many normal children remove the prompt or helper of their own volition as they become more skilled. Other children must be withdrawn gradually from the prompt.

Blind children begin learning Braille with large bumps and then, gradually, the size of the bumps is reduced. Young children learning to write are given paper with dark lines for structure at first. Both are examples of fading.

Pleasant Conditions and Consequences

A student is more likely to learn if the instructional conditions are pleasant.

This rather ideal situation can be promoted by:

1. Avoiding aversive conditions and consequences such as:

    a. Boredom -- repeating unnecessarily, waiting too long, non-challenging material. Boredom happens too frequently when a child has a problem with age appropriate material. Material at a lower level is often boring to the learner and serves only to fill time.

b. Unpleasant physical conditions -- too hot, too cold, too noisy, always being in the same place, too many distractions, etc.

c. Frustration -- unreasonable demands with no escape, continually failing, being asked to "pay attention" when it's not possible to see or hear. The list of what can cause frustration could go on and on. We must try to be alert to the signs and, if possible, avoid them.

d. Emotional hurting -- by not touching the learner, by making harsh comparisons, by harmful jokes, scapegoating, etc.

If these unpleasant conditions are not avoided, the student will soon learn to avoid the situation, the teacher, and the school. Avoidance could easily turn into adjustment problems and/or delinquent behavior.

2. Providing pleasant conditions and positive consequences.

a. Setting challenging tasks. Each task should really require some effort from the learner. Learning theory suggests that if a learner has about 50% chance of success he or she is more apt to continue doing the task. For a child with long standing learning problems, 50% may be a little low. But a 90% chance for success is too high. A challenge is necessary and is in itself motivating.

b. Giving feedback. A learner needs information regarding what he or she is doing -- the more immediate the better. Keep in mind the question "why." If you can explain to a learner "why" it is that he or she did the task either appropriately or inappropriately, and discuss what should be done differently, he or she will be more likely to do it better the next time, assuming that is your objective.

c. Rewarding the student's efforts. If the learner is trying, and is involved in the process of learning, praise the process.

At first give praise for effort immediately and every time, always referring directly to what is being performed. Gradually make the praise more intermittent.
This particular strategy can be both over-
done and phony. Be careful.

Given an understanding of the principles of motivation and learning listed here, the odds are with
you now.

A LEARNING STYLES PRIMER

Rita Dunn

Everybody has a learning style. You have one yourself, and if you're married, the chances are that your mate's style is very different from yours. Psychologists tell us that, while we feel comfortable with people like ourselves, we don't seem to marry them. As you read this article and begin to identify your own learning style, consider the style of your spouse (or someone else close to you), and you will see the two are opposite in many ways. Even in the same family, siblings often learn in drastically different ways. And children's learning styles tend to be extremely different from those of their parents. The next time you tell your children when, how, and how not to study or do homework, remember that you may well be misdirecting them. What works for you, usually doesn't work for them.

Since parents' learning styles are not necessarily reflected in their offspring, and since siblings usually are more different than similar, we cannot be certain whether learning style is biologically inherited or environmentally developed. Moreover, since learning style itself is made up of a number of different elements, its origin is complex. Indeed, the research evidence on the question differs from one element to another. For each element of learning style discussed below, the current consensus of researchers as to whether it is biologically or environmentally determined will be indicated.

Environmental Elements: Sound, Light, Temperature, and Design

Reprinted from PRINCIPAL, 60 (5): 31-34 (May 1981), by permission of author and publisher. Copyright 1981, National Association of Elementary School Principals. All rights reserved.

Well-designed and well-conducted research studies verify that, regardless of age, IQ, socioeconomic status, or achievement level, individuals respond uniquely to their immediate environment when they are trying to learn something new -- particularly if it is difficult. Many require absolute silence when they are concentrating; others can block out distractors and absorb information; and some cannot study in silence. People in the last group are so sound sensitive that when their surroundings are quiet, they hear all the extraneous noises they're usually not aware of, and those sounds actually prevent them from thinking. One recent investigation isolated students who could not tolerate sound when concentrating and others who required it. Statistically, both groups achieved significantly better when their preferences for quiet or sound (music to block out the environmental distractors) were matched correctly. Both groups did statistically less well when their preferences were mismatched.

People also respond differently to light. Some need brightly lit areas to learn, whereas others become fidgety, nervous, or hyperactive when the light is too bright for them. Members of the first group often become apathetic or sleepy when lights are dim, and those in the second are not able to internalize information until the lights are soft enough to permit relaxation.

Most students can describe the temperatures in which they function most effectively. In exactly the same room at the same time, some feel warm, others are cool, a few are cold, and many are comfortable. It is important to note that, unless individuals are at a harmony with their environment, it is difficult for them to concentrate.

Some youngsters can focus on what they are learning if they study in a "formal design" -- sitting on a straight chair at a desk or table, as found in a library, classroom, or kitchen. Others concentrate better and remember more when they study in an "informal design" -- relaxing on a lounge chair, couch, or bed or on the floor.

The preference for quiet or sound, and the ability to block out noise, are related to an individual's hearing sensitivity. Similarly, the need for bright, average, or dim light is a function of eye sensitivity, while temperature reactions depend on the thickness or thinness of one's skin. Whether a person remembers more when concentrating in a formal, rather than an informal, environment is undoubtedly an outgrowth of bodily needs. These environmental elements of learning style are hence thought to be biological and related to one's physical being.

Emotional Elements: Motivation, Persistence, Responsibility, and Need for Either Structure or Options

Students who are unmotivated and neither persistent nor responsible should be taught differently -- in fact, by diametrically opposite methods -- from those who are. Motivated, persistent, responsible youngsters should be told what they are required to learn (their objectives), what they may use as resources, how they may show that they have mastered their objectives, and where to get help if they need assistance. They appreciate feedback and deserved praise <u>after</u> their tasks have been accomplished. Unmotivated, less persistent and responsible pupils, on the other hand, require short assignments with very few objectives, frequent feedback, a great deal of supervision, and genuine praise <u>as</u> <u>they</u> <u>are</u> <u>working</u>.

We have learned a great deal about the elements of motivation, persistence, and responsibility during the past decade. For example, motivation is linked to achievement: the higher the individual's achievement, the more motivated he or she becomes. Motivation is also linked to a match of the student's learning style and the teacher's teaching style, and it changes from day to day, from class to class, and from teacher to teacher. Persistence and responsibility appear to correlate with conforming behavior, but many less persistent and responsible students do not learn through conformity.

Structure is another important element of learning style. Youngsters who require specific directions, sequential tasks, frequent feedback, and continuing support usually achieve well with a very structured instructional method (such as programmed learning), particularly if they are highly visual or visual/tactual and are able to work alone. If they are tactual/kinesthetic or peer oriented, on the other hand, programmed sequences may not hold their attention. But if they require structure, are tactual/kinesthetic

82

(but not highly auditory or visual), and find learning difficult, they probably will achieve better using multisensory instructional packages.

Students who are auditory or auditory/visual and who are motivated, self-structured, or responsive to options often perform best with contract activity packages (CAPs). That system also lends itself to use with youngsters who cannot tolerate flexibility, for the teacher who is using a CAP merely provides the necessary structure by requiring specific objectives, resources, activity and reporting alternatives, and due dates. If the students are peer oriented, the small-group techniques that are part of every CAP are also assigned.

The emotional elements of learning style appear to be an outgrowth of both the environment and each person's emotional makeup.

Sociological Elements: Learning Alone, with Peers, with an Adult, on in Several Ways

Some youngsters gain very little from even the most charismatic teacher or well-planned lesson; they need to learn by themselves, away from the distractions of other students, the teacher's pacing, the formal classroom design, or perhaps even the instructional strategy being employed. Different methods should be prescribed for those students, depending on whether or not they need structure and their perceptual strengths.

Small-group techniques such as circle of knowledge, team learning, brain-storming, case studies, or group analysis are effective teaching strategies for those who are peer oriented. Such youngsters are more concerned with what their classmates think than they are with their teacher's or parents' reactions.

Even students who respond well to adults in general should be matched with the teacher whose style -- be it collegial or authoritative -- is right for them. Research verifies that the closer the match between the student's and teacher's styles, the higher the grade point average and the more the student likes school.

Some learners do not achieve well with other people of any age and cannot work alone. Such youngsters may benefit from the use of instructional media and should have chances to work with computers, videotapes, films, filmstrips, and the like.

The sociological elements of learning appear to be environmentally based.

Physical Elements: Perceptual Strengths, Intake, Time of Day, and Need for Mobility

Perceptual strengths appear to develop on a continuum, with kindergarteners tending to be strongly tactual/kinesthetic. By about third or fourth grade, visual strengths begin to develop, and by fifth or sixth grade, most youngsters begin to become auditory. An auditory learner can remember about 75 percent of what is verbalized in a forty- to forty-five-minute lecture, while a visual learner remembers approximately 75 percent of what is seen during a class period of the same length.

Girls develop auditory skills earlier and faster than boys, a difference that is evident throughout the life span. For example, infant girls are able to recognize familiar voices at a younger age than can infant boys. Little girls develop a large vocabulary earlier than boys, who have more speech problems. And as adults, women tend to be more articulate than men, and tend to lose their hearing later in life.

Bearing those differences in mind, consider the two most popular methods of teaching children to read: phonics and word recognition. In the first, youngsters must hear the differences between sounds (at, fat, bat, cat, sat, hat, and so on); in the second, they must recognize the differences between letters and then relate them to meaning. Since the average kindergartener and first grader are neither strongly visual nor strongly auditory, a tactual/kinesthetic approach to reading -- such as tracing words in sand or correctly placing sandpaper letters into sequence -- is more successful with the very young. Several studies have shown that when the reading approach is matched correctly to individual children's perceptual strengths, they learn more words more easily and remember them longer. Although strong motivation can overcome perceptual weaknesses, many youngsters' motivation declines in direct proportion to their inability to master reading.

Another physical element in learning styles is intake, or oral ingestion. Some people eat, drink, smoke, or chew gum while they are engaged in cognitive studies, either to replace the nutritional energy that their concentration uses up, or to relax them from the tension of learning. Few schools permit students to nibble on raw vegetables or other nutritional snacks while they are learning, but that practice alone has helped many youngsters achieve higher grades.

The new science of chronobiology verifies the empirical observation that each person enjoys different peak energy times during the night or day. Extending this concept to the classroom suggests that students should be taught their most important subjects during the time when they are most alert. In fact, one study found that when students were scheduled for classes at a complementary time of day, school records showed a reduction in chronic truancy and lateness.

Another element that either facilitates or inhibits learning is mobility. Some people are able to remain seated for long periods, while others need to move around. We mistakenly label the movers hyperactive, but they may merely be particularly sensitive to sound, light, temperature, or design. They may be unable to learn through the particular perceptual mode that the teacher is emphasizing; or they may be self- or peer-oriented, rather than teacher-oriented. Or they may simply be unable to sit still for a sustained period at that particular time of day. Classroom activities that allow for movement and large-scale motor activity will be more effective with such students.

The physical elements of learning style appear to be biological in origin.

Psychological Elements: Global/Analytic, Hemispheric
    Preference, and Impulsive/Reflective

Many studies indicate that some youngsters learn sequentially, step by step, in a well-ordered continuum -- the way math, biology, and grammar usually are taught. Others cannot even begin to focus on the lesson without an overall gestalt of what will be taught. Such students require a visual image of the topic, an illustrative anecdote to involve them in it,

85

and motivation to pursue it. The first type of learning is called analytic; the second, global. When analytic learners are taught analytically, and when global learners are taught globally, both achieve significantly better than when learning styles and teaching styles are mismatched.

Reading this article, in which each element of learning styles is discussed in turn, in a sequential format, you are being introduced to the subject analytically. Many traditional classroom materials are similar in format and presentation. That's fine for the analytic learner, but what about the global learner?

Hemispheric preference, or cerebral dominance, is a newly recognized element of learning style. During the past few years, we have learned that students who use their left brain more than their right brain learn in extremely different ways than those who do the reverse. The left hemisphere of the brain, according to many researchers, shows a distinct advantage when it comes to analytic tasks like dealing with language or classifying objects, while the right hemisphere seems relatively more important in performing spatial tasks. In fact, some environmental elements of learning style, such as sound, light, and temperature, seem to correlate well with hemispheric inclinations.

Finally, learners differ in their degree of impulsiveness and reflectiveness. Impulsive youngsters call out answers without considering various possibilities, while reflective rarely volunteer information although they often know the answers. Verbal class participation is difficult for some and easy for others.

The psychological elements appear to be both biological and environmental in origin.

Putting Learning Styles to Work

In 1967 the State Department of Education in New York designed a program, in which my colleagues and I were involved, to develop effective teachers for underachieving youngsters in public schools. Through extensive observations, interviews, and experimental studies, we recognized the extent of individual differences among the students. Continuing research since

86

then has corroborated our belief that significant improvement in achievement, motivation, and discipline
occurs when students' learning styles are matched with
complementary teaching styles, instructional resources
or approaches.

Schools throughout the nation are now successfully using instruction based on learning styles. One
such school was Madison Prep, an alternative junior
high in New York City that, during its brief lifetime,
made effective use of individual learning styles. (For
fiscal reasons, Madison was recently rejoined to its
parent school.)

Working with the "worst" twenty youngsters from
one of the city's public junior high schools, a dedicated and enthusiastic teacher turned a dark basement
into a cheerful and personal educational environment.
Then, in a compatible physical setting, the group
tackled its first educational task: diagnosing each
student's individual learning style, based on response
to a questionnaire about how they learn best. Results
of the questionnaire were discussed with the students,
and each one's working preferences were charted on the
Learning Style Profile form.

Students and staff chose aerospace as an integrating theme or curricular base for almost all learning at the school. Hence, a literature sequence might
have included myths about flight, or a science activity might have focused on the physical structure of
birds and planes. Instructional assignments were based
on individual student characteristics, and a variety
of contract activity packages and programmed learning
sequences were designed. Weekly conferences were arranged for all students, along with frequent planning
and progress reviews.

Academic progress at Madison was astonishing: in
ten months, some students gained as much as two to
four years in reading and mathematics. Equally impressive was the students' change in attitude. As
Kenneth Dunn, superintendent of schools in Hewlett-
Woodmere, New York, and adjunct professor at St.
John's University, observed, "An esprit de corps has
developed. Students attend regularly and no one has
dropped out." This "remarkable cohesiveness and positive outlook" Dunn attributed to "mutual caring,
achievement, 'ownership' of the school, and a variety
of self-image builders -- all of which rest on the

87

solid foundation of recognition of individual learning styles."

And Madison Prep was not the only such school. Principals need only read about how P.S. 220 in Queens (with a 40 percent mobility rate among its students) obtained among the highest scores in the district, how a New York City teacher of learning disabled second graders increased their reading achievement, how another teacher helped kindergarteners achieve significantly better in reading, and how differently gifted students and others learn, to become convinced that it is important to recognize and work with individual learning styles.

Resources are available for principals who want to help their faculty increase their teaching effectiveness. An ordinary classroom, for example, can be redesigned in an hour -- at no cost -- to respond to the environmental learning styles of its students. Instructional materials can be developed through in-service as teachers learn to expand their teaching styles in response to various learning styles. And for those who need additional help in making that change, the technology is now available for identifying students' and teachers' styles and then matching them by computer.

If you want to know more about how to design, implement, administer, supervise, or evaluate a learning styles instructional program, there are several steps you can take. First, you can read more about the subject. (See "For Further Information," at the end of this article.) You can visit schools where such a program is working. You can, along with selected staff members, attend a training conference in New York this July. (For details, write Rita Dunn, Center for the Study of Learning and Teaching Styles, St. John's University, Grand Central Parkway, Jamaica, New York 11429.) And you can press for more recognition and coverage of the learning styles concepts in the publications and meetings of your professional organizations.

If your own leadership style is impulsive -- with high energy, motivation, and responsibility levels -- you'll do all of these things. If you are reflective, you may wait until the courts or your state legislature mandates it. Either way, your school eventually will become involved, for the research indicates that many students who previously did not achieve well are doing so now -- through learning styles.

For Further Information

Publications

Dunn, Kenneth. "Madison Prep: Alternative to Teenage Disaster." EDUCATIONAL LEADERSHIP 38 (Feb. 1981): 386-87.

_____, and Rita Dunn. "Identifying Individual Learning Styles." In STUDENT LEARNING STYLES: DIAGNOSING AND PRESCRIBING PROGRAMS. Reston, Va.: National Association of Secondary School Principals.

_____. TEACHING STUDENTS THROUGH THEIR INDIVIDUAL LEARNING STYLES: A PRACTICAL APPROACH. Reston, Va.: Reston Publishing Co. Division of Prentice-Hall, 1978. Explains all the techniques named in this article -- programmed learning, multisensory instructional packages, contract activity packages, circle of knowledge, team learning, and classroom redesign -- and provides samples at every level, primary through secondary.

Dunn, Rita. "Individual Instruction Through Contracts -- Does It Work With Very Young Children?" AUDIOVISUAL INSTRUCTION 16 (March 1971): 78-80.

_____. "Learning Styles." EDUCATIONAL LEADERSHIP 38: (November 1980): 191-92.

_____, and Gary E. Price. "Identifying the Learning Style Characteristics of Gifted Children." GIFTED CHILD QUARTERLY 24 (Winter 1980): 33-36.

Griggs, Shirley A., and Gary E. Price. "Learning Styles of the Gifted." In STUDENT LEARNING STYLES: DIAGNOSING AND PRESCRIBING PROGRAMS. Reston, Va.: National Association of Secondary School Principals, 1979.

_____. "Self-Concept Relates to Learning Style in the Junior High." PHI DELTA KAPPAN 62 (April 1981): 604.

Wheeler, Roberta. "An Alternative to Failure: Teaching Reading according to Students' Perceptual Strengths." KAPPA DELTA PI RECORD 17 (December 1980): 59-63.

Other Resources

LEARNING STYLES NETWORK NEWSLETTER, sponsored by the National Association of Secondary School Principals and St. John's University's Center for the Study of Learning and Teaching Styles. For information, write to Professor Rita Dunn, Learning Styles Network, St. John's University, Grand Central Parkway, Jamaica, New York 11429.

Instruments for identifying learning style: 1) THE LEARNING STYLE INVENTORY (LSI), reliable and valid for grades three through twelve. Specimen set $10. 2) THE PRODUCTIVITY ENVIRONMENTAL PREFERENCE SURVEY (PEPS), reliable and valid for adults. Specimen set $7. Both available from Price Systems, Box 3271, Lawrence, Kansas 66044.

PIAGET:
IMPLICATIONS FOR TEACHING

Patricia Kimberly Webb

The educational implications of Piaget's theory
are closely tied to his concept of intelligence as the
dynamic and emerging ability to adapt to the environment with ever-increasing competence (Piaget, 1963).
By what processes does the individual gain this proficiency, and how may the teaching-learning situation be
designed to maximize human potential? A brief review
of Piaget's basic assumptions will provide some insight into the processes of cognitive growth (Piaget
and Inhelder, 1969, Piaget, 1963), and examples drawn
from research and personal experience will illustrate
applications of this theory to educational practice.

Theoretical Assumptions

Piaget believes that four factors serve as pro-
pellants to mental development. Each is vital, as it
is the interaction of these components that results in
cognitive growth. First, maturation of both nervous
and endocrine systems provides physical capabilities.
Second, experience involving action on the part of the
learner aids in the discovery of the properties of objects and in the development of organizational skills.
Third, social interaction offers opportunities for the
observation of a wide variety of behaviors, for direct
instruction, and for feedback concerning the individual's performance. Finally, Piaget believes that within each person there is an internal self-regulation
mechanism that responds to environmental stimulation
by constantly fitting new experiences into existing
cognitive structures (assimilation) and revising these
structures to fit the new data (accommodation). Piaget
refers to these cognitive structures as schemas. A

Reprinted from THEORY INTO PRACTICE, 19 (2): 93-97
(Spring 1980), by permission of author and publisher.

balance, or equilibrium, between assimilation and accommodation maximizes cognitive functioning.

Piaget has identified a series of stages in the
process of cognitive development. These stages must
occur in a particular sequence, since each stage in-
corporates and restructures the previous one and re-
fines the individual's ability to perceive and understand. While suggested ages for each stage are indicated, intelligence and/or environment may cause variations. Certain patterns of behavior are characteristic of the way an individual will interpret and use
the environment at each of these stages.

While Piaget's research has generated many suggested implications for teaching, five issues have
been selected for discussion. These are stage-based
teaching, uniqueness of individual learning, conceptual development prior to language, experience involving action, and necessity of social interaction.

Stage-based Teaching

Several questions arise with reference to the use
of Piaget's developmental stages in teaching. What implications may be drawn from the general characteristics of each stage? Can or should a child's progres-
sion through those stages be accelerated? Does a unitary period of formal operations actually exist?

During the sensori-motor stage, from birth to
about two years, the child uses his senses and emerging motor skills to explore the environment. Verbal
interaction, an object-rich setting, and the freedom
to explore are of paramount importance at this time.
During the preoperational stage, from about two to
seven, the child is "perceptually bound;" he is unable
to reason logically concerning concepts that are dis-
crepant from visual clues. His thinking is hampered
by such factors as egocentrism (seeing things only
from his own point of view), centering (focusing only
on one attribute at a time), and inability to follow
transformations and perform reversals. Being confronted with the opinions of others and being actively
involved with objects and processes will help this
child to build the cognitive structures necessary for
logical thought.

As the child moves into the concrete operational

stage, from about seven to eleven years, he is able to
use this logic to analyze relationships and structure
his environment into meaningful categories. It is crucial for the child to have many interactions with concrete materials during this entire period, since the
ability to think abstractly is built on these understandings. Finally, during adolescence the individual
may pass into the period of formal operations and develop the ability to manipulate concepts abstractly
through the use of propositions and hypotheses. The
teacher should realize, however, that from 25 to 75
percent of all adolescents and adults have not attained formal operations, and many concrete interactions are needed for comprehension (Good et al.,
1979).

What problems may arise from a mismatch between
the level of the learner and that of the material?
Kirkland (1978) observed that in beginning reading the
preoperational child's centering may make her unable
to consider parts and wholes in words at the same
time. The child may regularly confuse "was" and "saw"
despite extensive drill. The child who cannot follow
transformations may not be able to sound out words.
The individual sounds of c a, and t may not be recognized as "cat" even when she "says it fast." Some research studies have indicated that there is a high
positive correlation between the ability to conserve
and beginning reading achievement.

Another attempt to match level to learner was the
University of Nebraska's ADAPT program (Accent on Developing Abstract Processes of Thought). Since many
college students cannot perform formal operations,
ADAPT was designed to provide concrete experiences in
math, science, and the humanities. After the freshman
year, these students scored significantly higher than
controls on a variety of measures (Tomlinson-Keasey
and Eisert, 1978).

Can a child's progress through the stages be accelerated? Piaget contends that for optimal comprehension, these changes should result from numerous experiences over a long period of time. Two reviews of
research illustrate both the possibilities and the
problems in acceleration attempts.

In an effort to determine what can be accelerated
fifteen training studies were classified in three
types: learning a specific Piagetian task, learning to

perform a specific mental operation, and moving a student from the concrete to the formal stage (DeCarcer et al., 1978). Conclusions were: (1) that an individual can learn a specific task or operation but often with limited retention and transfer and (2) that apparent shifts from concrete to formal operations may result from interim experiences unrelated to training and/or from test-wiseness if the same instrument was used for both pre- and post-testing.

Evans (1975) analyzed the teaching methods used in training studies. He categorized the approaches as verbal rule (direct verbal instruction), cognitive conflict (getting children to question their own perceptions), and task analysis (pretraining on subskills of a task). Use of verbal rule and cognitive conflict can result in the acquisition of conservation, but transfer may be limited. The relative success of task analysis seems to depend on the levels and interactions of subskills already possessed by the learner.

Educators may draw several implications from the findings of these studies. Rather than concentrate on the learning of specific Piagetian tasks and operations, the classroom milieu should be structured to encourage constant thinking on the part of students. Verbal rule, cognitive conflict, and task analysis all may be used in a wide variety of settings to increase the incidence of transfer. Better comprehension at a given stage may be a more appropriate goal than forced acceleration to the next cognitive level. Piaget feels that such piecemeal acceleration often results in distorted or incomplete conceptual development that may hamper future thinking.

While Piaget's first three stages appear to be universal, serious concerns have been expressed with reference to the period of formal operations. Berzonsky (1978), after an extensive review of research, suggested that formal operational thinking is not a unitary quality that can be applied to all areas of thinking. Abstract thinking appears to be linked only to those content areas in which an individual has had extensive training. Based on the work of Guilford and others, Berzonsky suggested a branch model. After concrete operations, an individual may acquire abstract thinking in behavioral, symbolic, semantic, and/or figural content areas depending on experience. The quality and type of educational opportunities during adolescence thus become crucial, since both the development and direction of formal operations depend on these experiences.

Uniqueness of Individual Learning

If a science lesson is presented to six students, each of them will have a different learning experience? Why is every learning experience unique? How does an individual's repertoire of schemas structure the learning for him? What is meant by high level and low level learning?

Each person's cognitive schemas are constantly being revised through the assimilation of new information and the refinement of mental structures to make fullest use of this input. Therefore, no two individuals can ever be at the same level of readiness for a given experience.

The particular schemas that an individual has developed and their levels of functioning will structure the learning situation in several ways: (1) what is noticed (we perceive selectively in terms of such factors as past experience, interest, level of difficulty, and novelty), (2) whether we fit in the new information accurately or distort it (the child learns that "es" is used to form plurals and says "mouses"), and (3) how much increase in competence results from the encounter (at an adequate readiness level, material is correctly incorporated into the schema thereby increasing the capabilities of that cognitive structure).

While Piaget contends that the child will restructure everything that he experiences in terms of his current cognitive schemas, Gagne' feels that meaningful structure can come from the environment (Strauss, 1972). Gagne' advocates curricula based on sequential hierarchies. The views of Piaget and Gagne' may or may not be in conflict depending on the particular situation. Gagne's prerequisite experiences may provide the necessary input for Piaget's schema accommodation thus rendering one learner ready for the experience. However, because of a difference in schema development, another learner may perceive these same prerequisites as boring, too hard, or unrelated to his needs and withdraw from the learning situation.

Intellectual growth occurs only when the learner

is doing thinking that is high level in relation to his own stage of development (Furth and Wachs, 1975). A given activity may be high level for one child and low level for another. A level that is too high may produce frustration, distortion, or rote learning; one that is too low can result in disinterest and boredom. When a task is presented, it is the child who makes the final determination as to whether it will be a low or high level task; she performs in terms of her own level. For instance, if she is asked to learn about geological land forms, she may understand the concepts and apply them to other instances (high level), or she may memorize without comprehension (low level). "Whether or not instruction is individualized, learning is!" (Wadsworth, 1978, p. 183)

Piaget believes that the child first internalizes concepts from his interactions with the environment and later develops the language to label and describe these understandings. He further contends that language actually may confuse comprehension. Many early childhood panics are based on a child's misunderstanding of things that are said. Another example is that of the student who becomes hopelessly lost after reading a stated problem in math because he can't conceptualize the relationships among numbers presented. Empirical support for the development of concepts prior to linguistic experience is found in several studies relating to deaf children (Evans).

Is language, then, of no value in the development of concepts? Piaget found that seriation may be improved by verbal training while conservation is not. By contrast, Bruner and others have found in many studies that the use of language facilitates conceptual development.

What implications for teaching may be drawn from the relationship between concept development and language acquisition? First, in all areas of learning, much concrete experience must precede abstract verbalizations. Second, task-oriented testing situations should be used so that the child's understanding will not be confused with his verbal ability. When I was teaching seventh grade, I was alarmed to note the high positive correlation between grades in reading and in social studies over a seven year period. Verbal loading in both teaching and testing could account for this finding. A third implication is that much learning can be accomplished without extensive use of oral language. When Furth and his colleagues established their model School for Thinking, most of the thinking games included in the curriculum did not involve the use of oral language (Furth and Wachs, 1975).

While these implications relate to all children, they are particularly crucial in the development of children who, for various reasons, are language disabled. The teacher should remember that use of language is not the same as concept development, and verbal explanations are not adequate substitutes for experience.

Experience Involving Action

If learning were viewed merely as an increase in knowledge, active participation on the part of the learner would not be so vital. However, if one accepts Piaget's concept that each learning involves a restructuring of the student's cognitive schemas, learner involvement becomes mandatory. How does direct experience aid in cognitive development? What criteria may be used in the selection of appropriate learning activities? When may activities not prove profitable?

In discussing the importance of experimentation in cognitive development, Wadsworth (1978) makes several important points. Most ideas are not completely wrong; they are merely incomplete. When the child makes an incorrect response and the teacher simply tells her the right answer, the child may discard all the reasoning connected to that wrong answer. What the teacher should do to promote thinking and cognitive growth is to help the child to analyze the problem again, keep the correct elements of her reasoning, and fill in the necessary details to correct the error. For example, when deciding whether an object will float or sink, heaviness is not totally wrong as a determinant; it is just not the only variable. When considering experience from this point of view, wrong answers can be as important as right ones.

Furth and Wachs (1975) suggested the following rationale for selecting worthwhile activities. (1) Let each child's success be measured in terms of bettering his own performance. Motivation is hard to maintain in the face of repeated failure. (2) Structure for individualization, not for convergence. Avoid activities that are so structured that there is only one correct

97

way to respond. (3) Provide activities that are challenging, but not overwhelming. (4) Arrange for most
of the students' time to be focused on activities, not
on the teacher. (5) Provide individual activities to
be accomplished in the company of peers. While individual effort is necessary for cognitive growth, peer
interaction provides encouragement and assistance.
(6) Become a thinking person yourself so that you can
model these qualities to your students.

Will the use of activities guarantee cognitive
development? Learning may not take place if such activities are not geared to the ability level of the
learner. Good (1979) found that college students capable of abstract thought learned science concepts
more readily if concrete objects were used. However,
students still in the concrete stage failed to comprehend these ideas despite the use of models. Activities
also may be too simple; Inskeep cautioned against the
overuse of manipulation after the students were capable of abstract reasoning (1972).

Necessity of Social Interaction

Piaget viewed social interaction as one of the
major forces in cognitive development. How do relations with others facilitate learning and mental
growth?

Peer interaction can be of great value for several reasons. First, students are apt to attach special significance to activities deemed important to
their peers. Second, peers can serve as models and/or
instructors for skills yet to be acquired. Third,
since peers are likely to be near the same cognitive
level as the learner, their explanations may be more
understandable than those of the teacher. Fourth, when
students at varying cognitive stages discuss problems,
the less advanced students may gain insights and correct inaccuracies in their thinking.

The more advanced students also profit from such
exchanges. In trying to explain a concept to others,
these students must think through their own reasoning.
In answering questions from the group, ideas may be
more clearly differentiated or expanded.

The effectiveness of group processes in facili-
tating learning has received empirical support. In one

study, children at different stages of development
shared their often contradictory views to problem situations. After these exchanges, many of the preoperational children advanced to the concrete operational
stage of thinking (Strauss, 1972). In another study,
students were placed in small classes and exposed to
many group experiences. In addition to scoring significantly higher than controls in logical and abstract
reasoning, these students showed marked gains in personality skills and social interactions (Tomlinson-
Keasey and Eisert, 1978).

Summary of Implications

　°Consider the stage characteristics of the student's thought processes in planning learning experiences.
　°Use a wide variety of experiences rather than
drill on specific tasks to maximize cognitive development.
　°Don't assume that reaching adolescence or adulthood guarantees the ability to perform formal operations.
　°Remember that each person structures each learning situation in terms of his own schemas; therefore,
no two persons will derive the same meaning or benefit
from a given experience.
　°Individualize learning experiences so that each
student is working at a level that is high enough to
be challenging and realistic enough to prevent excessive frustration.
　°Provide experience necessary for the development
of concepts prior to the use of these concepts in language.
　°Consider learning as active restructuring of
thought rather than an increase in content.
　°Make full use of wrong answers by helping the
student to analyze his thinking in order to retain the
correct elements and revise the miscomprehensions.
　°Evaluate each student in terms of improving his
own performance.
　°Avoid overuse of materials that are so highly
structured that creative thought is discouraged.
　°Use social interaction in learning experiences
to promote increases in both interest and comprehension.
　°Piaget's view on the role of a teacher can best
be summed up in his own words. "What is desired is
that the teacher cease being a lecturer satisfied with

99

transmitting ready-made solutions; his role should be, rather, that of a mentor stimulating initiative and research" (Good, 1979, p. 430).

References

Berzonsky, M.D. "Formal Reasoning in Adolescence: An Alternative View." ADOLESCENCE, 1978, vol. 13, no. 50, pp. 279-290.

DeCarcer, I.A. et al. "Implications of Piagetian Research for High School Science Teachers." SCIENCE EDUCATION, 1978, vol. 62, no. 4, pp. 571-583.

Evans, E.D. CONTEMPORARY INFLUENCES IN EARLY CHILDHOOD EDUCATION. New York: Holt, Rinehart, and Winston, 1975.

Furth, H.G. and Wachs, H. THINKING GOES TO SCHOOL: PIAGET'S THEORY IN PRACTICE. New York: Oxford University Press, 1975.

Good, R. et al. "Piaget's Work and Chemical Education." JOURNAL OF CHEMICAL ENGINEERING, 1979, vol. 56, no. 7, pp. 426-430.

Inskeep, J.E. "Building a Case for the Application of Piaget's Theory and Research in the Classroom" ARITHMETIC TEACHER, 1972, vol. 19 pp. 255-260.

Kirkland, E.R. "A Piagetian Interpretation of Beginning Reading Instruction." READING TEACHER, 1978, vol. 31, no. 5, pp. 497-503.

Piaget, J. THE ORIGINS OF INTELLIGENCE IN CHILDREN, New York: W.W. Norton, 1963.

Piaget, J. and Inhelder, B. THE PSYCHOLOGY OF THE CHILD, New York: Basic Books, 1969.

Strauss, S. "Learning Theories of Gagne' and Piaget: Implications for Curriculum Development." TEACHERS COLLEGE RECORD, 1972, vol. 74, no. 1, pp. 81-102.

Tomlinson-Keasey, C. and Eisert, D.C. "Can Doing Promote Thinking in the College Classroom?" JOURNAL OF COLLEGE STUDENT PERSONNEL, 1979, vol. 19, no. 2, pp. 99-105.

Wadsworth, B.J. PIAGET FOR THE CLASSROOM TEACHER. New York: Longman, 1978.

LEARNING DISABILITIES:
FUTILE ATTEMPTS AT A SIMPLISTIC DEFINITION

Roger Reger

Bateman (1964) was one of the first to give national attention to the term learning disabilities as
a way of referring to children who experience problems
in learning but who do not fit other classifications
of handicapping conditions. However, since 1964 not
much progress has been made in defining the term.

Recently at least two major journals in the field
of special education have seen fit to produce editor-
ial comment about the problem of definition. In Academic Therapy. Greenlee and Hare (1978) note, "Professionals find it difficult at present to agree upon a
single definition. Stating what the category is not
seems to be much easier than defining specific criteria for inclusion" (p. 346). In the Journal of
Learning Disabilities, Senf (1977) observes, "There is
another impediment to the orderly accumulation of
knowledge involving both research and practice: the
definition of those termed learning disabled" (p. 37).

Obviously there is a problem. After more than 10
years of struggling with defining what a learning disability is, it seems time to consider the effort that
such effort is futile. The effort may be futile as
long as the search continues along the path taken to
date. The underlying assumption among those who try
to define the term seems to be that somewhere in the
maze of complexities there is a hidden area of common-
ality, that within the population of children there is
a mysterious but as yet undiscovered homogeneity. The
major model used in conceptualizing learning disabilities is a discrepancy model -- a child performs lower

than is expected. The expected level of performance is almost always based on age and measured intelligence.

The Paradox

Despite all the definition problems, there exist today many programs for children classified as learning disabled. How is it possible to call children learning disabled and place them in programs designed specifically for the learning disabled if, in fact, there is no definition of learning disabilities? Part of the answer is that a definition does exist, at least enough of a definition to move programs forward. There is a saying, perhaps apocryphal, that according to aerodynamic theory the bumble bee is not supposed to fly because its size and weight are too large for its wings, but the bee flies anyway.

Even with definitional problems, there is an overriding need to provide special educational services for children who are not responding to the regular school program. This need has been so great and so apparent to such a large number of people that action has been taken without the sanction of acceptable ways of precise categorization and classification. As with the small town fire department that wanted a two-week notice before every fire, the population has been unable to meet the requirements for orderliness and predictability.

A Discussion

With the exception of people at the very extremes of human differences, there probably has never been a successful effort to sort people into discrete, unique categories that allow for precise predictability. Probably no test designer claims that any test in itself can slot people into absolutely discrete categories; some traits or characteristics are prominent or more likely to be observed in one person rather than another. Yet when it comes to learning disabilities, the continuing search is for the absolutely discrete: this child is learning disabled, and the evidence shows he is similar in characteristics to all other children classified as learning disabled and different from all others not so classified.

Even a casual historical perspective suggests that the unidimensional, single-factor trait discrepancy model of learning disability never will result in a satisfactory definition. Human behavior is multidimensional; each dimension interacts with every other dimension, and these are in constant interaction with multi-environmental factors. This is not to deny that gross predictions can be made about human behavior, especially from an actuarial viewpoint. However, it is not the gross behavior that is causing the definitional problem; it is the single-case, unique individual who has many characteristics in common with those who share the problems as well as those who do not share them.

Ultimately the term learning disabilities has to be defined in a certain context. It is not a discrete category. What is called a learning disability in one context is viewed a different way in another context. This is not unusual. The supposedly objective classification of mental retardation is subject to exactly the same conditions. In some school districts there will be more children classified as mentally retarded than in others. Indeed, even in the same school district one building will produce more mentally retarded children than other buildings while some may produce none. This is not necessarily due to actual differences in the children but due to attitudes, expectations, curriculum, professional sophistication, parental involvement, funding and service availabilities, and even to differences among the behaviors of such persons as school psychologists.

Consider only the attitude dimension. One school may have a permeating attitude that children in school should want to learn; if they do not want to or cannot learn, they do not belong there. Contrast this with a school having an attitude that all children belong in school, that each teacher is responsible for how each child learns, and that every child's needs will be accommodated. Typically in the first school, a psychologist will be expected to keep very busy testing children so that the nonresponders can be more appropriately placed. In the second school, the faculty will be seeking new materials, ideas, and services to help them fulfill their responsibilities. In the first school, removing a nonresponding child is the first priority; in the second, it is the last resort.

Why, then, are expectations about the definition

of learning disabilities greater than those for all other special education categories? In large part, undoubtedly, the reason lies in the illusory belief that all other categories have objective definitions. The child called "mentally retarded" is stereotypically similar in significant characteristics to all other children called "mentally retarded" and different in significant characteristics from all children not called "mentally retarded."

The Way It Is Done

The literature contains many estimates of the numbers of learning disabled children. These figures range from small percentages up to 30% or more. Nobody seems to know how the figures are derived; apparently they pop out of the heads of experts. Sometimes the figures are justified on the basis of the results of scores on achievement tests. An expert may decide that all children who score below average (which obviously would be 50%) are learning disabled, or some arbitrary cut-off area may be designated as the area of the learning disabled, such as one standard deviation below the average.

But the question remains: How, in fact, are children today really classified as learning disabled? Typically, the way it is done is conceptually quite simple. A child is viewed by parents and/or teachers as having learning problems in school. With or without a psychological evaluation (which typically functions to rule out mental retardation), a group of people meet formally or informally to review objective performance data and then make a subjective decision on classification.

The objective performance data usually are reading and math test scores, examples of work done in the classroom, observations of behavior from a management viewpoint, and comparisons in other ways with children of the same age and grade. The subjective decision is based on what the group feels is appropriate and inappropriate, the degree of differences, and significantly the probable chances of success with or without the classification (and presumed placement). Available services, whether or not special funding is available, and attitudes and personalities are also involved. The definition is based on the homeostatic needs of the particular educational and social environment, including the needs of the child.

If this description is reasonably accurate, there are implications on a large scale for legislation and funding. The only practical way to fund programs for children classified as learning disabled is on an actuarial basis: a certain arbitrarily defined maximum percentage of designated school populations would be fundable as learning disabled. This, in fact, has been recognized in Public Law 94-142. Test scores of various kinds may be used as rationalizations for different percentage allocations in different settings, such as larger cities compared with suburban or rural areas.

The problem is that without special additional funding many children would not receive the help they need. With a restrictive definition the results would be the same for some children who have problems, but do not fit the definition and thus would not be eligible for help under the learning disability category because their performance, even though failing in grade, still is consistent with "expectations."

By actuarial limitations on funding, each local school district would make its own decisions on the classification of children for receiving special educational services based on whatever specific criteria were considered locally appropriate. By this method all children requiring services would be eligible whether or not they fit into existing slots that too often are narrow and exclude children from service. The problem for each school would be to establish a local cut-off point for determining who needs special educational services.

The reason for funding limitations is that no legislature is going to provide special education funding for more than a limited percentage of the school population. While it may be possible to offer evidence that 50% of a school is learning disabled, such action strains the credibility of the school in the eyes of those who control purse strings. To the average legislator, handicapped children are a relatively small proportion of the population. They are aware that in one way or another almost every child could be called handicapped (by size, weight, popularity, parent status, etc.), but they also are aware that by calling all children handicapped, something significant is lost. A blind child elicits more legislative sympathy than a child who is reading at the 49th percentile.

This is not new; it is only a description of what has existed for the past few years. What is necessary is that the practices should be legitimately recognized and sanctioned, with perhaps some procedural guidelines provided. There are ways of funding special education programs without uniformly inclusive categorical definitions. Consider again the category of emotional disturbance, which has almost no definitional parameters unless one considers the opinion of a psychologist and/or psychiatrist as a "definition."

Many issues remain with definition. There is an issue about the implications of the disability presumption when a child experiences learning problems. The literature seldom or never touches upon the contribution made to learning problems of children not only by schools and teachers but also by parents. Since the middle of this century there has been a reaction against the Freudian assertion that psychological problems stem primarily from relationships with parents; the child disability notion continues to protect parents from responsibility for their child's learning problems. While finger-pointing to assess blame does little or no good once a problem has been discovered, it may be helpful in some instances if parent responsibility was recognized when it comes to remedial efforts.

Finally, the entire labeling process requires considerable review and change. Why is it necessary for a child to be labeled -- in effect, called a derogatory name -- before help can be offered? Add to this the stereotyping that follows labeling and the implications of stereotypical treatment rather than individualized treatment.

There is much to be initially done, most conceptually. While many people in the field want to get on with shovels and bricks -- and tests of statistical significance -- it is first necessary to have a conceptual plan. We are building something today, but we do not quite know what it is.

EVERY STUDENT A SUCCESS:
IMPROVING SELF-IMAGE
TO INCREASE LEARNING POTENTIAL

Lloyd P. Campbell

Educators agree that a negative self-concept is
one of the most prevalent factors in preventing youngsters from achieving their optimum learning potential.
Classroom teachers seeking a solution to such a problem find that far too often journal articles provide
appropriate description of the student with a problem
of self-concept, but typically offer little prescription as to how the teacher can assist the student to
overcome the problem and maximize learning.

The willingness of many students to become actively involved in classroom learning is contingent
upon the degree to which they feel they are an important and respected member of the class. It is imperative that the teacher provide appropriate opportunities, within the first few weeks of a new semester,
for the students to become more knowledgeable about
one another. One method that works extremely well is
to instruct students to identify recent successes they
have had. These could involve family, social, church,
work, or sports life. Most students can identify three
to four accomplishments that they will be willing to
share with classmates.

The class is divided into groups of four to six
students, and they are asked to share their successes
with their group members. Students enjoy this activity and often learn of important, unique, and even significant accomplishments of classmates. At the conclusion of this phase of the activity, the teacher can
create new groups by having two members from one group
join with two members of another group. The two

Reprinted from the NATIONAL ASSOCIATION OF SECONDARY
SCHOOL PRINCIPALS BULLETIN, 65 (441): 76-78 (January
1981), by permission of author and publisher.

members are responsible for introducing each other.

Accentuate the Positive

Another way to facilitate knowing and appreciating each class member is to spotlight members of the class (after entire class is reassembled). The teacher might say, "What do you think we (the entire class) should know about _____?" Classmates respond by sharing this person's strengths as they remember them. This exercise is an excellent way to accentuate the positive accomplishments of students and will often lead to promoting the development of friendships both inside and outside the classroom. This kind of student rapport produces a classroom where students appreciate both self and others, an environment which produces the greatest opportunity to maximize learning.

A second way to accentuate student success is through use of the bulletin board. Often overlooked by teachers, the bulletin board can be one of the most useful means to highlight student successes. A recommended approach is to utilize one of the classroom bulletin boards for "Very Important Persons." Each student in the class would be spotlighted during the semester. For example, if one had 30 students and a 90-day semester, a different student would be spotlighted every three days.

Appearing on the bulletin board would be the student's picture, a profile of past and present major achievements, and aspirations for the future. The student is responsible for designing, decorating, and completing all aspects of "putting his or her life before others." Being the VIP is a source of pride for each student and creates the kind of self-respect that promotes learning. Students look forward to finding out more about the lives of those whom they see and interact with each day.

A third approach to highlighting student success is the "Expert for the Moment" approach. Most students have some area of interest in which they spend a great deal of time -- the arts, sports, hobbies, travel, reading, etc. At some time during the semester each student might be assigned a day when he is to share his "expertise" in the most creative and appropriate fashion he chooses. The time for this activity can vary from five to 30 minutes and should be arranged with each student. Students will do such things as field questions from classmates, allow classmates to view collections (stamps, butterflies, coins, etc.). This approach to building positive self-concept in students is especially rewarding. Students get a chance to share something they do well in a way that emphasizes the uniqueness and worth of each person.

The suggestions for building positive self-concept in students as described in this article do more than that. These activities also build a respect for others, classroom rapport, and a camaraderie not found in the typical classroom. In such an environment, students become supportive of each other; therefore, learning opportunities are maximized. As described by Abraham Maslow in his Hierarchy of Human Needs, when one feels secure in his relationships with those around him, the task of learning becomes easier.

If teachers are serious about making <u>every</u> <u>student</u> <u>a</u> <u>success</u>, the careful use and planning of such activities as those described in this article can be a step in that direction. Such an effort can pay rich dividends for both the students and the teacher. Those teachers who want to build the kind of positive self-concept and classroom rapport described in this article are encouraged to implement these activities.

CAN SCHOOLS TEACH KIDS VALUES?

Amitai Etzioni

Complete the following sentence:

A cop stops a speeding car; he sees it's the President of the United States! He says...

Answer the following question:

Under what circumstances would you try to pass a toll machine without paying the fee?

_____Only if I were certain that I would not be caught.

_____If I felt I had a good chance of not getting caught.

_____Never, under any circumstances.

_____Only if I needed the money desperately, like for family food supplies.

Using such educational materials, often both somewhat provocative and somewhat inane (How likely is it that the patrolman would not notice the President until after he stops his limousine? How much food could money from a toll possibly buy?), teachers are trying to provide the hottest new item in post-Watergate curriculums: moral education.

A 1975 Gallup Poll of a random sample of adult Americans reports that 4 out of 5 favor instruction in morals and moral behavior in the schools.

Reprinted from TODAY'S EDUCATION, 66 (3): 29-39 (September-October 1977), by permission of author and publisher.

110

Behind the surprisingly broad consensus that schools need to provide more moral education is considerable disagreement as to what the nature of the problem is, what is to be taught, and how.

What parents, educators, and community leaders perceive as the problem moral education should address depends largely on their upbringing and whether their outlook on personal and political issues is liberal, conservative, or some mixture of both. Thus, many who term themselves conservatives are alarmed about the decline in religion while crime, sexual permissiveness, and rebellion against authority are on the increase. In contrast, many liberals identify as the nation's major moral defects what they see as a disregard for basic human rights and civil liberties, persistence of poverty, "social injustice," and exploitation by institutions.

Various groups use different cue words to signal their views regarding the underlying sources and appropriate remedies for the nation's ethical malaise. Thus, the American Bar Association refers to the need for "law-related" studies in schools, implying that the ethical instruction students require is in more respect for and obedience to the law.

On the other hand, the followers of Harvard's Lawrence Kohlberg favor the term <u>moral reasoning</u> (rather than compliance), which aptly conveys their view that at its highest level, morality is "creative," entailing the capacity to form and follow principles higher than the code of one's community. Thus, in a story used by Kohlberg to teach moral reasoning, Helga must decide whether or not to hide her friend Rachel from the Gestapo -- clearly a violation of the law of the land but an ethical act according to the "higher law" of conscience.

U.S. Office of Education officials, trying to sidestep the political booby traps risked in following one path or another, prefer terms such as <u>civic education</u>, <u>civic ethics</u>, or <u>citizen/moral education</u> - terms that presumably encompass some of everything.

It is impossible here to do justice to the plethora of educational philosophies, theories, and techniques competing with one another to shape how the schools are to take on moral education. Apologies to those whose favorite technique is left out in this brief Cook's tour.

Giving the Blue-Eyed the Blues. Jane Elliott, a third grade teacher at Community Elementary School in Riceville, Iowa, came up with a method sufficiently imaginative and arresting to become the subject of an ABC News documentary ("The Eye of the Storm") and a book (A CLASS DIVIDED by William Peters). But few schools seemingly have followed her lead.

In 1968, Elliott wanted to teach her students the injustice of discrimination, but she sensed that just talking about the arbitrariness and unfairness of race prejudice would be too academic to have much impact. Her inspiration was to appeal directly to the kids' capacities for empathetic insight by declaring a day of discrimination against the blue-eyed. She began by "explaining" the innate superiority of the "cleaner," "more civilized," "smarter" brown-eyed. She moved all the blue-eyed to the back of the room to the tune of self-satisfied snickers from the brown-eyed. She then informed the blue-eyed children that they would not be permitted to play on the big playground equipment at recess and could only play with brown-eyed children if they were invited. Throughout the day she was con-spicuously more tolerant of mistakes by brown-eyed children.

The brown-eyed lorded it over the blue-eyed, who soon showed signs of insecurity and loss of confi-dence. One blue-eyed girl, used to being popular, did poorly in class and walked around in a fog after being given the "treatment" by her erstwhile friends.

After reversing the roles, Elliott had every child write about how it felt to be discriminated against. Though to many adults the procedure may sound more than a bit heavy-handed, as far as the kids were concerned, the experience "took" and had a pro-found impact.

Moral Dilemmas. A tamer method of moral educa-tion is discussion of "moral dilemmas." Thus, the students in a Pittsburgh junior high school started their civics class one morning with a brief "moral di-lemma."

Sharon and Jill were best friends. One day they went shopping together. Jill tried on a sweater and then, to Sharon's surprise, walked out of the store wearing the sweater under her coat. A moment later, the store's security officer stopped Sharon and demanded that she tell him the name of the girl who had walked out....

(This dilemma appeared in Barry K. Beyer's article: "Conducting Moral Discussions in the Classroom," SOCIAL EDUCATION, April 1976. It is based on a story created by Frank Alessi.)

The teacher confronted the class: Should Sharon tell?

George: Sharon could say, "I don't even know her. I just walked in the store off the street, and I don't even know where she lives. I just met her."
Teacher: So what she ought to do is lie for a friend. Right?
George: Yah.
Teacher: What is going to happen if everyone lies whenever they feel like it, whenever it suits their convenience?...Peter.
Peter: If everyone goes around shoplifting, if someone goes and steals a whole bunch of things from somebody's store, then you go back to your store and see everything from your store missing, do you know what kind of life that would be? Everybody would just be walking around stealing everybody else's stuff.
Teacher: Mary Lu, do you want to comment about what he said?
Mary Lu: Yah, but everybody doesn't steal and everybody wouldn't, and the thing is that the store owner probably has a large enough margin of profit anyway to cover some few ripoffs he might have.
George: But the store can't exist if everybody is stealing, there are so many people, and it is getting worse and worse every day....

What educators who favor this approach stress as important about such dialogues is that a discussion rather than a lecture takes place and that the teacher refrains from pronouncing his or her values and tolerates a free expression of students' viewpoints.

Also, they believe -- and are backed up by some data -- that such give-and-take improves students' awareness of moral issues, improves their ability to reason out moral issues, and leads to higher levels of moral reasoning.

113

The scholar most often cited by students of moral reasoning, Professor Kohlberg, suggests that children move from an amoral stage toward ever greater concern with the needs and feelings of others, a sense of justice, reciprocity, and equality. Children at first believe in doing what is right only because (and as long as) violations entail punishment or conformity generates pleasure. As their capacity for morality develops naturally with age and is developed by education, they learn to behave in ways that will gain the apporoval of others. Finally, at the highest levels, they come to understand the intrinsic virtue of being law-abiding and ethical.

Kohlberg argues, and to some extent has demonstrated, that it is useless to try to get children at the most primitive stage of moral development to understand principles or modes of reasoning at the highest level. At the same time, it is possible, through proper classroom dialectics, to help children move up one stage at a time in their levels of moral reasoning.

Kohlberg's critics maintain that the link between reasoning morally and acting morally is weak, that the focus on developing the cognitive side of morality neglects the affective side, the moral commitment. This, they say, is better achieved by more emotive techniques, such as setting examples to emulate, fostering identification of the child with educators, and encouraging the right values in the child's peer group.

One vainly looks for data to provide a definitive answer as to which approach is better, as this is a field in which rhetoric is abundant and facts extremely rare. Kohlberg, though, has more data to support his view than have his critics -- which is not to say that he has much. In the end, it may well turn out that both emotional and cognitive development and education are needed.

In discussion groups conducted for 150 children, aged eight and nine, at Brentwood College in the United Kingdom, the children were told: "There are 12 in a lifeboat after a shipwreck. Four must go overboard if any are to survive." The 12 included a child of eight, a priest, an artisan, a scientist, a dog, etc. Invariably the teacher went overboard, never the child, often not the dog. It is questionable not only whether one wishes group discussions to enforce such views, but whether one wishes to encourage children to accept the _implied_ ethical notion that you do throw people overboard rather than go down with them and not kill. What is a child to learn from these extreme situations to apply to everyday life? That self-interest sanctions killing?

Values Clarification. The main champion of this approach, Sidney B. Simon of the University of Massachusetts, has just about lost count of the hundreds of schools that have purchased the "values clarification" kits he and his associates have designed.

One such school is the William W. Niles Junior High School, a school with predominantly minority students, located in the Bronx. According to Claudia Macari, assistant principal for guidance, and Mildred W. Abramowitz, principal, one of the teaching techniques they employed went something like this:

Exercise one: "Write down 20 things you love to do." Pause. "Now that you have made your lists, star the five things you love to do best of all." Pause. "Place a check after the things you love to do alone." Pause. "Place a cross after the things you love to do with other people." Pause. "Circle the things that cost you less than $3 to do." Pause. "Write the date of the last time you did each of these things."

Macari and Abramowitz explain that the purpose of having the students choose the five out of 20 things they like best is to make them aware of what it is they value. The whole idea of values clarification is _not_ to instill or introduce any particular values, new or old, but to help students discover those they already have. Having to decide which 15 items to leave out, which five to include, leads the youngsters to an understanding of the concept of values, i.e., of the choices inevitably involved. Moreover, the theory stresses that "exercising" one's values via such paper and pencil exercises will help students hold on more firmly to their values. As with other facilities, so with the capacity to form and sustain values: If you don't use it, you lose it.

The other questions in this exercise aim at helping a person gain insight into what he or she values and why (e.g., Do you prefer to do things with others or by yourself? Do the things you like to do cost a lot of money?)

115

There are no right and wrong answers in values-clarification exercises. Any and all answers are considered "right" as long as one can give a reason for them. Asked whether a youngster might not therefore end up reaffirming "wrong" values, such as thievery, the designers of the approach reply, "...our position is that we respect his right to decide that value."

Critics point to this moral neutrality as a main weakness of the approach. Granted that preaching a code and testing students to see if they subscribe to it may well be inappropriate, ineffectual, or both, does it follow that teachers must imply that all values are equally valid? Others claim that it is precisely this principled amorality of the values-clarification package that is the chief reason for its popularity in the public schools, which are thereby protected from having to choose whose values to teach. At the same time, whatever directions for teacher neutrality the kit contains, each teacher is in fact free to lead the discussion of each exercise as he or she sees fit -- and to decide just how neutral to be if confronted with a classroom full of 13-year-old Machiavellians.

Actually, it seems to me, few teachers can hide their feelings on views when issues such as abortion, women's rights, and injustice to minorities are discussed in the classroom. Body language, tone of voice, allotment of more time to speak to kids who have the desired answer, if not outright statements of advocacy, are sure to cue the class as to what side of the issue the teacher is on. Whatever limited teacher training comes with the moral education kits cannot hope to neutralize teachers' ethical feelings or put them completely out of view.

Nor may this be as important as the advocates of the kits believe it to be. Pupils are exposed to a variety of views of different teachers, coaches, parents, peers; they can well evolve their moral positions out of the competing variety of positions they face, rather than in an artificial moral vacuum.

Several educators have emphasized that schools "impact" children not only -- and indeed probably not even primarily -- via the curriculum taught in class, but by the way the schools themselves are structured. It has long been understood that children learn from their parents by emulation -- as is acknowledged in the well-known saw of the parent who himself sets a bad example: "Do as I say, not as I do!" The same notion is applicable to the ethics taught in school: The way teachers, administrators, coaches, and other school officials interact with children teaches ethical values by example -- or sets some contrary example of petty tyranny, hypocrisy, or see-no-evil mentality. These comprise the school's "hidden curriculum."

After talking to students, I find that the core of the hidden curriculum revolves around such subjects as grades, athletics, and exploitation of some students by others (e.g., extortion). School officials' attitudes and actions regarding these topics often do not convey the importance of standing up for ethical principles in the face of the pressures of self-interest or pragmatic expediency.

For example, in two schools in an Eastern state, administrators became aware that some minority pupils had formed gangs which collected a quarter a day in protection money from younger, mainly white children. For a long time, however, officials in both schools looked the other way. Why? Well, they said, they were afraid that an active effort to find out which children were in the extortion rings and punish them would open them up to charges of "police tactics."

Finally some gang members were caught in both schools. In one school, the principal sent the boys to the guidance counselor, who in turn handled the matter by asking them if perhaps their families were poor and badly needed the money. Upon establishing that they were "needy," he warned them not to extort money again.

The other principal's main concern was that it was a "no-win" situation. As he put it, "If we kick them (the extortionists) out of school, the black community will be up in arms, and we already have our hands full with everything from drugs to alcoholism to vandalism, etc." After being caught, the extortionist pupils were first suspended; then, when minority parents protested, reinstated; then, when white parents were outraged, sent to an experimental school; then, when the minority parents charged "exile," back to the original school. The principal felt no need to apologize for setting policy according to which group protested most at the time. The main issue, as he saw it, was not what to do about extortion or how his failure to do anything credible about it would affect the kids, but how to negotiate a political tightrope without falling into the vengeful hands of either set of outraged parents.

As for grades, they seem to have lost legitimacy for a large number of students. But at the same time, many students believe that nothing less than their life's fate hangs on getting into the "right" college, which in turn depends on having high grades. But since they see good grades as having little real meaning, they view what they do to get them as similarly unimportant. Thus, for quite a few students the notion that cheating on exams or term papers is a serious ethical issue is about as quaint as is the medieval scholastic debate over how many angels can dance on the head of a pin to modern theologians.

With sports, how seriously ethical issues are taken appears to vary with the sport; each sport has its own informal rules of fair play that range from just somewhat to great deal looser than the official code. Two students who play tennis said that they did believe the assistant coach wanted them to play it fair, "gentleman style," but they were somewhat unclear how strongly he felt that way.

Basketball players told me that they are trained to keep a keen eye on the referee and push another player out of the way only when the referee is not looking, although "really digging your elbow into the other guy" is going too far. Football seems to be the focus of the most intense pressures to win -- and hence the greatest temptations to win at any price. Football players expressed the feeling that the coaches want them to win any way they know how, short of pulling a face mask.

Traditionally, one of the major justifications for lavishing large sums of money on sports programs in the schools, especially competitive team sports, has been that athletics are "character-building." And indeed they very likely are -- the question that needs greater attention, however, is, "What kind of character are they building?"

The hidden curriculum's emphasis on high grades and winning in sports suggests that grades and sports are still important tools for instilling the American "success ethic;" likewise, it would seem that stimu-

118

lating the drive for success is still a major mission of the American school. The success ethic is scarcely very ethical, however, if it builds into its creed in school and afterward an attitude toward the meaning of competition and reward such as the oft-quoted motto: "Winning is not the most important thing, it's the only thing." Competition may well build character and be compatible with an industrious society. Unbounded competition, however, is incompatible with any ethical code or social order; it puts self above all.

Of all the approaches to moral education, the one that focuses on the reform of the hidden curriculum is likely to be both the most relevant and the most difficult to accomplish, because teachers and students are less aware of its moral implications than they are of the formal curriculum and because its roots lie in what the community values most. It is hence far from accidental that when Kohlberg tried to apply his ideas about how best to foster higher levels of moral reasoning in the schools, he ended up having to set up an experimental alternate school. (The school is run on participatory principles. Each pupil and staff member has one vote and "no major decisions or commitments are made without consulting the entire community.")

While this solution is entirely suitable to Kohlberg's experimental purposes, most of America is probably far from ready for such a radically egalitarian approach to the public school's authority structures. Most schools require reforms if they are to provide a just allotment of grades which pupils perceive as relevant, sports played to learn respect for rules (not just to win), the hidden curriculum as much as possible in line with what is taught in ethics classes.

The objection may well be raised that a school structured to produce more ethical youth would of necessity fail in its major mission of adequately preparing its students for later life. Such a view is especially likely to be espoused by those who believe that the American success ethic, though indeed subtler now than in its nineteenth-century form, still owes a lot to the unapologetic amorality displayed by Tammany boss George Washington Plunkitt, who, in defining what he called "honest graft," said "I seen my opportunities and I took 'em."

One could counter this criticism somewhat stiffly and stubbornly perhaps, by steadfastly maintaining that the schools have a duty to educate their students morally -- over and above whatever the prevalent societal standards are. At the very least, then the students will have some principles to compromise later on, and though their standards may fall, they may nonetheless not stoop so low as they would have if they started out with no such scruples. True, most schools cannot proceed very far in promoting values not shared by the community at large. Hence, ultimately, whether via the hidden curriculum or the conventional one, before the schools can effectively provide moral education, the surrounding community must care about morality and work to reform itself.

What is thus required now is for all concerned to get together to focus on the question: How can our schools be restructured to make them sources of ethical experiences rather than, as they too often are, training grounds for cheating, intolerance, coping with bureaucratic or arbitrary authority?

The present period seems especially opportune for attempting such a change. We are now in an era in which various elements of society have had to confront questions of ethicality, of how to formulate and move toward higher standards of conduct. The schools can act as either accelerator or brake on this ethical drive.

Part 3

TECHNIQUES OF TEACHING

AND TESTING

COMPETENCY TESTING:
A SOCIAL AND HISTORICAL PERSPECTIVE

Vito Perrone

An Introductory Statement

The kinds of testing that have come to dominate discussions of educational standards in our schools grow out of a twentieth century belief that language, intelligence, achievement, and the like are subject to assessment through a series of relatively simple multiple-choice, paper and pencil exercises. While doubts about these testing practices -- their underlying assumptions and validity -- are escalating rapidly among educators, students, and parents, use of these testing practices also is increasing.

The current debate over testing in the United States is beginning to focus on the minimal competency movement and a range of related procedures governing grade promotion and high school graduation -- not because other testing practices in the schools are benign, but because competency testing programs have become very popular among state legislatures and departments of education and are being advocated as vehicles for bringing about an overall improvement in the quality of the schools. In order to make a discussion of this latest effort more intelligent, let us place it within a larger historical perspective, as well as raise some of the related measurement problems and educational dilemmas that need more thorough examination.

Current Context for Competency Testing

What is the basis upon which thirty-five states, either through legislative mandates or state education

Reprinted from EDUCATIONAL HORIZONS, 58 (1): 3-8 (Fall 1979), by permission of author and publisher.

agency regulations, have instituted competency testing? Winsor Lott, Chief of the Bureau of Elementary and Secondary Educational Testing, New York State Department of Education, provides a straightforward response that epitomizes the related national literature:

> There are probably two reasons for the current interest in basic Competency Testing throughout the Nation. First, there is concern that schools are awarding high school diplomas to individuals who lack some of the basic skills, who can't read and write, for example. In addition, because of the cost of education, there is a continuing interest in accountability. Here it seems (that) various state legislatures...are demanding proof that the schools are doing a good job and that taxpayers are getting something of value for their investment. (Personnel and Guidance Association Newsletter, 1977, p. 2.)

The foregoing statement relates to the erosion of confidence in the schools that has characterized the decade of the 1970s, with the debate over test score-accountability declines and educational costs representing popular strands. Shalock, a serious student of the competency education movement, in the statement below suggests that "technological" advances also have contributed to the current level of interest:

> Another condition that has contributed is the remarkable progress that has been made over the past decade in the technology of instruction, assessment and information management. The emergence of the performance or goal based instruction movement, the concept of mastery learning, and the development of criterion tested instructional materials are cases in point....The information storage and retrieval capabilities now available through computer technology, and the evaluation strategies for data management and utilization in decision making makes it possible to apply effectively the instruction and assessment capabilities previously unavailable to schools (Shalock, 1976, pp. 1-2).

The "current context" is outlined above in high relief -- clearly, the context is larger, more subtle, and more complex. Readers should, however, keep this high relief in mind as we turn now to an historical review.

Historical Perspective

Before directing this discussion to efforts to use tests to certify whether individual students have succeeded with various levels of education or to determine basic educational standards that exist in schools, it is important to comment on historical perspective in general. Public education in the United States has a history almost as long as the republic itself, yet we lack extensive historical accounts of schools and their interaction with the culture at large. In large measure, this is the case because educators have not seen historical perspective as critical to the improvement of schools. If we had, for example, better descriptions of school curricula, organizational patterns, and instructional processes, as well as the political, economic, and social factors that influenced them, we might have a better grasp of what educational reform demands. Lacking historical perspective, we enter often into what are viewed as new directions for reform without a sufficient base or inclination for examining earlier but similar efforts and their contexts. Competency testing is among a number of contemporary examples and the one that we will use to illustrate the point.

The Boston schools, in 1845, instituted a common secondary education certifying examination, and the New York Legislature, in 1877, established a system of examinations "to furnish a suitable standard of secondary school graduation." By the turn of the century, most states had testing programs affecting promotions and graduations. To be sure, these early examinations were not of the multiple-choice variety (that technology developed most notably in the post-1910 period) but their effects were not dissimilar. What were the consequences of this early testing?

The certifying examination had, for the most part, negative consequences for minorities and the poor. Their failure rate tended to be high, and few went into the secondary schools. At the turn of the century, such a circumstance was not viewed adversely by educators, politicians, or societal leaders. A wide range of social, cultural, and racial inequalities was

124

tolerated, and testing was accepted as a legitimate means for selecting students into and out of educational opportunities. Equality of educational opportunity as a matter of public policy is, after all, a post-World War II development.

Was it disastrous at the turn of the century for an individual not to complete high school? In the face of what has been said, this needs some comment. While the completion of the secondary school clearly opened up many opportunities inaccessible to those without a high school diploma, the lack of a high school diploma did not prevent the majority of individuals from gaining an economic livelihood or place them in a radically different social position than most of those around them. After all, less than 10 percent of those who began school in 1900 completed secondary education. As school attainment increased after World War I, not having the high school diploma became a larger burden, but it was almost 1950 before it became an absolute catastrophe. In 1950, 52 percent of the eighteen- and nineteen-year-old population (for the first time a majority) completed high school. This attainment figure peaked nationally in 1965 at 76 percent and has remained stable since. But throughout the twentieth century, the poor and minorities have carried most of the burden of limited school attainment.

It should be noted that this overall increase in school attainment took place as statewide examination systems that related to promotion and retention began to decline in number. By 1950, they had virtually disappeared. Accompanying the increased levels of attainment, and the growing commitment in America to expanding educational opportunities for all Americans, school programs became more diverse. A natural consequence of this diversity was that high school diplomas lost whatever common meaning they had. Surprisingly, this consequence went unnoticed, to be interpreted in the 1970s as a sudden decline in standards.

What effect did the certifying tests have on curriculum? The evidence is that the tests influenced significantly what was taught. The diaries of early twentieth-century teachers were filled with accounts of the long periods in which they prepared students for the state examinations, giving up in the process what they considered to be more engaging for the stu-

dents. The REGENTS INQUIRY INTO THE CHARACTER AND
COST OF PUBLIC EDUCATION IN NEW YORK STATE reported in
1936 that the Regents Examination had, in effect, become the curriculum. What did not appear on the examination was not taken seriously by teachers or students. The broad goals of locally established curricula were given little attention. Madaus and Airasian,
who have examined the history of certifying examinations in the United States as well as in Australia and
Europe, comment:

> Faced with a choice between one set of ob-
> jectives which are explicit in the course
> outline and a different set which are ex-
> plicit in past certifying examinations,
> students and teachers choose to focus on
> the latter. This finding holds true over
> different countries and over many decades.
> Most studies have found that the proportion
> of instructional time spent on various ob-
> jectives was seldom higher than the pre-
> dicted likelihood of their occurrence on
> the external examination (Madaus and Aira-
> sian, 1978).

And what can one say for the interest in "technological advances" that Shalock suggests is a basis
for the interest in competency testing. Technological
advances such as systems analysis, instruction by objectives, objectives-referenced testing, and mastery
learning have earlier antecedents if no greater theoretical support. (1) They are part of a longterm fas-
cination in the twentieth century with applying science to education. One has only to read Callahan's
classic EDUCATION AND THE CULT OF EFFICIENCY (1962) to
gain some historical perspective about how little such
efforts have contributed to the improvement of public
schools. (2)

Have we not had other periods where the schools
and their standards were under attack? The nineteenth
century produced a number of examples that generally
resulted in greater centralization of schools and increased levels of uniformity of school practice. Testing was a related phenomenon. (3)

Within the past half-century, we have experienced
two major debates about the quality of schools. Each
has touched off, curiously, different responses. The
first was precipitated by the Russian launching of

Sputnik in 1958, continuing through much of the 1960s. While there were some who argued for the reestablishment of state testing programs and instructional uniformity, the prevailing response was to put money into improving the quality of teacher training and instituting a wide range of curriculum development programs. At a time when governance of schools was local in nature, teacher training (preservice and inservice) and curriculum development were obvious responses. (4) On the other hand, the response to the debates in the 1970s over the quality of schools is testing. Why the difference? In large measure, this has occurred because the nature of educational governance is changing. It is clearly more complex now, with more authority resting at the state and federal levels than has ever been the case. Removed as state and federal legislators and bureaucrats are from the complexity of classrooms and the social consequences of school programs, testing has gained a simple appeal.

What does the new wave of testing emanating from state legislatures and state departments of education look like in relation to previous efforts? Walter Haney noted in several National Consortium on Testing papers that minimal competency testing programs are "not aimed at improving the quality of education for all students but instead are aimed at those toward the bottom of the educational heap." And who is at the bottom? A Congressional Budget Office Study recently reported that among high school seniors in 1972, "21 percent of the white students and 60 percent of the black students were in the lowest quartile (based upon grades, test scores, etc.)." Minority students are more often retained than nonminority students, tend as a result to be older in the secondary schools, and are more often in nonacademic programs. In Florida, for example, 30 to 40 percent more blacks are in nonacademic high school programs than whites and 20 to 50 percent more blacks than whites failed the Florida Functional Literacy Test. There is sufficient evidence already on record to demonstrate that the new wave of testing for purposes of promotion and graduation is having its most negative effect on minorities and lower socioeconomic populations. In a major publication, TESTING...GROUPING: THE NEW SEGREGATION IN SOUTHERN SCHOOLS? (Bryan and Mills, 1976), the Southern Regional Council presented its concerns about the growing interest in competency testing among the southern states.

Judging from the results of the competency testing efforts, little appears to have changed since 1900. The only difference is that in 1900 public policy had not yet coalesced around such directions as equality of educational opportunity. Does this new wave of state testing suggest that the more recent public policy commitments are faltering? It has that appearance to me!

Is "teaching to the tests," "a narrowing of curriculum," a consequence of the new wave of state testing programs? On the basis of his inquiry in Florida, Tyler reported that:

> We were told that many teachers interpreted
> the emphasis on basic skills to mean that
> they must devote most of their attention to
> routine drill. This usually results in a de-
> crease in the student's interest in schooling
> and it diminishes the time that should be de-
> voted to the meaning and the application of
> those skills (Tyler, 1979, p. 30).

During the recent Florida court case (decided against the State of Florida) in which the Functional Literacy Test and the withholding of diplomas were under question, considerable testimony was given that indicated that remediation programs established for those not succeeding on the examinations were geared almost entirely toward test items that were on the examinations. Preparation for the tests had become, for many students, the curriculum of the schools.

In a major review conducted by this author and colleagues of how teachers functioned in a Michigan school district where test scores carried major significance, it was clear that the curriculum had been narrowed, teaching to the tests being the principal curricular activity. Teacher after teacher noted that test scores were going up while the overall quality of education in the district was declining.

Schaffarzick and Walker, in summarizing the data over the past twenty years on curriculum and testing (1974), noted that it has consistently been the case that test scores reflected the degrees of emphasis placed upon the specific information asked for in the tests. Different curricula bring about, as they reported, different patterns of achievement. To follow the major research is to understand that the drive

toward minimal competency testing is a drive toward
less diversity of curriculum at a time when no significant consensus exists about what curricular patterns
ought to exist in schools.

In 1900, the victim was the student. We see a
similar consequence today. Improving education in
1900 was viewed by those supporting a growing "scientific" movement as a technical question. The nature
of existing competency programs suggests that improvement still is viewed as a technical question. That we
have not learned from our experience is disheartening!
To the degree that states expend their energies and
resources toward every-child testing programs under
the veil of accountability or minimal competency testing, they are engaged in an effort with limited educational potential and one that will most likely do little to reestablish broad public confidence in and understanding of schools and schooling. The same can be
said for all other technical efforts that tend to reduce the diversity of educational practices and programs.

Educational Dilemmas and Competency Testing

In order to provide readers with a sense of the
complexity, I have posed in this closing section a
number of questions that might help give some form to
later articles in this issue of EDUCATIONAL HORIZONS.
In large measure they serve to add to some of the earlier issues that have been raised.

How valid are the tests? Testing programs that
depend on a multiple-choice and norm- or criterion-
referenced format are relatively new in American society. While they often purport to measure one's abil
ity to read, for example, it must be clear to most
educators that they cannot represent reading as reading is commonly understood; they are at best weak indicators of reading. Persons who read very well may
select "wrong" answers from among the limited choices
available for a host of reasons that may have little
to do with their ability to read. The literature is
full of descriptions of the drawbacks that multiple-
choice formats possess; namely, single correct responses, ambiguity, cultural and linguistic bias, etc.

As another example, does competency in writing
mean knowing rules of grammar and spelling, or does it

mean the ability to make oneself clear in a written statement? In most of the tests that exist, grammar and spelling dominate. The problems multiply when efforts are made to use existing technology to make judgments about functional literacy, life-skill competency, and the like.

How are cutoff scores to be determined? If tests are used to determine promotion or high school graduation, how are cutoff scores to be determined? There is, as yet, no empirically based process for determining cutoff scores. Those that now exist are largely arbitrary, certainly subjective.

At this point, cutoff scores are being established on a political basis; for example, how many students can be held back, not given a diploma, without a serious public response? Another concern that needs to be raised in connection with the establishment of minimal standards is will the minimal standards become maximum standards?

What effect are external standards likely to have on teachers? Will their roles in schools be reduced even further, leaving them as technicians? If teachers are not free to respond to children, to particular occasions, to enter into significant inquiry into learning with children, are they likely to remain enthusiastic about their work? All of the evidence indicates that teachers in technician roles lose their commitment to intensive learning. Teaching becomes "merely a job." If we haven't learned anything else over the years, we have learned that the teacher is the critical factor in what happens for children in classrooms. And what can be said about a related concern, that of student intentions? Hampshire framed it well when he wrote: "A man becomes more and more a free and responsible agent the more he at all times knows what he is doing, in every sense of this phrase, and the more he acts with a definite and clearly formed intention" (Hampshire, 1960, p. 91). Spady and Mitchell introduce a similar concern, arguing that:

> It is not enough for state legislatures, school boards, administrators or even teachers to have clearly specified goals -- students will only achieve a higher level of devotion to their learning goals if they themselves have identified this as important and as an appropriate basis for channel-

ing their energies and actions...narrow
and constraining performance demands destroy vital student motivation (Spady and
Mitchell, 1977, p. 13).

How narrow are the external standards to become?
Because of our limited conception of human behavior
and our likewise limited ability to measure it, external standards, when established with mandates for
quantitative measurement, quickly turn to those things
easily conceived and measured. Broader, more diffuse
goals dealing with human action are difficult to
translate into specific behaviors. And even when the
translation is accomplished, the inferential leap from
behaviors to objectives tends to be great, and, in the
process, the intentional quality of human action is
lost.

So many more questions, concerns could be raised.
In spite of the questions and concerns, however, the
movement propels itself forward, not yet having to
face a substantial challenge. Cremin, in his latest
book, PUBLIC EDUCATION, writes that:

...good theory...should convey a sense of
the richness and complexity of the phenomenon
it seeks to illumine. And it is precisely
a sense of richness and complexity that has
been missing from the educational discussions
of recent years (Cremin, 1978, p. x).

Nowhere is Cremin's concern more evident than in
the competency education movement as it now is unfold-
ing. This writer's hope is that the complexity will
be realized and will become a source of critical debate before we are all led further down a trail filled
with little potential for educational improvement.

Reference Notes

1. Readers interested in this technological orientation might wish to review the following: Leon Les-
singer, EVERY KID A WINNER: ACCOUNTABILITY IN EDUCA-
TION, New York: Simon & Schuster, 1970; Richard Hos-
trop et al. (ed.) ACCOUNTABILITY FOR EDUCATIONAL RE-
SULTS, Handen, Conn: Linnett Press, 1973; PHI DELTA
KAPPAN, December 1970 issue; Bela Bethany, INSTRUC-
TIONAL SYSTEMS, Palo Alto: Fearon, 1968; Robert Gagne
(ed.), PSYCHOLOGICAL PRINCIPLES IN SYSTEM DEVELOPMENT,

New York: Holt, Rinehart and Winston, 1966; Robert Mager, PREPARING OBJECTIVES FOR INSTRUCTION, Palo Alto: Fearon, 1962; John Carrol, "A Model of School Learning," TEACHERS COLLEGE RECORD, May 1964; Benjamin Bloom, "Learning for Mastery," UCLA EVALUATION COMMENT, May 1968; Benjamin Bloom, HUMAN CHARACTERISTICS AND SCHOOL LEARNING, New York: McGraw-Hill, 1976.
2. Readers might wish also to read the long debate between Boyd Bode and Franklin Bobbit over this direction. In his 1924 book, HOW TO MAKE A CURRICULUM, Boston: Houghton Mifflin Company, Bobbit described the curriculum maker as a "great engineer." Bode's basic response can be found in his MODERN INSTRUCTIONAL THEORIES, New York: Macmillan, 1927. Lawrence Cremin, in his TRANSFORMATION OF THE SCHOOL: PROGRESSIVISM IN AMERICAN EDUCATION, New York: Knops, 1961, has several chapters devoted to our penchant for using "science" in the service of the schools.
3. Michael Katz, THE IRONY OF EARLY SCHOOL REFORM: EDUCATIONAL INNOVATION IN MID-NINETEENTH CENTURY MASSACHUSETTS. Cambridge, Mass: Harvard University Press, 1970, represents a particularly useful case study of the Boston schools and the centralization-decentralization struggle.
4. As noted earlier, the drive to increase school attainment in the twentieth century brought about a diversity of school programs. To achieve greater diversity, local control of schools took on greater meaning and state testing programs, especially for promotion and retention, declined.

References

Bryan, M.M., & Mills, R. TESTING...GROUPING: THE NEW SEGREGATION IN THE SOUTHERN SCHOOLS? Atlanta: Southern Regional Council, 1976.

Callahan, R. EDUCATION AND THE CULT OF EFFICIENCY. Chicago: University of Chicago Press, 1962.

Cremin, L. PUBLIC EDUCATION. New York: Basic Books, 1978.

Hampshire, S. THOUGHT AND ACTION. New York: Viking Press, 1960.

Madaus, G. & Airasian, P. MEASUREMENT ISSUES AND CONSEQUENCES ASSOCIATED WITH MINIMAL COMPETENCY TESTING. National Consortium on Testing, May 1978.

PERSONNEL AND GUIDANCE ASSOCIATION NEWSLETTER, New York, Spring 1977.

Schaffarzick, H.D. & Walker, D. "Comparing Curricula," REVIEW OF EDUCATIONAL RESEARCH, 1974, 44 (1), 83-111.

Shalock, H.D. ALTERNATIVE MODELS OF COMPETENCY BASED EDUCATION. Salem, Oregon: Northwest Educational Laboratory, 1976 (N.I.E. Contract #400-76-028).

Spady, W. & Mitchell, D. "Competency Based Education: Organizational Issues and Implications, EDUCATIONAL RESEARCHER, February 1977.

Tyler, R. "The Minimal Competency Movement: Origin, Implications, Potential and Dangers, NATIONAL ELEMENTARY PRINCIPAL, January 1979, p. 30.

MINIMUM COMPETENCY TESTING: A PROPONENT'S VIEW

Jacob G. Beard

Since 1976, a considerable amount of space in educational journals has been devoted to the conceptualization and definition of "competency-based education" and "minimum competency testing." These two concepts are related; but for the purposes of this paper minimum competency testing will be discussed without exploring the full range of issues involved in competency-based education. Minimum competency testing involves the administration of proficiency tests in order to certify that minimum competency or proficiency exists with regard to a well-defined set of knowledge or skills. In Florida, as in most states, students are required to demonstrate the ability to apply the basic skills of reading, writing, and arithmetic to the solution of problems encountered in everyday living. The tests include basic knowledge and skills learned by most students at or below the eighth-grade level, and do not attempt to cover the full range of topics included in the high school curriculum. However, New York State's new Regents Competency Testing Program will include "high school-level material" in their minimum competency test scheduled for the graduating class of 1981 (New York State, 1979).

These testing programs usually are included in a larger educational program that makes provisions for diagnosis and attempted remediation of achievement deficiencies before, in some but not all cases, ultimately denying the student a regular high school diploma. Making the diploma contingent upon passing the test has created a great deal of controversy and has resulted in litigation in the State of Florida.

Why Competency Testing?

The competency-based education movement was de-

Reprinted from EDUCATIONAL HORIZONS, 58 (1): 9-13 (Fall 1979), by permission of author and publisher.

scribed by Spady (1977) as "a bandwagon in search of a definition." The magnitude of the bandwagon effect is seen in the fact that over thirty states recently have moved to initiate some type of competency testing program, with several others in the process of doing so, according to a report prepared by the Education Commission of the States (Pipho, Note 1).

The minimum competency testing movement is fueled from several sources. It has widespread popular appeal to citizens and politicians who see it as a way of holding schools accountable and forcing them "back to the basics." These groups are convinced that the quality of public education has been eroded over a period of years and that high schools are graduating significant numbers of students who are unable to read and write, and, consequently, unable to support themselves through gainful employment. This view has been suggested or reinforced by educators' reports of declining test scores. Furthermore, reports of grade inflation have raised doubts about the achievement standards that teachers use in evaluating and grading students.

Teachers and school administrators also generally support minimum competency testing because it operationalizes previously vague concepts of accountability, and because it motivates low-achieving students to study. The lack of such motivation has been a source of frustration to teachers and has caused serious discipline problems in the schools. The imposition of minimum competency requirements adds credibility to the teachers' claims that the underlying instructional objectives are worthwhile by attaching a specific reward to their mastery.

The basic concepts involved in minimum competency testing have been derived from instructional systems theory and use criterion-referenced testing methodology. While many of the testing programs incorporate only to a small degree the basic principles of "competency-based education" and "credit by examination," they nevertheless reflect the initial attempts of legislators and administrators to incorporate these theories into school practice.

The current interest in minimum competency testing can be viewed as merely a part of the evolutionary trend in American educational systems toward a more behavioristic approach. The trend already has resulted in widespread interest in behavioral objectives, criterion-referenced testing, individualized instruction, and, more recently, competency-based education. Therefore, these testing programs are not a unique fad. Rather, they fit into the overall scheme of things and are the product of educational theory, although the products may not always be recognizable by the theorists.

Possible Effects of Minimum Competency Testing

The proponents and opponents of minimum competency testing have attributed a large number of possible effects to its implementation. The number of effects is so large that if they were taken seriously, one would be forced to conclude that the movement is of immense significance and will revolutionize education. The truth is that the effects of current programs, positive and negative, are largely unknown, but probably of less immediate significance than one would infer from the arguments.

The following effects have been claimed in litigation (Civil Action, Note 2) or mentioned by educators in published articles or papers (Mitchell and Spady, 1978; Pinkney, 1979; Blau, Note 3; and others):

°<u>Discrimination against minority students</u>. While educators have debated the positive and negative effects of minimum competency testing, the most serious challenges have been brought by legal groups representing black children. The class-action suit brought on behalf of black children who failed Florida's test against the Florida Board of Education and the Board of Public Instruction of Hillsborough County charged that the statutory scheme under which the test is required was racially discriminatory and a deprivation of due process. The plaintiffs charged that placing those students who failed in remedial programs "carries forward the effects of prior and continuing racial discrimination and unfairly penalizes, stigmatizes and resegregates black students who have suffered the effects of prior and continuing racial discrimination in the public schools" (Civil Action, Note 2).

The defendants claimed that a major purpose of the program was to identify students who had not learned to apply the basic skills of reading, writing,

136

and arithmetic; and to provide remedial instruction so
the students would not suffer the ill effects which
absence of such skills would occasion in the everyday
world. The state legislature had appropriated 36 million dollars during the preceding two years for remedial instruction, and Hillsborough County had had a
remedial program in operation for approximately four
years. The defendants brought several witnesses from
the school districts who testified that the program
had had a beneficial effect on learning of the basic
skills in their schools.

The plaintiffs also argued that insufficient time
for remediation had been allowed the graduating class
of 1979, since the law was passed in the spring of
1976 and the first of three administrations for this
class occurred in October 1977.

The court adjudged the legislative act that established the minimum competency testing requirement
for graduation to constitute a violation of the equal
protection clause of the Fourteenth Amendment to the
United States Constitution for black students who fail
the test before the 1982-83 school year. The schedule
for the implementation of the statute was found to be
a violation of the due process clause of the Fourteenth Amendment, and the state was enjoined from use
of the functional literacy test as a requirement for
high school graduation until the 1982-83 school year.
That is the first year in which black students would
generally have been enrolled in integrated schools
throughout their twelve years of education.

The memorandum opinion in this case should be
studied carefully by those responsible for implementing minimum competency testing programs affecting high
school graduation. It should be noted that the legis
lative act and the schedule were found to be unconstitutional. Many other claims of test inadequacy were
considered by the court and not found in themselves to
be of significant magnitude to prevent its usage.

°Increase in drop-out rates. Opponents of minimum competency testing programs claim that final failure rates are understated because significant numbers
of students who initially fail the tests drop out of
school to avoid the experience of remediation and the
possibility of not eventually receiving the diploma
even after remediation efforts. Empirical support of
this argument has not been presented, and the super-

intendent of one medium-sized Florida school district testified in the Florida court case that an initial analysis showed that the drop-out rate had declined for the past four years. Certainly, the drop-out rates of states implementing these testing programs should be monitored closely to insure that low achievers are not merely dropping out, an occurrence that would be inconsistent with the purposes of such programs and would falsely give the appearance of increasing academic achievement.

°<u>Stigmatization of failures.</u> These tests have been created, in part, as a response to claims that schools are graduating illiterate students, and the tests are sometimes called "functional literacy tests." The term "functional literacy" has two major problems associated with it: (a) it is a term having multiple meanings and for which there is no consensus among scholars as to its exact definition; and (b) it is a term that generally communicates to the public-at-large so well that it is over used and over interpreted. Opponents of these programs claim that students who fail the tests are burdened with the stigma of illiteracy, which is harmful and serves no useful educational purpose. Proponents of the programs, while they may feel that the term is reasonably descriptive of the results, would like to replace it with a less emotion-laden one that operationally describes the test results. The Florida Cabinet, meeting as the State Board of Education, officially changed the name of Florida's "Functional Literacy Test" to "Student Assessment Test - Part II" (Minutes of the Florida Board of Education, Note 4).

°<u>Adverse economic effects.</u> Opponents of minimum competency testing programs argue that many, and perhaps most, jobs require a high school diploma for entrance, and that to deny persons the diploma is to reduce seriously their opportunities for earning a living. Proponents claim that it is the education that the diploma represents, rather than the diploma itself, which makes persons employable, and that the employment process is facilitated by associating standards of achievement with the diploma.

°<u>State testing and local curriculum control.</u> Minimum competency testing programs typically are administered from the state level, whereas curricula are determined at the local district level. This raises questions about such tests' curricular validity, that

138

is, correspondence of the test content to the curriculum content for the various districts and schools. Such tests can deal only with content that is included in the curricula of all schools. Tests of basic reading and arithmetic skills are more likely to have curricular validity than tests that deal with the broader range of high school subjects, because the basic skills are prerequisite to most academic learning.

Some freedom of districts to determine what is taught in the schools must be relinquished to the state level when statewide testing programs are established. However, local control of curriculum has been a myth for some time, because the curriculum for most schools is rather fully determined by state and national policies. Indeed, the idea of each school district's separately determining a largely unique curriculum simply is not consistent with current practice.

°<u>Motivation.</u> Proponents of minimum competency testing claim that the programs result in heightened motivation to learn, especially on the part of those students in the lower portions of the achievement range. Many of these students have been moved through the grades by social promotion and do not necessarily associate progress through the grades with academic achievement. Teachers have experienced a great deal of difficulty in maintaining academic standards in the classes in which these students are enrolled and have come to feel that they are alone in their struggle to maintain any sort of academic standards. It became evident in Florida that most high school students attach great value to a diploma, and they and their parents became aroused when the prospect of their receiving one was threatened. Suddenly, the school system moved from a condition where little concern was expressed for low achievers to one in which the legislature, school administrators, teachers, pupils, and parents were striving to remedy these academic deficiencies.

°<u>Development of alternative instructional systems.</u> The idea of "performance-based education" or of awarding "credit by examination" is one for which the time is approaching. Time-based programs, such as those employed in most elementary, middle, high school and college programs, have come under increasing attacks by the supporters of "flexible scheduling," "performance-based education," and other alternative instructional systems. A basic premise of such systems is that credit is given for accomplishment of instructional objectives rather than for spending time in programs. The requirement that minimum competency be demonstrated is consistent with such instructional systems.

The minimum competency testing program and the necessary accompanying remedial instruction program require the implementation of instructional systems and individualized instruction. These concepts have heretofore been attempted but have had little success in achieving widespread or long-term implementation. However, Florida's program has stimulated and virtually necessitated the establishment of such systems, which include instructional objectives, the provision of instruction, and assessment of mastery of those objectives for students on an individual basis. The concepts of diagnosis and prescriptive learning have been made more real than ever before.

°Neglect of average and above-average learners. A concern that frequently is expressed by school personnel is that minimum competency testing programs lead to a preoccupation with low-achieving pupils at the expense of the average and above-average achievers. The remedial programs also have the effect of raising per-pupil expenditures for low-achieving students over that for regular students. Such expenditures would be justified if the programs do, in fact, have a profound and lasting beneficial effect on these individuals. However, the lasting effects of minimum competency testing remain to be proven. There is no evidence that neglect is occurring, but school officials should insure that the total program is kept in perspective.

°Meaning restored to the high school diploma. Citizens have been shocked to learn that high schools throughout the country have been awarding diplomas to pupils who cannot read, write, or do basic arithmetic. These citizens, through their elected representatives, are attempting to hold the school system accountable by imposing minimum competency testing programs. They are becoming increasingly reluctant to fund systems that, in their eyes, have neither established or maintained minimum academic standards. Their response has been simple and straightforward and has not been governed by sociological and psychological theories. They are insisting that the diploma represent some minimum level of achievement.

°Problem posed by private schools. Private
schools operate independently of the state school system in most states -- Florida, for example -- and establish their own requirements for the high school diploma. Therefore, these schools may not require passing the state's minimum competency testing program for
graduation. Black citizens and pupils resent the white
flight to the private schools, especially those established since desegregation, and suspect that students
remaining in the public schools are being discriminated against through this testing requirement. One of
two possible effects could result: (a) the minimum
competency test requirement could be extended to all
private as well as public schools; or (b) a new generation of private schools could emerge for the express
purpose of bypassing the minimum competency laws.

The preceding set of issues and their possible
effects on educational systems are all important. Some
are more important to a particular political or professional group than others but all must be considered
by educators in implementing a minimum competency
testing program.

Implications for Educational Systems

It is quite clear that there is widespread public
concern about education in America today. This public
concern should be harnessed and directed toward the
overall improvement of goals, purposes, activities,
and products of our public schools.

Minimum competency testing programs can make genuine contributions to the improvement of our schools
if they are carefully conceptualized, developed, and
implemented. However, there is a danger that testing
programs may be thrust upon educational systems that
are not prepared to incorporate them properly into
their organizational structures. Mitchell and Spady
(1978), drawing on Cremin's work in school reform
(1964), cogently addressed this problem. School reform
"has always been partial and incomplete, producing organizational and program elements which are inconsistent and contradictory. Only if the historical alternatives are understood within a theoretical framework
and subjected to systematic research can educationally
effective and politically acceptable outcome-based
educational programs be developed."

Our schools are complex organizational structures and even well-intended efforts to improve them in one area may very well prove to be at the expense of another. New goals and objectives must be considered carefully and the schools' organizational structure related to the desired outcomes. Such a revised structure may require new arrangements, new kinds of instructional materials, new testing strategies, new skills for teachers, and new teacher training programs.

Minimum competency testing is being demanded by citizens and their elected representatives, it is consistent with educational theory, it offers opportunities for making needed changes in our educational system, and, most important, it reflects a determination to insure that every effort is made to provide each of our citizens with those basic skills necessary for independent functioning in our society. The proponents and opponents of current efforts to initiate such programs must not be forced into polarized and untenable positions. Rather, educators must profit from different views and use the energy behind the movement to better our schools.

References

Cremin, L.A. THE TRANSFORMATION OF THE SCHOOL. New York: Vintage Books, 1964.

Mitchell, D.E. & Spady, W.G. "Organizational Contexts for Implementing Outcome Based Education. EDUCATION RESEARCHER. 1978, 7(7), 9-17.

New York State's Plan to Set Graduation Standards. PHI DELTA KAPPAN, 1979, 60, 555.

Pinkney, H.B. "The Minimum Competency Movement in Public Education. THE CLEARING HOUSE, May 1979, pp. 413-416.

Spady, W.G. "Competency Based Education: A Bandwagon in Search of a Definition. EDUCATIONAL RESEARCHER, 1977, 6(1), 9-14.

PEER TUTORING AS A STRATEGY
FOR INDIVIDUALIZING INSTRUCTION

Ann C. Candler, Gary M. Blackburn,
and Virginia Sowell

Classroom teachers often wish for more time and/
or more assistance in meeting the needs of individual
students. One strategy which students and teachers
may employ in an effort to meet individual student
needs is peer tutoring. Simply stated, peer tutoring
involves students helping each other. Tutoring of
this kind is not a new idea. In fact, it is a teach-
ing/learning strategy which has occurred both in
school and out for many years. Somehow, it seems very
natural to ask a peer for assistance in solving a
problem, learning new information, or understanding a
concept.

Peer tutoring offers a number of advantages for
the teacher as well as for the tutor and tutee. The
greatest advantage of peer tutoring is that it is a
flexible instructional strategy which frees the
teacher to work with students needing extra help.
While the teacher works with one student or groups of
students, other students can work in pre-arranged tutoring groups.

Regular education and special education classmates can work together. Elementary pupils can benefit
with working from older students or with classmates on
a different instructional level.

Peer tutoring can be employed for practice, instruction, and/or review purposes in the various academic areas. Furthermore, it is a strategy conducive
to the development of motor, craft, and language development activities. Many different learning tasks
lend themselves to peer tutoring strategies. Workbook

Reprinted from EDUCATION, 101 (4): 380-383 (Summer
1981), by permission of authors and publisher.

assignments, reading practice, academic games and small group discussions are great activities for peer tutoring arrangements.

In the past, peer tutoring has frequently been left to chance, or at best, has been used as an incidental instructional strategy. However, the importance of the systematic planning and implementation of peer tutoring cannot be overestimated. Teachers who utilize peer tutoring freely admit that the strategies and techniques which they implement are effective because of advanced planning and preparation. Through such organization, teachers structure situations which allow all participants to experience success. Advance planning and preparation allows the teacher to recognize and therefore avoid some of the possible difficulties which may arise. Further, unavoidable difficulties can be minimized through such arrangements.

As a teacher prepares for peer tutoring, he/she should give careful consideration to (a) the selection of tutors and tutees, (b) the matching of tutors with tutees, and (c) the training of tutors. These considerations may make the difference between having a successful or unsuccessful program.

As the teacher begins to formulate his/her peer tutoring program, careful selection of potential tutors and tutees is important. In the initial stages of a tutoring program, the teacher would be well advised to select those students who will be most likely to react favorably to the peer tutoring situation. This immediately rules out those students with serious behavior and/or emotional problems. While students with serious problems can be included in the tutoring program later, it is probably best to avoid such students until the program is established. Wait until the teacher and students have some opportunities for success before tackling more difficult situations.

In selecting students to serve as tutors, an important factor for consideration is behavior. The teacher should select students who can and will follow directions in unsupervised settings. Further, the students who are selected to serve as tutors should be students who relate well to other students. Attention to these two aspects of a potential tutor's behavior can avoid or minimize discipline problems and interpersonal conflicts during initial peer tutoring sessions.

A second consideration in selecting students to serve as tutors is mastery of the material to be covered in the tutoring session. This does not mean that tutors must have high IQ's, but they should have mastered the material to be covered in the tutoring session. When the tutor understands the material to be covered in the tutoring session, the chances of misinformation are reduced. Also, a tutor who understands the material covered in the tutoring session will have less need for teacher supervision and/or direction during the session.

These basic considerations in the selection of tutors do eliminate certain types of students as tutors. However, it is not necessary to employ only "perfect" students as tutors. Essentially, the diligent student who is well-liked will qualify as a potential tutor. Potential tutors may themselves have problems. A poor self-concept, shyness, and/or underachieving may be problems which will not interfere with peer tutoring. In fact, selecting students with such problems may have the added advantage of assisting the tutor in overcoming his difficulty.

The other important student in a peer tutoring relationship is the tutee. The best potential tutees are students who want help. Often these are the students who need additional practice, are not self-directing, are easily distracted, and/or need adaptations of the learning task. Another potentially good tutee is the student who needs assistance because he/she has been absent from school. Students such as these may or may not have serious learning problems. The severity of the tutee's learning problem is not a serious concern as long as the concept to be covered in the tutoring session is within the ability of the tutee. More important than the level at which the tutee is working or the severity of his/her learning problem is the tutee's willingness to accept help.

After selecting potential tutors and tutees, the teacher must then give consideration to the important process of matching tutors to tutees. The most important consideration in matching tutors to tutees is selecting students who can work well together. Students who work well together are more than just students getting along in a social sense. In fact, pairing two students who are just socially compatible may mean disaster for the tutoring session if the session becomes a social issue. Therefore, in addition to match-

145

ing students who get along, a variety of other student characteristics should be considered in the process. From an academic standpoint, it is important to match a tutor who has mastered the skill which the tutee lacks. It is probably wise to pair students of the same sex in one-to-one tutoring sessions. This can avoid a variety of problems depending on the ages of the students involved. An empathetic tutor might be of great assistance to a tutee who is shy and withdrawn not only academically but also socially. Likewise, there might be similar favorable outcomes when a shy tutor is matched with a more outgoing tutee.

Once the tutors and tutees have been identified, it is important to prepare them for the role each is about to assume. While this preparation need not be an elaborate and complex process, it is important. The preparation process should include an explanation of the role of the tutor, the procedures to follow in tutoring and a carefully observed peer tutoring session or two. Through the provision of these three elements, the tutor is given the opportunity to demonstrate his ability to work as an effective tutor.

Step one of the preparation process is an explanation of the role of the peer tutor. Most tutors will already have a basic understanding of what a tutor does; however, the purpose of the preparation is to specify the things a tutor should or should not do. Tutors should know in advance how to handle various situations which may arise. The importance of aiding the tutee in completing assignments rather than doing the work for the tutee should be stressed. Further, the tutor should be aware that his/her role does not include discipline. Should a discipline problem arise during the tutoring session, the tutor should call the teacher or some other individual to handle the situation.

In addition to delineating the role of the tutor, it is necessary to explain the procedures to be followed in conducting peer tutoring sessions. The procedures can be divided into the three phases of a tutoring session. First, the tutor must learn how to prepare for a tutoring session. Second, he/she must know how to conduct a tutoring session. Finally, the tutor must know what to do after the session.

Preparation for a tutoring session will include finding out the assignment for the session and making sure he/she understands the material. Some teachers may wish to employ some sort of simple form in making tutoring session assignments. If this is the case, the tutor should know where his assignment sheet is kept. Further, tutors should know where all the supplies and/or equipment needed in tutoring sessions are kept and how to utilize each piece. For most tutors, the equipment will include little more than pencils, worksheets, number lines, math counters, etc. However, if tape recorders, film projectors, and other such equipment will be employed in tutoring sessions, the tutors should know how to operate each item. Along with finding out the assignment for the session, the tutor should get together all the materials to be used in the tutoring session as a part of the preparation for a session.

ASSIGNMENT SHEET

Objectives:

Materials to use:

Directions:

A tutor should also be acquainted with the procedures for conducting a tutoring session. This may include the use of reinforcement of correct responses, types of activities to be included in a session, and appropriate places to conduct tutoring sessions. The exact information included in this part of the tutor training process will vary greatly from classroom to classroom. However, complete information regarding each of the above topics may save time in the long run.

The tutor should also know what to do once the tutoring session is complete. This should include replacing all materials and equipment in the appropriate places and providing the teacher with information re-

garding progress made during the session. There are
many methods of letting the teacher know what progress
was made during the session. These include a brief
narrative written by the tutor, an individual conference between the teacher, tutor, and tutee (if appropriate), and/or the written work which was the assignment for the session. Obviously, these range from complex to simple and from time-consuming to fast. Therefore it is probably best not to always employ any one
technique. Probably, an infrequent conference supple-
mented by the written work which was assigned for each
session is sufficient. Whatever the progress reporting
technique selected, the tutor should know what to include and when and/or where to put the report. That
is, if the report consists only of the written assignment, the tutor should know where to put it. If the
report is a written narrative, the tutor should know
when to write the report, basically the types of information to include, and where to put the report. If
the report is an individual conference, the tutor
should know when the conference will be held. Advance
scheduling of such conferences can avoid unnecessary
interruptions during instructional periods.

Implementation of the peer tutoring strategies in
an actual tutoring session is the final phase of the
tutor training program. During this phase, the tutor
works with the tutee in actual tutoring sessions. The
primary difference between this session and later sessions is the close teacher supervision required in
this session. Certainly, the tutor will never be completely without direction or supervision during peer
tutoring. However, once the tutor has demonstrated
the ability to conduct tutoring sessions, the teacher
can reduce the amount of supervision. During the time
when the tutor is demonstrating his/her ability to
conduct tutoring sessions, the teacher should be close
by and not deeply involved in other teaching activities. After the tutor has demonstrated his/her ability, the teacher may wish to work with a different
group of students during the tutoring session. Thus,
the purpose of peer tutoring -- to provide for additional individualization of instruction -- is accomplished, and the total instructional program is enhanced.

IMPROVING LEARNING STRATEGIES
WITH COMPUTER-BASED EDUCATION

Robert M. Caldwell

Parallel advances in teaching and technology have
made it necessary for educators to redefine the nature
of the learning experience and to devise ways to make
contacts between the learner and the learning experience more meaningful, more efficient, and more productive. New delivery systems are needed that will be
able to make information available to students whenever and wherever it is needed.

This need has been met in part by advances in the
development of educational television, satellite communication and self-paced media. Few of these, however, hold the potential for individualizing instruction and for making information readily available as
does the computer. Computer technology and its related
instructional capabilities have the ability to:

1. Provide interactive instruction where learners
become active participants in the learning process instead of mere receivers of information.

2. Provide alternative learning paths within lessons or within courses to aid in student learning.

3. Offer independent pacing for individuals so
that they may progress through courses at a rate that
is suited to their learning style.

4. Give learners controlled reinforcement.

5. Evaluate student performance quickly and accurately to provide data on the degree to which learn-

Reprinted from THEORY INTO PRACTICE, 19 (2): 141-143
(Spring 1980), by permission of author and publisher.
Published by the College of Education, The Ohio State
University.

ers have mastered predetermined objectives and to aid in providing information that will help improve the effectiveness and efficiency of the course.

6. Store massive amounts of information about students for use by teachers in counseling and for use by students themselves in self-evaluation.

These capabilities have been applied to educational functions in a variety of ways. Computer Assisted Instruction (CAI), Computer Managed Instruction (CMI) and Computer Aided Instruction all describe specific uses of the computer in the educational process. In recent years, the term Computer Based Education (CBE) has become widely accepted to mean any use of the computer to support educational activities. That support can take several forms, but its primary purpose is to assist in individualizing instruction.

One aspect of computer support is using the computer directly as a teaching machine. Here the computer directly presents and reinforces specific instructional content. In this process, commonly known as Computer Assisted Instruction (CAI), the computer's influence is brought directly into the classroom. This direct interaction may take the form of a drill-practice routine for an individual student or a complex simulation requiring a group of students to work together to solve a "realistic" problem. A third form is the direct presentation of new information to an individual student. This is called a tutorial presentation.

Computer Managed Instruction (CMI) uses the computer to assist in classroom management. This function includes using the computer to aid in test administration and scoring, diagnosing student abilities, maintaining class records, and prescribing appropriate materials and methods for instruction based on student progress through a course of study. CMI allows for the easy flow of students through programs where each is following a course of study designed to meet his individual learning needs. Learners engage in learning activities which might include a variety of media and many diverse learning contacts. In either case, the computer monitors the learning sequence and provides students with formative evaluation and a record of their progress.

Computer Based Education, then, is not merely a

fixed system of hardware, software, and courseware, but an entire educational environment which is characterized by specific applications of the educational and computer technologies which aid in the learning process. It is a complete system which offers an extensive array of learning alternatives not possible through conventional teaching strategies and materials. In addition, it is the only two-way communication medium available. As learners gathering information, we cannot interact with newspapers and print media or with a television; even in an audience listening to a lecture we rarely have an opportunity to talk with the speaker. Only with computer based education can we expect every learner to follow a computer assisted lesson and "talk back" to it in a way that shapes learning experiences.

The computer, therefore, offers a dynamic new tool for developing a range of cognitive skills and for helping learners develop useful learning strategies. Unfortunately, much of what passes for courseware today neither helps to develop higher level cognitive processes nor challenges the student to use learning strategies commonly associated with higher order learning. Most courseware utilizes a "drill and practice" format where the computer asks a question and requires the student to respond by means of a forced choice question. Many programs which claim to be "tutorial" in nature are no improvement. They often print expository text which is followed by question asking and answering. This sort of instruction has its use but attends to only one form of learning strategy, rote memorization. It implies that the computer's power lies only in its ability to present text and ask questions. This form of instruction only serves to recreate the very worst of what presently occurs in a traditional classroom while ignoring all other kinds of classroom activity which can help develop learning styles and learner independence.

It should be pointed out, however, that drill and practice is not without its benefits: First, the questions asked can be controlled on the basis of the student's progress, therefore individualizing the learning experience. Second, the use of the computer accurately defines a sequence of instruction that pupils can manage and provides immediate feedback on their responses. Third, the learner has control over the pace of learning.

These are advantages to instruction which are hard to ignore or ridicule as being trivial. A growing body of literature, in fact, can be offered to support the usefulness of drill and practice for improving instruction, particularly with disadvantaged learners whose most commonly employed learning strategy is rote.

The computer can present in tireless fashion vocabulary, rules, facts, or any content which can be committed to memory and virtually ensure its mastery using adaptive branching and reinforcement. What it does not do, however, is allow learners to ask questions. They are not asked to organize what they are learning in their own way. They are not encouraged to explain things in their own words, to offer opinions, or to apply what they learned to a new situation. It is possible to include these activities in the design of dynamic, interactive courseware but this is rarely done.

Through the use of dialogue and simulation in instructional design, a course developer can help learners develop the following learning strategies:

Physical: Well designed programs can help learners note physical similarities and differences in content. This is particularly helpful in language learning where learners must see how words change form but retain features of root words.

Elaboration: Here the computer can classify material to be learned so that it is more meaningful. This is done by tracking previously learned knowledge and representing it at opportunities where it can be used to solve new problems.

Grouping: One of the mind's most powerful techniques for organizing information is spatial analogy. When we want to imprint a train of thoughts in our memories, we associate each of these thoughts with a familiar environment. In order to recollect the sequence of ideas, we sort through those environments where we had deposited them earlier. An effective dialogue uses the computer to help the learner sort out the different types of information stored earlier. In this way, learners are taught to use information for their own goals and purposes rather than for defining what teachers expect them to know.

Using the computer to develop these learning strategies reduces the probability that learners will see learning as a trivia contest which demands recall of ritual responses. Instead it allows for practice in challenging what others call "facts," assembling data into theories and testing them, and solving new problems in novel ways. In a world where computers are clearly more accurate "memorizers," we must find ways to measure the development of information processing skills, not new ways to measure how much information a learner is able to store. Research is badly needed to investigate the effects of dialogue and simulation in computer based programs on the movement of learners from one level of learning strategy to higher ones.

In summary, new approaches to designing computer based instruction can serve to disrupt present patterns of computer use which reinforce the tendency to place students in passive roles so that the process of learning is taken on by others. Instead of operating under the assumption that knowledge must be inserted into the heads of learners, instructional designers must develop programs which help students access information in a way that contributes to meaningful learning patterns. We should train students to be able to recognize their own limitations in knowledge and in skills for acquiring new knowledge, and to take effective action in overcoming them. In short, we must exploit the power of the computer to encourage individual thought, inquiry and learning.

SUCCESSFUL TEACHING STRATEGIES
FOR THE INNER-CITY CHILD

Jere Brophy

The Seventies produced a great deal of progress in research on teaching. Sophisticated research designs and classroom observation systems were developed and significant funding from such sources as the National Institute of Education and Project Follow Through made it possible to study large numbers of classrooms around the U.S. The outcome has been a consistent set of findings on the elements of effective basic skills instruction, especially for inner-city students.

Teachers and teacher educators should be aware of these research findings for several reasons. First, these findings spring from large-scale classroom research; they do not rely solely on untested theory. Second, the instructional implications of the data are feasible and realistic for teachers with classes of 20 to 40 students; they do not require special facilities or equipment, full-time aides, or other hard-to-come-by resources. Third, the instructional implications are generally applicable, because they have been derived from observations of typical public school teachers and typical students engaged in ordinary school activities.

The research to which I refer includes several large-scale correlational studies, showing that teachers who teach students basic skills effectively differ systematically in their classroom behavior from those who do not (1). Follow-up experiments have demonstrated that teachers can be trained to use those classroom behaviors that are associated with student learning gains; moreover, students taught by teachers with this kind of training outperform comparable stu-

Reprinted from PHI DELTA KAPPAN, 63 (8): 527-30 (April 1982), by permission of author and publisher.

dents of teachers without such training (2). Findings from research of the Seventies do not agree in every respect, but this body of research has given consistent support to certain principles, on which I shall now focus (3).

Teachers Make A Difference

Academic achievement in the late Sixties was commonly viewed as a product of intelligence and home background -- unrelated to quality of instruction. Teachers were said to have little or no impact on students' achievement, a conclusion that contradicted both common sense and most people's own school experiences. Nonetheless, some people still believe this today.

The research of the Seventies has clearly disproved this notion by establishing that some teachers are reliably more effective than others in producing student learning gains on standardized tests of basic skills, even when students' initial achievement levels are taken into account. Stable individual differences in teacher effectiveness are observable despite change in class size and composition, group dynamics and other factors unique to certain classes, and teacher health and welfare (which vary from year to year). I shall review here eight teacher characteristics or behaviors that are associated with success in producing student learning gains.

1. Teacher expectations, role definitions, and sense of efficacy. A congruent set of expectations and attitudes underlies the specific behaviors of effective teachers. These teachers accept the responsibility for teaching their students. They believe that the students are capable of learning and that they are capable of teaching them successfully. If the curricula, instructional methods, or evaluation devices that they intended to use do not work, they find others that will work (4). If something is not learned the first time through, they teach it again. In general, these teachers treat student failure as a challenge; they do not write off certain students as unteachable because they lack ability or experiential background. These attitudes are characteristic of effective teachers in any setting, but they are vital for teachers working in inner-city schools.

155

2. Student opportunity to learn. Students of
effective teachers learn more than other students, in
part because they are given more opportunity to learn.
Effective teachers allocate most of their available
time to instruction, and they organize and manage
their classrooms to insure that the time is actually
spent in this fashion. Thus the students of effective
teachers spend many more hours on academic tasks each
year than do students of ineffective teachers. Sometimes the annual difference amounts to several hundred
hours (5). Effective teachers view time as a precious
commodity that must be used wisely to achieve learning
outcomes.

3. Classroom management and organization. Careful allocation of time is not enough; it must be
backed by an effective classroom learning environment
and by group management that maximizes student engagement in academic activities. Organization of the
classroom environment begins before school starts in
the fall with the arrangement of physical space and
seating patterns to complement the teacher's instructional objectives and methods.

Once the students arrive, effective teachers take
time right away to instruct them on classroom procedures and routines (6). They show their students what
to do, provide practice, and follow through with reminders and periodic review. In the early grades, effective teachers begin the year with detailed instruction on how to make smooth transitions between activities, to sharpen pencils, to obtain equipment, to get
help with assignments, and to check their work. Older
students usually require less formal instruction on
classroom procedures and routines, but they do require
a clear understanding of the teacher's expectations
and consistent follow through. Effective teachers at
all grade levels make sure their students know what
they are supposed to do, and realize that they will be
held accountable for meeting these expectations.

Effective teachers also use effective group management techniques (7). They plan lessons carefully
to provide a smooth, continuous focus for students'
attention. They accomplish transitions between activities quickly and efficiently. They give students assignments of appropriate difficulty and sufficient
variety to maintain their interest. Students know
what to do if they need help and what options are
available to them if they complete their assignments

early.

Effective classroom organization and group management techniques minimize disruption. Students are likely to remain attentive and engaged when their teacher presents appropriate activities, keeps these activities moving at a good pace, and monitors students' responsiveness to them. Careful preparation of the physical environment, early instruction on classroom procedures and routines, and continuous review and maintenance throughout the year lead to a classroom environment that promotes learning (8).

4. Curriculum pacing. To learn efficiently, students must be engaged in meaningful tasks. Variety and a degree of challenge help to motivate learning, but the key variable seems to be the match between students' present achievement levels and the difficulty levels of their assigned tasks. Students learn best when they proceed rapidly but in very small steps. If they are consistently given work that is too difficult, they are likely to give up and become "motivation problems."

This general principle has been well known for some time, but recent research indicates that students require a very high success rate in order to progress efficiently. There is disagreement on this point, however. The literature on achievement motivation suggests that a 50% success rate is optimal, at least for youngsters who do not fear failure. This has sometimes been taken -- inappropriately -- to mean that classroom questions and assignments should be geared to a 50% success rate. Other writers have reached a similar conclusion from their belief that higher-level thought questions are more valuable that lower-level "fact" questions or from their belief that learning is likely to be repetitive, boring, or pointless if it is "too easy." On the other hand, advocates of mastery learning demand at least an 80% success rate on assignments and advocates of programmed learning expect the success rate to approach 100%. New research supports this position; findings show that teachers who aim for success rates of 90% to 100% on student assignments produce more learning than teachers who tolerate higher failure rates. The importance of success rate to learning has led one group of researchers to define "academic learning time" as the time students spend engaged in academic tasks with very high rates of success (9).

Very high success rates (90% to 100%) are especially important for seatwork assignments, when
students are expected to work independently without
frequent monitoring by or assistance from the teacher.
Somewhat lower success rates can be tolerated in large
group instruction, since the teacher is present to
monitor students' responses and to provide immediate
feedback. Even in this case, a teacher should aim for
70% to 80% correct answers, especially when working
with inner-city students (10).

Thus the students of effective teachers are exposed to and progress through more material than other
students, and the pacing of classroom activities and
of progress through the curriculum is generally brisk.
But they move along in small steps, and they experience consistent success along the way. This approach
is not only effective but probably essential for
teaching basic skills to most students, because so
much of the curriculum in the early grades is cumulative and students are expected to work independently
for much of the time.

5. Active teaching. Effective teachers of inner-
city students are more than instructional managers who
distribute and correct assignments. They actively
teach their students in large and small groups -- demonstrating skills, explaining concepts, conducting
participatory and practice activities, explaining assignments, and reviewing when necessary. If they are
first-grade teachers working with reading groups, they
introduce new words, point out important phonetic features, and work with students on word analysis and
story comprehension (11). If they are fourth-grade
mathematics teachers, they spend time with the class
developing key concepts or skills, and they make sure
that students understand the assignment thoroughly before they release them to work independently (12).

Students who receive much of their instruction
directly from the teacher generally do better than
those who are expected to learn on their own or from
one another. To learn independently, students must be
able to read, understand, and follow directions. They
must be able to identify key concepts and to correct
their own errors. Furthermore, they must be willing
and able to sustain sufficient levels of concentration
and effort. No youngsters in the early grades and
probably only a small percentage of older students
possess this combination of skills and motivation. Yet

the emphasis of the Sixties and early Seventies was on
teacher-proof curricula and individualized learning
packages that changed the teacher's role from instructional leader to instructional manager. The notion
that there was too much "teacher talk" in classrooms
and not enough "student talk" compounded the problem.
The research of the Seventies suggests that these attempts to change the teacher's traditional role were
mistaken.

6. Teaching to mastery. Following active instruction in new content, effective teachers provide
opportunities for practice and application, monitoring
individual students' progress and providing feedback
and remedial instruction. Their students consistently
experience high success rates because these teachers
make sure that new knowledge and skills are mastered
to the point of overlearning. Basic skills are taught
in hierarchically sequenced strands; thus success at
any given level usually requires mastery of skills
taught earlier and ability to apply them in new situations. But students typically cannot retain and apply
skills unless they have first overlearned them. It is
vital to teach to this level of mastery consistently,
if consistent success is the goal.

Curriculum theorists and teacher educators often
criticize teachers -- especially those in inner-city
schools -- for placing too much emphasis on low-level
objectives. The term "low-level" implies that such
objectives are trivial and easily mastered. Neither
claim is true. National and state assessment data
regularly reveal that vast numbers of students have
failed to master even fundamental objectives in such
areas as reading and mathematics. Yet everything we
know about learning complex and hierarchically organized skills tells us that higher-level objectives will
not be readily comprehended, let alone mastered, until
lower-level objectives are not only mastered but overlearned to such a point that they can be combined and
applied in the learning of more complex material. Thus
it is not surprising that effective teachers spend
much of their time asking factual questions and supervising practice of basic skills. There appear to be
no shortcuts to efficient performance on higher-level
objectives.

7. Grade-level differences. I have said that
effective instruction in the basic skills involves determination to teach these skills thoroughly, careful

allocation of classroom time to this purpose, organization and management of the classroom to involve students in academic activities, programming for brisk curriculum pacing and easy success, active instruction and supervision of students, and teaching to mastery. These principles constitute a general model for instruction in basic skills, but they require qualification or elaboration when differences in students, subject matter, or other factors are taken into account. Grade level is one such factor.

Students in the early grades require a great deal of one-to-one interaction with the teacher, who provides them with opportunities for overt practice with feedback. For the sake of efficiency, most of this dyadic instruction occurs during small group instruction. Nevertheless, it is important that the teacher monitor the progress of and interact with each student regularly. In reading groups, for example, teachers who call on students to read or recite in a predetermined order tend to be more effective than teachers who call on students randomly (13). The ordered method provides structure for students who may need it, and cuts down on the distractions caused by students who are trying to coax the teacher to call on them. Perhaps more important, this method insures that all students participate regularly and somewhat equally. Earlier research on teacher expectations as they are communicated to students showed that most teachers who think they are calling on students randomly actually call on higher-achieving and assertive students more often than on low-achieving or shy students (14). As a result, those students who most need opportunities for practice with feedback have fewer opportunities to participate actively.

Students in the higher grades have less need for overt practice and individualized interaction with the teacher, because they are better able to learn by attending to the teacher's presentations to the class and through interactions with their peers. Thus presentations to the whole class become the usual mode for introducing new material, and remedial activities take place in small groups. The teacher's need to interact overtly with each student gives way at this level to the need for more briskly paced lessons directed to the class as a whole. In fact, in the higher grades it is often counterproductive for teachers to interrupt large-group activities for any length of time in order to deal with concerns specific to individual students, because this may lead to loss of lesson momentum and student attention.

Even in the higher grades, however, teachers must monitor students' independent work closely and provide necessary assistance and feedback. Students left on their own too long are likely to become distracted or to develop misconceptions about the content -- even if they do remain on task and are able to produce correct answers (15). Inner-city students in particular profit from structure and teacher guidance.

8. A supportive learning environment. It is important to note that effective teachers maintain a strong academic focus within the context of a pleasant friendly classroom. Highly effective teachers clearly stress cognitive objectives, but they do not come across as slave drivers, and their classrooms do not resemble sweatshops. They maintain high standards and demand that students do their best, but they are not punitive or hypercritical (16). Instead, students perceive effective teachers as enthusiastic and thorough instructors whose classrooms are friendly and convivial (17). Such teachers are supportive of students, especially those who may be inhibited, frustrated, or alienated.

Much of this support is instructional. Students who have difficulty mastering material receive more structured learning experiences, more detailed and repetitive explanations, more frequent and individualized opportunities to respond and obtain feedback, shorter and more closely monitored assignments, and more continuous general direction and supervision. Support also takes more personal forms. Effective teachers obtain maximal performance from discouraged students not by demanding it (with implied rejection or punishment for failure to deliver), but by fostering such performance gradually through praise, encouragement, expressions of appreciation for effort, and attention to evidence of genuine progress. Their long-range goals include turning these students into confident independent learners. In the meantime, they are willing to provide the students with whatever extra direction and support they may need.

The research of the Seventies is encouraging, because it demonstrates that all students, including inner-city students, can be taught effectively. It is also reassuring, because it validates many of the practices that teachers have found to be effective in their own classrooms. The instructional implications of this research seem simple, but this does not make them easy to implement.

Effective teachers -- teachers who do all the things I have mentioned above -- are not "ordinary" teachers. They are probably brighter and more dedicated than average. They are certainly better organized and more efficient classroom managers, better prepared and more thorough instructors. The successes represented by their students' test scores are the cumulative result of daily planning, thorough preparation, and simple hard work. Teachers cannot realistically expect consistent success if they are not willing and able to supply these ingredients.

There are limits, however, to what even the most dedicated and talented teachers can accomplish on their own. It is difficult to maintain an academic focus when classroom activities are frequently interrupted by announcements on the intercom or hallway noise. More can be done with a class of 20 students than with a class of 40, and more can be done when the class contains only one or two disruptive students than when it includes six or eight. Issues of school funding, policy, and administration influence the effectiveness of teachers.

The research of the Seventies has revealed a great deal about effective instruction of inner-city students in basic skills. But these findings will not necessarily prove easy to implement in classrooms. In any case, they can provide only part of a successful response to the challenge of creating effective inner-city schools for the Eighties and beyond.

References

1. Jere E. Brophy and Carolyn M. Evertson, LEARNING FROM TEACHING: A DEVELOPMENTAL PERSPECTIVE (Boston: Allyn & Bacon, 1976).
2. Linda M. Anderson, Carolyn M. Evertson, and Jere E. Brophy, "An Experimental Study of Effective Teaching in First-Grade Reading Groups," ELEMENTARY SCHOOL JOURNAL, March 1979, pp. 193-223.
3. Jere E. Brophy, "Advances in Teacher Effectiveness Research," JOURNAL OF CLASSROOM INTERACTION,

Winter 1979, pp. 1-7.

4. Brophy and Evertson, LEARNING FROM TEACHING: A DEVELOPMENTAL PERSPECTIVE.

5. Charles Fisher, David Berliner, Nikola Filby, Richard Marliave, Leonard S. Cahen, and Marilyn D. Dishaw, "Teaching Behaviors, Academic Learning Time, and Student Achievement: An Overview," in Carolyn Denham and Ann Lieberman, eds. TIME TO LEARN (Washington, D.C.: National Institute of Education, 1980).

6. Edmund T. Emmer, Carolyn M. Evertson, and Linda M. Anderson, "Effective Classroom Management at the Beginning of the School Year," ELEMENTARY SCHOOL JOURNAL, May 1980, pp. 219-31.

7. See, for example, Jacob Kounin, DISCIPLINE AND GROUP MANAGEMENT IN CLASSROOMS (New York: Holt, Rinehart and Winston, 1970).

8. Linda M. Anderson, Carolyn M. Evertson, and Edmund T. Emmer, "Dimensions in Classroom Management Derived from Recent Research," JOURNAL OF CURRICULUM STUDIES, October/December 1980, pp. 343-56.

9. Fisher et al., "Teaching Behaviors, Academic Learning Time, and Student Achievement: An Overview."

10. Brophy and Evertson, LEARNING FROM TEACHING: A DEVELOPMENTAL PERSPECTIVE.

11. Anderson, Evertson, and Brophy, "An Experimental Study of Effective Teaching in First-Grade Reading Groups."

12. Good and Grouws, "The Missouri Mathematics Effectiveness Project: An Experimental Study in Fourth Grade Classrooms."

13. Anderson, Evertson, and Brophy, "An Experimental Study of Effective Teaching in First-Grade Reading Groups."

14. Jere E. Brophy and Thomas L. Good, TEACHER-STUDENT RELATIONSHIPS: CAUSES AND CONSEQUENCES (New York: Holt, Rinehart, and Winston, 1974).

15. Stanley H. Erlwanger, "Case Studies of Children's Conceptions of Mathematics -- Part One," JOURNAL OF CHILDREN'S MATHEMATICAL BEHAVIOR, Summer 1975, pp. 157-283.

16. Brophy and Evertson, LEARNING FROM TEACHING: A DEVELOPMENTAL PERSPECTIVE.

17. Tikunoff, Berliner, and Rist, AN ETHNOGRAPHIC STUDY OF THE FORTY CLASSROOMS OF THE BEGINNING TEACHER EVALUATION STUDY KNOWN SAMPLE.

WHAT ABOUT HOMEWORK?

Elizabeth E. Yeary

Homework. It's making a comeback as a hot topic
in education circles -- riding into prominence on the
coattails of the back-to-basics movement. In many
parts of the country, school boards are debating about
making their systemwide homework policy more strin-
gent.

Some of the debate results from parental pressure
on school systems to work students harder. In some
districts, administrators take the initiative in push-
ing for more homework. For example, several months
ago, as a result of pressure from principals, the San
Francisco Unified School District School Board instituted a new homework policy for secondary schools. It
says that "homework should be assigned in all academic
subjects and that it should be completed outside of
regular school hours." The previous policy had only
"encouraged" teachers to assign homework.

A junior high school student in the district,
writing in his school paper, wondered whether the new
policy was "hastily designed to please angered parents
or for the benefit of students." He also wondered
whether teachers would start assigning busywork just
to fulfill the requirements.

In January of this year, the AMERICAN SCHOOL
BOARD JOURNAL asked its readers, who are primarily
school board members and administrators, "Should homework be mandated?" Of those responding, nearly 63
percent said that homework guidelines should be flexible and that school boards should encourage teachers
to assign homework but leave them to make the actual
decisions about it. Only 18 percent favored requiring
homework four nights a week. Eight percent wanted to

Reprinted from TODAY'S EDUCATION, 67 (3): 80-82 (September 1978), by permission of author and publisher.

mandate homework and place the issue on the bargaining table and into the teachers' contract. The other 11 percent felt that mandatory homework was not likely to be worth student or teacher effort.

Most teachers interviewed for this article would agree with the majority in the SCHOOL BOARD JOURNAL survey that teachers should make the decisions about homework. Almost all said they gave homework on weeknights but usually not on weekends or holidays. Although they claimed many parents were pressuring for more homework, the majority of the teachers interviewed said that they had not increased the amount of homework they assigned. Many said the quality of student homework had deteriorated over the past few years.

Only one teacher interviewed for this article -- a business education teacher in a high school in a disadvantaged neighborhood on the West Coast -- said he gave no homework. He claimed most teachers in his school did the same, because if they assign it, students won't, or can't, do the work.

A May 4, 1978, NEW YORK TIMES article reported a similar situation in the New York City schools. According to the article, teachers in that city "agree that students are being asked to do less homework and of a less challenging nature. And what they do turn in, even in schools where lengthy homework assignments are still given...is of low quality." The article goes on to say that some teachers in slum-area schools say they want to assign more homework than they do but that they have low expectations of pupil performance and that students either cannot or will not complete homework they are assigned.

Why the fuss about homework? Does it really make a difference in student achievement? Back in 1961, the editors of TODAY'S EDUCATION asked June Grant Murly to find out. An associate professor of education at the University of Pittsburgh at the time, Murly discovered the following:

"There is little conclusive evidence available concerning the positive or negative effects of home study, either the regular assigned homework or the voluntary assignment. Although many articles have been written about homework or home study, most of them express a subjective viewpoint."

One of the more recent studies on homework -- and one that made headlines in daily newspapers as well as education periodicals -- is a study by the National Assessment of Educational Progress (NAEP). Following a nationwide assessment of mathematics in 1976, NAEP asked 10,000 17-year-olds questions about their after-school activities, primarily about watching television and doing homework. The 17-year-olds represented a wide sampling of racial and ethnic groups.

The findings: In general, students who reported doing the most homework and the least television viewing performed best on the assessment. For example, those students who answered an average of 80 percent of questions correctly said they watched less than one hour of television a night and did more than 10 hours of homework a week. Those who said they received no assigned homework performed poorly on the assessment regardless of how much -- or how little -- television they said they watched. They answered an average of only 50 to 55 percent of the questions correctly.

Two other findings of this survey relate specifically to homework:

1. Those who said they had reading materials in their homes scored consistently higher on the mathematics assessment than those who said they did not. Seventeen-year-olds with newspapers in the home averaged 8 percentage points higher; those with encyclopedias or other reference books, 10 percentage points higher; and those with magazines, 13 percentage points higher than those who did not.

2. Not having a specific place to study at home did not make much difference in student performance on the assessment.

Whatever the research findings, teachers can safely assume that most of them will continue to assign homework and will continue to struggle with those who refuse to do it. Many teachers believe the struggle with homework delinquents would end if they and their colleagues observed the following don'ts:

Don't give assignments hastily at the end of a class period or at the end of a school day. Be sure students understand what they are supposed to do and why an assignment is important.

Don't give homework that includes concepts and ideas that you haven't explained in class or that you have explained but that many students don't understand.

Don't overload students with homework in the subject or subjects you teach. Some schools avoid problems in this area by establishing a homework schedule -- science and social studies homework on Mondays and Wednesdays, math and English homework on Tuesdays and Thursdays -- or a certain number of minutes of homework in each subject a night.

Don't forget that students need time for family and other out-of-school activities, such as Scouts, religious and civic groups, socializing with friends, part-time jobs, recreational reading, and, yes, television.

Don't assign humdrum, mechanical, and unchallenging work. Dr. Lee Salk's column, "You and Your Family," in the March 1978 issue of McCALL'S features a letter by a parent asking for advice on homework. The parent says her 10-year-old complains that her homework is boring and consistently puts off doing it. Dr. Salk replies that if this child procrastinates only about homework, "in all likelihood her homework itself is a problem. ...If homework is boring or uninteresting, even the most highly motivated child would want to put it off for as long as possible."

But what if students turn in homework that is not up to their ability? Or don't turn in anything at all?

In the first case, John Payne, a sixth-grade teacher in New Orleans, recommends talking to the backslider in private, comparing homework with classwork. He may ask the student to redo the work.

Edith Shannon, a former Jonesboro (Arkansas) Senior High School teacher, now retired, recommends a technique she calls Second Bounce. If a student's first effort is unacceptable, the student can submit a second version, making corrections on the basis of the teacher's comments. If the second version is entirely correct, the student suffers only a 10 percent penalty on the grade.

This procedure requires double work for the

167

teacher and the student, but it has benefits. Shannon says, "Instead of merely glancing at his grade and chucking the paper into the wastebasket, the student really reads the comments on the paper and acts upon them."

If a student turns in a homework assignment that is almost totally wrong, Shannon advises, staple some-one's correct copy to the wrong one and ask the student to make a careful copy of the correct one. The student who copies gets only partial credit for the assignment, of course.

If students simply don't turn in the work, John Payne calls the parents or penalizes the students on the report card. Almost all teachers interviewed for this article agree with Payne on notifying parents about missing homework. Parents -- if they follow up on homework -- can be a great ally of the teacher and the school. Not all the teachers lower students' grades, however. Some prefer having students come in after school to do the assignment.

In 11 Los Angeles schools involved in Jesse Jack-son's PUSH for Excellence (EXCEL) program, pledges produce homework. Students sign pledges promising to study each evening between 7 and 9 p.m. No interrup-tions from radio, television, or telephone. Parents also sign pledges to encourage home study and enforce the no-interruption rule. Fred Ollie, liaison with EXCEL from the Los Angeles Unified School district, says the pledges have produced improvements in home-work in all 11 schools.

PROMOTING EXCELLENCE
THROUGH MASTERY LEARNING

James H. Block

Mastery learning is a topic currently creating much controversy and excitement in national and international education circles. The controversy centers around mastery learning's views about human potential to learn and teach; the excitement around mastery learning's classroom practices.

This article provides an introduction to mastery learning. (See Anderson and Block, 1976; Block, 1971, 1974; Block and Anderson, 1975; Block and Burns, 1976; Bloom, 1976; and Torshen, 1977, for more detailed treatments.) First, the article defines what mastery learning is. Then it examines how mastery learning works. And lastly it indicates how well mastery learning works.

What Is It?

What is mastery learning? It is two things.

First, mastery learning is an optimistic theory about teaching and learning. Essentially this theory asserts that any teacher can help virtually <u>all</u> students to learn excellently; the teacher can help "dumb" students to learn like the "fast" students, "retarded" students to learn like the "gifted" students. Such teaching, the theory contends, not only improves many students' chances for long term social and personal prosperity, but many teachers' chances as well. In particular, the students acquire those basic intellectual, manual, and emotional competencies which

Reprinted from THEORY INTO PRACTICE, 19 (1): 66-74 (Winter 1980), by permission of author and publisher. Printed by the College of Education, The Ohio State University.

ensure that they can and want to undertake life-long learning. And the teachers acquire some basic pedagogical skills and career rewards which ensure that they can and want to keep teaching.

Second, mastery learning is an effective set of individualized instructional practices that consistently help <u>most</u> students to learn excellently. Some of these practices are of the group-based/teacher-paced variety where students learn cooperatively with their classmates and where the teacher controls the delivery and flow of the instruction. The genotype for these practices would be Bloom/Block's "Learning for Mastery" (LFM) strategy (see Block and Anderson, 1975). The remainder of these practices are of the individually-based/student-paced variety where students learn independently of their classmates and where each student controls the delivery and flow of the instruction. The genotype for these practices would be Keller's "Personalized System of Instruction" (PSI) (see Keller and Sherman, 1974).

Like other individualized instructional strategies, such as IPI, IGE, and PLAN (see Talmage, 1975; Gronlund, 1974; Hambleton, 1974), both varieties of mastery learning strategies assume that virtually all students can master a great deal of what they are taught in school if the "...instruction is approached systematically, if students are helped when and where they have learning difficulties, if they are given sufficient time to achieve mastery, and if there is some clear criterion of what constitutes mastery" (Bloom 1974, p. 6). Unlike other individualized approaches, however, mastery approaches are designed for use in the typical classroom situation where the teacher already possesses a curriculum where s/he must get through in a fixed period of calendar time, where inordinate amounts of instructional time cannot be spent in diagnostic-progress testing, and where student learning must be graded. Moreover, mastery approaches rely primarily on human beings for their success rather than on machines and other technological devices: teachers decide what goes on in the classroom and use their own instructional techniques and materials and students guide their own learning as well as the learning of others. Finally, at least one variety of these mastery approaches, viz., the group-based/teacher-paced variety, can be implemented without changes in school and classroom organization.

How Does It Work?

How do mastery learning strategies work? Let us describe the group-based/teacher-paced "Learning for Mastery" strategy. This strategy reflects all the basic mastery learning concepts and ideas. Moreover, it has proven to be one of the easiest mastery learning strategies to implement. We shall begin by describing the various steps in implementing the strategy. Then we shall examine the basic mastery learning concepts and techniques that underpin these steps.

The "Learning for Mastery" strategy is designed for use in instructional situations where the calendar time allowed for learning is relatively fixed and where students must be taught largely in groups. This strategy attempts to minimize the time a group of students needs to learn excellently so that it is within the fixed amount of calendar time available for instruction. This is accomplished through two distinct sets of steps. One set -- the Preconditions -- occurs outside the classroom and prior to the instruction; the second set -- the Operating Procedures -- takes place inside the classroom and during the instruction.

Preconditions for Mastery Learning

Defining Mastery. The teacher who wishes to use a "Learning for Mastery" approach begins by formulating what is meant by "mastery" of the subject. Ideally, the teacher would first define what material all students will be expected to learn. This entails the formulation of course objectives. Next, the teacher would prepare a final or summative examination (Bloom, Hastings and Madaus, 1971) over these objectives for administration at the course's close. Lastly, the teacher would set a summative examination score indicative of mastery performance. Students who perform better than this predetermined standard would be graded "masters"; those who do not would be graded "non-masters."

In actual practice, though, teachers have found it useful to use their old course achievement tests as working definitions of the material that each student will be expected to master. They have also found it convenient to administer one or more of these tests throughout the course for grading purposes. Finally, rather than grade the student's performance on a mas-

171

tery/nonmastery basis, the teachers have found it useful to fix an absolute grading scale wherein mastery corresponds to a grade of A and nonmastery corresponds to a grade of B, C, D, or F. The teacher forms this scale by determining the level of performance that students traditionally had to exhibit on the course examinations in order to earn an A, B, C, D, or F. All students who achieve to a particular level using mastery learning methods then receive the grade that corresponds to this level.

Planning for Mastery. Now the teacher breaks the course to be taught for mastery into a sequence of smaller learning units, each of which typically covers about two weeks' worth of material. In practice, these units correspond roughly to chapters in the course textbook or to a set of topics.

Next, the teacher sequences these units. After all, the teacher has broken the whole course into pieces, s/he must now recast the pieces into a whole. Teachers of mathematics and sciences have tended to sequence their units linearly so that the material in each unit transfers directly to the next unit. Teachers of arts, humanities and social sciences, however, have tended to sequence their units hierarchically so that the material in each unit transfers but not necessarily to the next unit. It may transfer to a subsequent unit.

Then, for each unit the teacher develops perhaps the single most important component of the mastery learning strategy: the unit feedback/correction procedures. These procedures will serve to monitor the effectiveness of the group-based instruction and to supplement it where necessary to better suit the learning requirements of certain students.

First, the teacher constructs a brief, ungraded diagnostic progress test or "formative" evaluation instrument (Bloom, Hastings and Madaus, 1971) for each unit. These tests are explicitly designed to be an integral part of each unit's instruction and to provide specific information or feedback to both the teacher and the student about how the student is changing as a result of the group-based instruction.

Next, the teacher specifies a score or performance standard on each formative test which, when met, will be indicative of unit mastery. Usually a score of 80 to 90 percent correct on a formative test indicates that the student is not having learning problems.

Finally, the teacher develops a set of alternative instructional materials and procedures or "correctives" keyed to each item on each unit's formative tests. Typically these correctives have consisted of cooperative small group study sessions, individual tutoring by classmates, or alternative learning aids such as different textbooks, workbooks, audiovisual materials, academic games/puzzles, and affective exercises.

Each corrective is designed to reteach the material tested by certain items on the unit formative test, but to do so in ways that will differ from the unit's initial group-based instruction. The correctives may present the material in a different sensory mode or modes or in a different form of the same mode than the group-based instruction. They may involve the student in a different way and/or provide not only different types of encouragements for learning but also different amounts of each type. Hence, should a student encounter difficulty in learning certain material from the group-based instruction unit, he can then use the correctives to explore alternative ways of learning the unmastered material, select those correctives best suited to his learning requirements, and overcome his learning problems before they impair subsequent learning.

Operating Procedures for Mastery Learning

<u>Orienting for Mastery.</u> The teacher is now ready to teach. Since students are not accustomed to learning for mastery or to the notion that they all might earn A's, the teacher usually must spend some time at the course's outset orienting them to the procedures to be used -- what they are expected to learn, how they are generally expected to learn it, and to what level they are expected to learn. My experience has been that this orientation period -- combined with continual encouragement, support, and positive evidence of learning success -- is crucial in developing in most students the belief that they can learn and the motivation to learn.

The typical orientation periods have stressed the

following:

1. The students are going to learn by a new method of instruction designed to help all of them learn well rather than just a few.

2. Each student will be graded solely on the basis of his performance on the final examination(s).

3. Each student will be graded against a predetermined performance standard and not in relation to the performance of his classmates. The standard of A work has been indicated.

4. Each student who attains this standard will receive an A.

5. There will be no fixed number of A's. Accordingly, cooperation with classmates in learning need not hurt a student's chances of earning an A. If a student and his classmates cooperate, and all of them learn well, then all will earn A's.

6. Each student will receive all the help he needs so as to learn. So if a student cannot learn in one way, then alternative ways will be readily available.

7. Throughout the course, each student will be given a series of ungraded diagnostic-progress tests to promote and pace his learning. He should use the information provided by these tests to locate misunderstandings and errors in learning.

8. Each student with learning problems will be given a number of alternative learning procedures or correctives to help him overcome his particular errors and misunderstandings.

9. The student should use his choice of the suggested correctives to "correct" these errors and misunderstandings before they accumulate and impair his subsequent learning.

Teaching for Mastery. Following this orientation period, the teacher teaches the first learning unit, using his/her customary group-based teaching methods. When this instruction has been completed, and before moving to the next unit, the teacher then administers the unit's formative test to the entire class. Next, each student usually corrects his/her own test. Finally, using a show of hands to discover the test results, the teacher certifies those students who have achieved the unit mastery standard and identifies those who have not. The former students are free to engage in enrichment activities and/or to serve as tutors for their "slower" classmates; the latter are asked to use the appropriate correctives to complete their unit learning.

The teacher then announces when the group-based instruction for the next unit will commence, and both sets of students are given responsibility for making use of the opportunities provided. If the teacher desires to postpone the start of the next unit, the students are given in-class as well as out-of-class time to discharge their respective responsibilities. If the teacher does not desire to postpone the start of the next unit, then the students must use out-of-class time.

The teacher repeats this cycle of initial instruction, diagnostic-progress testing, and certification or individual correction, unit by unit, until all units have been taught. The cycle is paced so that the teacher covers just as much material as would ordinarily be covered. Two pacing options are possible. If all the student enrichment/tutoring or correction responsibilities are to be discharged outside of class, then the teacher may pace each unit's instruction as in the past. However, if some or all responsibilities are to be discharged in class, the teacher can adjust the pace of the instruction, allowing more time for the early units and less time for the later ones. Essentially, the teacher borrows time that would ordinarily be spent on later units and spends this time on the earlier units. The assumption is that this borrowed time will not be needed later if students learn for mastery earlier.

Grading for Mastery. The teacher finally administers the course summative examination and awards A's or their equivalent to all students whose test scores are at or above the predetermined mastery performance standard. Those students who score below this level are awarded grades appropriate to the level they have achieved.

Some Basic Concepts

As noted earlier, some basic concepts about instruction underlie each of the preceding steps. Figure 1 indicates these concepts and the associated mastery techniques.

At the most general level, the conceptual level, mastery learning strategies are *systematic* approaches

Figure 1.   Mastery Learning: How Does It Work?

CONCEPTS   TECHNIQUES

General

   A. Approach Instruction Systematically:
      It should provide bridge between
      whom and what you teach
      1. Match instruction to outcomes....Base instruc-
                                          tion on outcomes
      2. Match instruction to learners....Provide mul-
                                          tiple instruc-
                                          tional methods

Specific: Extra Classroom

   B. Be PROACTIVE, not REACTIVE
      1. Clarify outcomes............Pre-define mastery
                                     and make it explicit
      2. Provide for appropriate
         help in learning............Pre-plan instruc-
                                     tion for mastery
      3. Provide for appropriate
         learning time...............Pre-plan instruc-
                                     tion for mastery

Specific: Intra Classroom

   C. Manage LEARNING, not LEARNERS
      1. Provide STUDENT ORIENTATION....Orient students
                                        to mastery learn-
                                        ing
      2. Vary HOW and HOW LONG each
         student is taught as neces-
         sary..........................Use pre-planned
                                        instruction to
                                        teach for mastery
      3. PERSONALIZE GRADING............Grade for mas-
                                        tery

to instruction. They attempt to build a strong bridge
between what the teacher desires to teach and whom
s/he wants to teach. First, the instruction is matched
to the course outcomes the teacher seeks, i.e., all
mastery strategies are outcome-based. Then, the in-

struction is matched to the learners to be taught, i.e., all mastery strategies provide multiple methods for each student to attain each of these outcomes.

At a more specific level, the extra classroom level, mastery learning strategies are proactive approaches to instruction. Much of the teacher's time, effort, and energy is spent in planning outside of class for possible inside of class contingencies. Thus, when these contingencies occur the teacher is ready for them. S/he need not waste valuable time, effort, and energy reactively manufacturing all solutions on the spot.

Proactive teaching, from a mastery learning perspective, entails several stages. One stage is the definition of the learning outcomes the teacher is seeking. Obviously if the teacher has no clear idea of where his/her instruction is headed, then s/he is more likely to be seduced by fruitless pedagogical detours.

Outcome definition is a two step process. First, the practitioner must implicitly define what all students will be expected to attain and at what levels. Second, the practitioner must make his/her implicit definitions more explicit so they communicate clearly to the teacher what must be taught and to the students what must be learned.

Both of these steps are accomplished in mastery learning strategies in the process of defining mastery. When the mastery practitioner formulates the course instructional objectives and constructs a special course final or "summative" examination based upon them, the practitioner has explicated what all students will be expected to attain. And when s/he sets some mastery grading standards on the summative examination, the practitioner has explicated what levels all students will be expected to attain.

A second stage in proactive teaching is the provision of appropriate help in learning. Oftentimes, student learning problems at one point in the classroom instruction stem from unresolved problems from earlier points. So these earlier problems must be identified and corrected as they occur.

This identification and correction is accomplished in mastery learning strategies through the pre-planning of the classroom instruction. First, the teacher breaks the entire course into smaller learning units. Each unit is long enough to convey a number of skills, ideas, concepts and appreciations but small enough to allow the close monitoring of each student's learning as the unit, i.e., the course, unfolds. Second, the teacher sequences these units so that the material in one unit is used over and over in the subsequent units. This procedure helps ensure that if this material is taught well once, then the material will not be forgotten and will be available for later use. Finally, the teacher formulates a plan of mastery instruction for each unit consisting of (a) the <u>original instruction</u> whereby the unit's material will be taught initially -- typically this instruction will be similar in content and delivery, if not identical, to the teacher's customary group-based instruction; (b) a <u>feedback</u> instrument (pencil and paper or otherwise) whereby each student's learning from the original instruction can be described diagnostically and prescriptively; (c) a <u>mastery standard</u> whereby sufficient and insufficient learning progress can be judged; and (d) the <u>correction</u> whereby the unit's material can be taught in a variety of ways different from the original instruction. This plan enables the teacher to monitor student learning as it unfolds on a unit by unit basis and to exercise a necessary measure of quality control should the learning ever unfold less than excellently.

A third stage in proactive teaching is the provision of appropriate learning time. Clearly, if each student is to be provided with appropriate help in learning, then sufficient time must be found to make use of this help. All students cannot be allowed the same amount of learning time, if this time is insufficient for most students.

The provision of appropriate learning time is also accomplished through the pre-planning of the classroom instruction. This pre-planning helps, first, to increase the quantity of time that each student spends in learning. Essentially, it constrains each student to spend as much time as is necessary to master the material in one unit before attempting the material in the next one. For many students, this means spending far more learning time in class and/or outside of class than is customary. They can no longer passively settle for mediocrity or worse in their learning; they must actively pursue excellence. The pre-planning helps, second, to increase the quality of the time that each student spends in learning. Essentially, it helps to ensure that no student spends unnecessary time learning by methods that are poorly suited to his/her learning requirements. If any student cannot learn excellently from the original instruction, the student can learn excellently from one or more correctives. S/he need not waste time restudying the ineffective original instruction.

And at the most specific level, the intra-classroom level, mastery strategies are <u>management of learning</u> approaches to instruction. They propose that inside the classroom "...the function of the teacher is to specify what is to be learned, to motivate pupils to learn it, to provide them with instructional materials, to administer these materials at a rate suitable for each pupil, to monitor students' progress, to diagnose difficulties and provide proper remediation for them, to give praise and encouragement for good performance, and to give review and practice that will maintain pupils' learning over long periods of time" (Carroll, 1971, pp. 29-30).

The management of learning is executed in three basic stages by mastery practitioners. In the orientation stage, they indicate in a concrete fashion how and toward what ends students will be taught. Obviously, no instructional technique can succeed if the ground in which it is sown is not properly prepared.

In the teaching stage, they then vary, as necessary, how and how long each student is taught by using their pre-planned instructional units. The original instruction for each unit gives all students a chance to learn excellently from one method of instruction over one period of time. The feedback instrument and mastery standard indicate those students for whom the original instruction and the initial learning time were sufficient and for whom they were not. The unit's correctives provide these latter students with the opportunity to master the material not mastered from the original instruction using additional methods of instruction and additional learning time as necessary.

In the grading stage, the practitioner evaluates students on a more personal basis. Students are graded for what they actually have learned. In short, they are graded for mastery. Such mastery grading is de-

signed to engage what White (1959) has called "competence motivation," i.e., the intrinsic desire to compete against oneself and the material to be learned,
and to disengage what I (Block, 1977) have alluded to
as "competition motivation," i.e., the extrinsic desire to compete against others. From the standpoint
of developing the talent of all students, rather than
a few, the engagement of the former motivation makes
much more sense than the engagement of the latter.

How Well Does It Work?

How well, then, does mastery learning work? As
numerous practitioners have discovered, mastery learning represents a particular commitment about education, i.e., an innovative philosophy and set of practices for its improvement (Dunkin and Biddle, 1974).
But is this commitment, like so many others, "attrac-
tively argued but unsupported by data" (Dunkin and
Biddle, 1974, p. 51) or supported by data that indicates it works 51 percent of the time and fails 49
percent of the other? The answer is No! Mastery
learning strategies may not work quite as well as
their advocates propose, but they do work very well
indeed.

Let us review the mastery learning research according to criteria set out by Dunkin and Biddle for
evaluating any commitment (1974). These are:
1. that a given teaching practice is occurring at
present in typical classrooms;
2. that an alternative teaching practice can be
encouraged by changes in teacher education programs;
3. that the alternative teaching practice produces more desirable classroom processes or (prefera-
bly) products in pupil growth than the present practice" (Dunkin and Biddle, 1974, p. 52).

Classroom Usage. There can be no question that
mastery learning ideas and practices are presently occurring in many typical classrooms. Indeed, as I
(Block, 1979) note in a special issue of Educational
Leadership on mastery learning, with the help of dedicated practitioners and administrators, of innovative
teacher inservice and preservice programs, of progressive national and international educational organizations (e.g., ASCD, NEA, NASA, UNESCO, IEA), of leading
educational publishers (e.g., McGraw-Hill, SRA, Random
House, Westinghouse Learning Corporation), and of pow-

erful news media (e.g., New York Times, CBS Television), mastery learning has helped reshape the face of contemporary educational practice. Not only are mastery learning ideas being widely implemented here, they are also being widely implemented abroad.

Two trends in the classroom usage of mastery learning are now obvious. One trend is the growing use of mastery learning ideas and practices on a large scale basis. Mastery learning is being used with a greater number of subjects, classes, teachers, and schools than ever before. Whereas in the early part of the 1970s, the typical experiment involved one subject, class, teacher, and school, the current experiments often involve many subjects, classes, teachers, and schools. Indeed, in North America it is not uncommon to find entire school districts (e.g., Chicago, Denver, District of Columbia, New Orleans, Vancouver) actively plumbing the value of mastery learning for their particular educational situation and especially for purposes of Competency-Based-Education (Spady, 1978). What is true here is even more true abroad. Countries such as South Korea, Indonesia, and Australia already have large-scale tests of mastery learning under way with the South Korean tests involving several million students in all the subjects grades 1-9. About 10 to 20 other member nations of the IEA (International Study of Education Achievement) should have additional large-scale tests off the ground by 1981-82.

The second trend is the growing use of mastery learning ideas and practices on a more adaptive basis. Mastery learning is being used by more variety of subjects, classes, teachers, and schools to meet particular needs. Whereas in the early part of the 1970s, the typical experiment involved:
    (1) subjects that were basic, required, "closed," and oriented toward convergent thinking;
    (2) classes that were small and "regular";
    (3) teachers who were inexperienced, behaviorally or cognitively oriented, and "majority" members; and
    (4) schools that were suburban, elementary-level, academically-oriented, and public;

the current experiments increasingly involve:
    (5) subjects that are intermediate or advanced, elective, "open," and oriented toward divergent thinking;
    (6) classes that are large and "special" (e.g.,

handicapped, bilingual);

(7) teachers who are experienced, humanistically oriented, and "minority" members; and

(8) schools that are urban and rural, secondary and tertiary-level, technically/professionally oriented, and private.

Teacher Training. There also can be no question that mastery learning ideas and practices can be taught to teachers. Teachers both here and abroad have participated in countless local, regional, state-wide, and national preservice and inservice teacher training workshops and credentialing courses. Moreover, the experiences gleaned from these workshops and courses have already been packaged in a variety of how to do it manuals perhaps the best known of which are Block and Anderson's (1975) MASTERY LEARNING IN CLASSROOM INSTRUCTION, Keller and Sherman's (1974) THE KELLER PLAN HANDBOOK, Okey and Ciesla's (1975) MASTERY TEACHING, and Torshen's (1977) THE MASTERY APPROACH TO COMPETENCY-BASED EDUCATION. More courses and workshops and how to do it manuals are bound to appear.

Nor can there be much question that once teachers are taught for mastery they can use their training in the classroom. Okey (1975), for example, taught 20 inservice teachers and 20 preservice interns how to teach for mastery and then followed them back to their classrooms. He found that students noted a perceptible change in their teachers' and interns' behavior when they taught for mastery. For example, students saw the teachers and interns as telling them what they were expected to learn, allowing them different amounts of learning time, and using diagnostic tests to monitor their progress.

But there is a distinct question as to whether inexperienced preservice teachers use their training as effectively as experienced inservice ones. Okey (1975), for example, found that inservice teachers were far more likely to elicit greater learning from their students under mastery learning conditions than preservice interns. And my own experience, as well as that of others, has been similar. Perhaps this is because learning how to teach for mastery requires less in the way of the acquisition of a whole new set of teaching skills and more in the way of orchestrating and supplementing the skills one already has. Preservice interns would tend to have fewer classroom skills to orchestrate than inservice teachers.

Student Outcomes. Lastly, there can be little question that mastery learning ideas and practices promote student growth. Indeed, the impact that mastery learning ideas and practices have had on student cognitive and affective development has been remarkable.

Consider, for example, a recent review by Block and Burns (1976) of some 40 rigorous studies of student outcomes under mastery and nonmastery approaches to instruction. This review's findings echoed the general findings of earlier and later reviews. Block and Burns (1976) reported the following:

Learning Effectiveness. Mastery taught students typically learned more effectively than their nonmastery taught counterparts. Whether learning was measured in terms of student achievement or in terms of student retention, they almost always learned more, and usually significantly more, and they learned more like one another.

Learning Efficiency. Mastery taught students also typically learned more efficiently than their nonmastery taught counterparts. Whereas in the nonmastery taught classrooms some students learned several times as fast as other students, in the mastery taught classrooms individual differences in learning rate were substantially less. In fact, in these latter classrooms individual differences in learning rate seemed headed toward a vanishing point in which even the "slowest" students would learn roughly as fast as the "fastest" students.

Learner Affect. Lastly, mastery taught students liked their learning, their teaching and themselves better than their nonmastery taught counterparts. They virtually always responded more positively than their counterparts, for example, on measures of interest in and attitudes toward the subject matter learned, of self-concept (academic as well as general), of academic self-confidence, of attitudes toward cooperative learning, and of attitudes toward the instruction. Whether their more favorable affective responses were just momentary expressions of enthusiasm or more permanent ones that would carry over into their subsequent work was, however, indeterminable.

Summary

This article has provided an introduction to the topic of mastery learning. Specifically, the article addressed three questions: what is mastery learning, how does it work, and how well does it work?

We have learned that mastery learning is essentially an optimistic theory about teaching and learning and an effective set of individualized instructional practices for implementing this theory in the ordinary classroom setting. At the heart of this theory is the assertion that any teacher can help virtually all of his/her students to learn excellently.

We have also learned that mastery learning works on the basis of three large assumptions about what constitutes teaching for excellence. The most general of these assumptions is that the teacher must approach his/her instruction more systematically in the sense that the instruction should definitely bridge what is to be taught to whom is to be taught. This means that the instruction for mastery learning is outcome-based and provides multiple ways for each student to reach each outcome.

A more specific assumption is that the teacher must become more proactive in his/her instruction in the sense that more time, effort, and energy is spent outside of class readying for possible inside of class contingencies. This means that the teacher pre-defines and explicates mastery in learning so that the classroom outcomes s/he is seeking are clear. And the teacher pre-plans the classroom instruction for mastery learning so that it consistently provides appropriate help and learning time for each student.

The most specific assumption is that the teacher must concentrate more heavily on the management of learning in the classroom. This means the teacher orients students to learning for mastery so that they are clear about how and what they will be taught. The teacher also uses the preplanned classroom instruction for mastery learning so that how and how long each student is taught varies appropriately. And the teacher grades for mastery learning so that each student is graded on a more personal and less competitive basis.

Lastly, we have learned that mastery learning has

worked very well indeed. Mastery learning ideas and practices are being widely used in classrooms both here and abroad and their use is on the rise. They are also being widely disseminated to preservice and inservice teachers. When the ideas and practices have been learned and used, they have consistently promoted student growth. Students have not only learned more effectively and efficiently, they have also felt better about their learning, their instruction and themselves.

Much that we have learned about mastery learning theory, practice and research will, of course, seem "old hat" to some educators. After all, an optimistic faith in all students' capacity for excellent learning, an approach to instruction that is systematic, proactive and learning oriented, and an approach that consistently promotes student cognitive and affective growth have long been the trademarks of the paragons of the teaching profession. What should be "new hat," however, is the message that mastery learning theory, practice and research now offer these trademarks of our best teachers to all our teachers. Surely, at a time when public confidence in the teaching profession is low, such a message cannot be ignored.

References

Anderson, L.W., and Block, J.H. "Mastery Learning." in Treffinger, D., Davis, J. and Ripple, R. (Eds.) HANDBOOK ON EDUCATIONAL PSYCHOLOGY: INSTRUCTIONAL PRACTICE AND RESEARCH. New York: Academic Press, 1976.

Block, J.H. (Ed.) MASTERY LEARNING: THEORY AND PRACTICE. New York: Holt, Rinehart and Winston, 1971.

Block, J.H. (Ed.) SCHOOLS, SOCIETY, AND MASTERY LEARNING. New York: Holt, Rinehart and Winston, 1974.

Block, J.H. "Motivation, Evaluation, and Mastery Learning." UCLA EDUCATOR, Winter 1977, vol. 19, no. 2, pp. 31-36.

Block, J.H. "Mastery Learning: The Current State of the Craft." EDUCATIONAL LEADERSHIP, vol. 37, no. 2, November 1979, pp. 114-117.

Block, J.H. and Burns, R.B. "Mastery Learning." In Shulman, L. (Ed.), REVIEW OF RESEARCH IN EDUCATION, vol. 4. Itasca, Ill.: F.E. Peacock, 1976.

Bloom, B.S. "An Introduction to Mastery Learning Theory." In Block, J.H. (Ed.), SCHOOLS, SOCIETY, AND MASTERY LEARNING. New York: Holt, Rinehart and Winston, 1974.

Bloom, B.S. HUMAN CHARACTERISTICS AND SCHOOL LEARNING. New York: McGraw-Hill, 1976.

Bloom, B.S., Hastings, J.T., and Madaus, G.F. HANDBOOK ON FORMATIVE AND SUMMATIVE EVALUATION OF STUDENT LEARNING. New York: McGraw-Hill, 1971.

Carroll, J.B. "Problems of Measurement Related to the Concept of Learning for Mastery." In Block, J.H. (Ed.), MASTERY LEARNING: THEORY AND PRACTICE. New York: Holt, Rinehart and Winston, 1971.

Dunkin, M.J., and Biddle, B.J. THE STUDY OF TEACHING. New York: Holt, Rinehart and Winston, 1974.

Gronlund, N. INDIVIDUALIZING CLASSROOM INSTRUCTION. New York: Macmillan Publishing Co., 1974.

Hambleton, R.K. "Testing and Decision-Making Procedures for Selected Individualized Instructional Programs." REVIEW OF EDUCATIONAL RESEARCH, 1974, vol. 44, pp. 371-400.

Keller, F.S., and Sherman, J.G. THE KELLER PLAN HANDBOOK. Menlo Park, Cal.: W.A. Benjamin, 1974.

Okey, J.R. "Development of Mastery Teaching Materials" (Final Evaluation Rep., USOE G-74-2990), Bloomington: Indiana University, August 1975.

Okey, J. and Ciesla, J. MASTERY TEACHING. Bloomington: National Center for the Development of Training Materials in Teacher Education, Indiana University, 1975.

Spady, W.G. "The Concept and Implications of Competency-Based Education." EDUCATIONAL LEADERSHIP, 1978, vol. 36, pp. 16-22.

Talmage, H. (Ed.) SYSTEMS OF INDIVIDUALIZED EDUCATION. Berkeley, California: McCutchan, 1975.

Torshen, K.P. THE MASTERY APPROACH TO COMPETENCY-BASED EDUCATION. New York: Academic Press, 1977.

White, R.W. "Motivation Reconsidered: The Concept of Competence." PSYCHOLOGICAL REVIEW, 1959, vol. 66, pp. 297-333.

IN DEFENSE
OF GRADE INFLATION

Ralph J. Kane

Nearly everyone agrees that grade inflation has beset every level of our educational system, but no one has publicly identified the source of this menace. Well, I confess. For nearly two decades as a high school teacher, I have unashamedly given A's and B's to dozens of youngsters of less-than-average academic ability. Furthermore, I continue to do this. But before you condemn me as a heretic, let me advise you that a lot of teachers have commited the crime.

Teachers, by the thousands apparently, have abandoned the old method of norm-referenced grading. This system, more commonly known as "grading on the curve," produces a few winners and a few losers, leaving most students in the middle to be smothered by the deadening verdict of mediocrity. You probably grew up with this system, and if you remember it with fondness, no doubt you were one of the winners.

As a young teacher in the 1950's, I accepted the principles of norm-referenced grading without question. Then during the 1960's and the early 1970's, something happened to the mood of the country. We began to scrutinize the dominant values that we had labeled the "Protestant Ethic." In the process, we abandoned nothing; we merely softened and humanized what we already had -- a greening, if you will. Work as an end unto itself lost some of its sanctity, while the needs of the individual gained ascendance over the demands of institutions. Naturally, the schools could not ignore this shift in public sentiment.

Slowly but surely, the practice of grading kids with unequal ability by the same standards struck

Reprinted from TODAY'S EDUCATION, 67 (4): 41 (November 1978), by permission of author and publisher.

teachers as being a bit obscene. We had limited the number of acceptable grades, so one student's gain necessarily meant another student's loss. Finally, we realized that grades given under such conditions do not represent honest achievement in terms of real learning. They merely inform the student whether he or she has beaten someone out of an A or B. So without manifestos, we quietly moved toward more humane methods of evaluation.

Today many teachers, including myself, give all students a reasonable chance to make an A. They assign students a set of expectations well within their reach. Students soon learn to compete only against themselves. To be winners, they don't have to defeat their classmates. Many youngsters who would have given up when faced with certain defeat under the old system now work close to their full potential.

Of course, this means that more students get better grades than ever before because we have enlarged the winner's circle. It also means that some students will not possess all the knowledge or skills normally associated with high grades. Some university professors will be appalled when they encounter these students. But in my opinion, the final products of higher education -- our teachers, scientists, doctors, and lawyers -- are more intelligent and better trained than ever before. So what's there to get so excited about?

No doubt, much of the alarm about grade inflation stems from a problem of semantics. Grades and standards are not the same thing. They may not even be closely related. When a teacher consistently grades low, it does not necessarily indicate that he or she has high standards. More likely, it reflects a breakdown in the instructional process. If low grades could raise standards, I would be among the first to endorse them.

I have never given a class all A's, but I hope to before I retire from my teaching career. And when I do, I'll be darned if I will apologize to anyone.

STUDENT NONPROMOTION AND TEACHER ATTITUDE

Maurice Miller, Catherine C. Frazier,
and D. Dean Richey

A return to a minimum competency standard in the public schools and a general "back to the basics" point of view have brought renewed vigor on the part of those who favor nonpromotion, or retaining students at a particular grade level. While there are those who question whether any student should ever be retained (Miller, 1978), others propose that, with proper consideration of available data, retention may be the most suitable decision for some students (Light 1977). Research regarding retention is not very supportive of the concept, yet the practice is widespread. It is, therefore, necessary to examine what research has to say about this practice and to try to understand why it is still promulgated.

School plays an extremely important role in the total development of the child -- second only to the home (Jersild, 1952). If the school is a place where the child faces failure, rejection, and daily reminders of limitations (Purkey, 1970), and if retention serves as a negative indicator to the child, it impedes the child's total development. In fact, several researchers (e.g. Lloyd, 1971) have indicated that retention rate -- even in the first three grades -- is a significant predictor of later dropout rate. (This is interesting, considering the sometimes-heard comment that if retention is to take place it should be in the first three years of school.)

Research has consistently contraindicated retention. Typical research findings include:

1. Although the main reason given for retaining a student is lack of subject matter mastery, research

Reprinted from CONTEMPORARY EDUCATION, 51 (3): 155-157 (Spring 1980), by permission of authors and publisher.

shows that retention does not bring significantly greater gains in subject matter mastery.

2. Fear of possible failure does not make students work any harder.

3. Greater homogeneity of achievement within a grade level does not result when retention is practiced.

4. The more times the student is retained, the lower will be his self-concept.

5. Students retained have more adjustment-socialization difficulties.

6. Teachers and peers tend to develop unfavorable attitudes toward students retained.

7. Low grades and retention may also bring unfavorable attitudes from the child's family.

8. Retention may be justified in the case of a child who has been absent a great deal, or for the very immature child (Frazier, 1978).

In order to assess teachers' awareness of these findings, and to specify their current attitudes toward retention, a survey instrument was developed using descriptive and attitudinal items based on previous research findings.

Subjects

Teachers participating in this study were 150 elementary, secondary, and special education teachers enrolled in summer courses at a university located in middle Tennessee. The survey was administered within university classes, thus ensuring 100 percent return. Of the 150 teachers surveyed, 43 taught in grades K-3, 28 taught grades 4-6, 37 taught at the secondary level, and 42 were special education teachers in a variety of settings. In terms of age as a measure of experience, 60 were in the 20-25 age range, 46 between 26-30, 21 between 31-39, and 23 were 40 or over. Also, 31 were male and 119 were female.

Results

Sixty-nine percent of all teachers indicated that they had asked that a child be retained -- sixty-three percent indicating this happened in the previous two to three years. Eighty-one percent stated that their school did not have a written policy on retention, while seventy-five percent felt a school should have a written policy. Over a third of the teachers (37 percent) reported that they had not read any research or literature regarding retention.

Twenty attitudinal items on the scale were based on findings in the research literature or dealt with current issues. Items were responded to on a five-point Likert-type scale ranging from (1) strongly agree to (5) strongly disagree. The items with significant variation will be discussed here.

Item 12. "The threat of retention can make students work harder." Twice as many males as females agreed with this item, with female responses fairly evenly spread across the range. Secondary level teachers, also, tended to agree with this statement, while special educators and primary teachers tended to disagree.

Item 14. "Handicapped children should not be retained." More male teachers agreed than did female teachers, with forty-six percent of the females undecided.

Item 15. "Retention promotes behavior problems." Teachers in the 31-39 and 50 and over age group tended to agree; teachers who were 26-30 disagreed; and teachers in the 20-25 and 40-49 age groups had responses spread across the range.

Item 16. "Retention discourages learning rather than encouraging it." Ten percent of the males strongly disagreed, while only five percent of the females did so. Five percent of the females strongly agreed, but no males did. Teachers in the 26-30, 31-39, and 40-49 age groups tended to disagree, while teachers 50 and over tended to agree.

Item 19. "There is a typical personality profile among all children who are retained." Females tended to disagree, while males' responses were fairly evenly spread.

191

Item 20. "Children who have been retained are rejected by their peers." Sixty-nine percent of the females strongly disagreed, with thirty-seven percent of the males disagreeing.

Item 21. "Self-concept should be considered in retention decisions." Only three percent of the secondary teachers strongly agreed, while thirty to forty percent of all others strongly agreed.

Item 22. "Decision to retain a child should be made solely by the teacher." Thirty-two percent of the males agreed, but only twelve percent of the females did. Teachers in grades 7-12 agreed more often than the other levels of teaching.

Item 25. "All children retained should be referred to special education." Teachers in the over 4 age groups agreed with this item more frequently than the other groups.

Item 26. "Retention serves a useful function in helping children learn to adjust to failure." Female teachers tended to disagree. Also, secondary teachers agreed more often with this item than did the other groups.

Other items teachers generally disagreed with included retention's usefulness in promoting subject-matter mastery, the existence of a particular personality among retained students, and the use of absences and mild deficits as criteria for retention. Thus, on these items, teachers were generally in agreement with the research. With the items questioning whether children should be retained only in grades K-3, teachers strongly disagreed, as they did with the statement "No child should ever be retained." Thus, these teachers were at variance with some strong professional opinion, but in agreement with popular opinion.

Items with which the teachers tended to agree related to immature children being retained, retention contributing to school dropouts, children being involved in their own retention decisions, and minimum competency tests increasing the number of retentions. The teachers were in general agreement with research and professional opinion on these matters.

Because of the variety of teacher opinions stated on these items, no general conclusion can be reached

reached regarding these teachers' attitudes about retention. On some items teachers were in general agreement with research or current opinion. On other items there were strong pockets of disparate feelings. Speaking very broadly, female primary teachers in the 30 and 40 year old groups were most open-minded and most in agreement with research findings. Secondary male teachers were most close-minded and indicated more strongly that retention was academically useful and that there was a particular personality profile among students retained. Interestingly, most teachers felt that the individual child's self-concept and attitude should be considered in the retention decision.

Although teachers generally agreed that retention does not promote subject-matter mastery and that it may be detrimental to the child's self-concept, most teachers were in favor of retention as a practice and did, in fact, retain students. This raises the question of why they continued the practice. Perhaps they felt the weight of presumed opinions held by the public or by other teachers.

Since teachers continue the practice of retention even though research has been unable to show any benefits from it, there is a need for inservice programs acquainting teachers with the research and with alternative possibilities. At the very least, schools need to have written guidelines for teachers to follow.

References

Frazier, C.C. TEACHER ATTITUDES TOWARD RETENTION. Unpublished master's thesis, Tennessee Technological University, 1978

Jersild, A.T. IN SEARCH OF SELF. New York: Columbia University, 1952.

Lloyd, D.N. PREDICTION OF HIGH SCHOOL DROPOUT OR GRADUATION FROM THIRD GRADE DATA. National Institute of Mental Health, 1971 (ERIC Do. No. ED 085 623)

Miller, T.L. Light's Retention Scale (Review). JOURNAL OF LEARNING DISABILITIES, 1978, 11, 529.

Purkey, W.W. SELF-CONCEPT AND SCHOOL ACHIEVEMENT. Englewood Cliffs, N.J.: Prentice-Hall, 1970.

Part 4

MOTIVATING STUDENTS

AND MANAGING BEHAVIOR

WHAT CAN SCHOOLS DO ABOUT VIOLENCE

Francis A. J. Ianni and Elizabeth Reuss-Ianni

What are the nature and extent of violence and crime in American schools?

°What role do schools themselves play in producing, aggravating, or reducing crime?

°How can changes in schools, as distinct from changes in society, remedy the problems we seem to be having with social controls?

In 1978, we worked on the Safe School Study conducted by the National Institute of Education. This and similar work of ours and of others provide the statistics and examples we use in discussing these questions.

Research indicates that during the sixties both acts of violence and property destruction in schools increased. After the school year 1971-72, both rates leveled off. Most of the studies indicate that assaults on teachers increased from 1956 to 1974 but leveled off thereafter; that robberies and assaults increased in the early seventies; and that vandalism increased in the mid-sixties and leveled off after 1970 or 1971. The studies do not indicate that the rates of the offenses we call violence and vandalism are currently growing worse.

Some characteristics of communities over which schools have little control seem to be related to higher rates of crime and disruption in schools. For example, the proportion of schools seriously affected by violence declines with community size, from 15 percent in large cities to 6 percent in suburban and 4 percent in rural areas.

Reprinted from TODAY'S EDUCATION, 69 (2): 20-23 (April 1980), by permission of authors and publisher.

It seems clear, however, that schools do not simply reflect community crime rates. In a number of schools we studied, the incidence of school violence and vandalism had declined while crime rates in the schools' immediate communities had soared. In some of these schools, parents reported that they felt their children were safer within school than outside it. Teachers and administrators in these schools also said they felt safer in the schools than traveling through the surrounding communities.

The role of the school in structuring the disruption which takes place within it is also apparent in the fact that, except for trespassing and breaking and entering, most reported offenses in schools are committed by current students.

Of the characteristics over which schools have some control, the age-grade structure seems to be the one that is the most directly related to the nature and extent of crime in schools. To a lesser extent, it seems that disproportionate racial and ethnic balances in a school can bring victimization of the smaller groups.

Seventh graders are most likely to be attacked or robbed; twelfth graders are least so; and at age 13, the risks are apparently highest. We believe that moving out of the more protective elementary school context into the less self-contained structure of junior high school is the major factor here.

Most offenses in schools involve victims and offenders of the same race (58 percent). But the fact that 42 percent of offenses are interracial indicates that interracial conflict is a serious problem. The smaller the size of a minority group in the school, the greater the likelihood that members of other racial groups will commit offenses against members of the minority.

Studies have found that a number of other school-specific factors are related to school crime and disorder.

Crowding is one important factor. Schools which had major disruptions in the late sixties and early seventies often had more students than they were designed to serve. According to many teachers and parents, later reduction in the number of students in these schools was accompanied by a decline in violence and disruption.

In our observations we found that the location of violence and disruption were usually crowded areas -- stairways, hallways, and cafeterias. Many staff told us that control of students was easier in classrooms, where students can be identified as individuals, than in the disorder of the halls and stairs during change of classes.

School size in general is another important factor. Large schools have a higher incidence of more and serious crime and disruption than smaller schools.

In small schools, students are individually identifiable. A number of administrators, teachers, counselors, and security personnel whom we interviewed said that in a small school "there is no place to hide." In some of these schools, the principal knew not only each student but each student's family as well.

In large schools, in the absence of some form of identification, it is impossible to identify outsiders. In schools on split sessions, school personnel can never be certain who is and who is not supposed to be in the building at a given time.

Not only can students be easily identified in small schools, but they are more likely to identify with the school, with other students, and with teachers and to join in the activities and programs of the school. This characteristic, which seems quite close to what was called "school spirit" in an earlier day, is difficult if not impossible to develop in large, urban secondary schools which have 4,000 or 5,000 students.

While school spirit has usually been portrayed as a student characteristic, large school size also reduces the ability of the teachers to relate to the students. It thus seems to help cause the considerable apprehension teachers feel in urban schools.

Students unable to identify with a large school as a whole frequently claim control over particular portions of the school and even over "turfs" on the sidewalks outside of the school in much the same way that prisoners set up territories in prison yards.

These territorial claims are often based on ethnicity. In these cases, they not only reduce interaction among ethnic groups but are a source of potential conflict.

According to the Safe School Study, classrooms are the safest places, considering the amount of time spent there. Students' risk of violent encounter is greatest during the time between classes, especially in senior high schools. More than half of all thefts, on the other hand, occur during class. Next to classrooms, lockers are the sites of most thefts.

Nationwide, 1 out of 6 secondary school students in the Safe School Study reported avoiding three or more places in school because he or she believed them to be hazardous. When students' uneasiness reaches the limits of tolerance, they stay away from school altogether.

Students who have actually been victims of attack or robbery in schools are more likely than other students to say that they are afraid both on the way to school and in school. They are also more likely to say that their own grades are low or below average.

Victimized students are likely to be having behavioral problems in school and are twice as likely as others to report having been expelled from another school.

They are also more likely to report that they are punished by their parents if they get into trouble in school. If these perceptions are accurate, both home and school are less supportive and more punitive to students who are victimized than to other students.

Teachers, administrators, and students report that not only do the victims of attack and robbery share many characteristics with students who have been identified as offenders, but they are more likely than nonvictims to be offenders themselves.

Teachers and administrators we have interviewed complain that a small group of youngsters -- the term most frequently used was "hard core" -- produces most of the violence and disruption in schools. Many teachers and administrators estimate that this group is "about 10 to 15 percent" and that the other 85 to 90 percent of students are seldom either victims or offenders.

To some extent these reports may be the result of that sorting of youngsters by which the school seems to modify patterns of social relations by defining some youngsters as uneducable and violent. The hard core may, however, represent an actual deviant group within the school community. Members of this group do not seem to come from any specific racial, ethnic, or socioeconomic background. School staff commonly describe them as students who have difficulty academically, are frequently in trouble in the community, and come from troubled homes.

Teachers, administrators, and students, however, indicate that this group of troublesome students can find allies among other students when specific situations arise. Thus school violence and disruptive behavior can be described as interactive: A small group of students frequently causes problems and at times sets off a chain reaction among other students.

The schools are often unable to deal with this group of troublesome students. The most common treatment reported is suspension, but very few educators say that suspensions are effective either as deterrents or as treatment. Staff members often complain about the unavailability of adequate counseling or psychiatric help. More and more, school systems are transferring troublesome students to other schools. School staff often suggested, however, that these students require special training and socialization experience.

What makes school disorders most significant for education is the effect on the climate of the school. In addition to the actual costs in terms of people and dollars, crime and disorder in schools disrupt learning. Since schools are charged with much of the responsibility for socialization, school disruption can have a lasting effect on youth and can spread out into the community and into the future. Also, crime and disruption and the potential for it can have serious effects on teachers, who find their fear for personal safety is detrimental to effective teaching. A safe school is necessary for effective learning and efficient teaching to take place.

The responsibility for prevention and control of school crime has always rested more heavily on the school than on the community. Historically, this un-evenness is based on the doctrine of in loco parentis. The parent delegates some authority over the child to the teacher. The doctrine covers the school's right to discipline the child.

In recent decades, schools have emphasized the more positive developmental aspects of discipline, and students have challenged the more negative forms in the courts. One of the legacies of the considerable media attention to school crime and disruption, how-ever, is that today interest in reestablishing the school's right to use the more negative aspects of discipline is growing.

At the same time, new interest has arisen in the more positive kind of school discipline -- that which arises from good governance. The governance procedures which shape behavior are usually expressed in school rules and regulations. They are even more frequently found in informal social control: the importance or lack of importance attributed to academic excellence, the structure of order, and the development of an identification with the mission of the school. These elements are, we believe, the important components of the governance structure of a school.

Evidence is abundant that school governance thus broadly defined is the major factor determining the level of crime and disruption in schools. Students' perception of the school as maintaining order and teachers' perception of their own ability to maintain order in class are positively related to lower losses, measured in dollars, from vandalism and theft. So are good coordination and mutual support between adminis-tration and faculty.

Also, school crime and disruption are reduced in schools where students say they can identify with the teachers and have access to them and where ethnic and racial harmony are great.

Conversely, where teachers' behavior shows a lack of respect for students and where competition among students is strong, property losses tend to increase.

We are going to describe a specific pattern of school governance with a number of very distinctive features. These features were the most frequently cited reasons for success in the schools we studied which were safe and just as obviously absent from those which were not. More important, the same features were reported to be responsible for the improvement in turnaround schools -- those which had reversed a pattern of violence and disorder.

The most obvious and most frequently cited factor was the leadership style of the principal. Often the turnaround point in a school that was once considered unsafe and out of control was the arrival of a new principal. Wherever principals were described as dynamically moving the schools forward, students, community residents, and school staff frequently cited their educational leadership and the new educational programs they installed.

Visibility and availability to students and staff are two other characteristics of the principals in schools which have made a dramatic turnaround from periods of violence. Conversely, in schools which remained in difficulty, the principals were most frequently cited as the major problem. Often they were described as "unavailable and ineffective."

The principal's ability to initiate a structure of order in the school was equally important. A number of recent research findings indicates that a firm, fair, and consistent structure of order is an important determinant of success in many areas of education, from the teaching of reading to the establishment of a climate conducive to learning.

In such a governance system, discipline and sanctions, as well as rewards, are handed out in an even-handed fashion. Students and faculty are aware of the consequences of specific acts and aware that exceptions are rarely, if ever, made. In unsuccessful schools, on the other hand, rule enforcement in the academic areas tends to be highly arbitrary and seems to serve disciplinary rather than educational ends.

Of particular importance was the principal's responsiveness to teachers' and students' opinions about school policy. In some cases, this meant a receptivity to participation by students and teachers in making decisions; in others, a willingness to make known how decisions would be made and a practice of following these procedures with openness and honesty.

A number of characteristics of teachers also seem

to be important in those schools where a successful
governance program is part of the structure of social
control. High self-esteem, job satisfaction, and general agreement with the principal's educational and
procedural styles indicate the high morale common in
successful schools. Teachers in such schools report
that they are in those particular schools because they
want to be there.

Cohesiveness among teachers and a sense of identification with students are other characteristics
frequently mentioned. Generally, high faculty morale
seems to be associated with a strong sense of school
spirit among students.

Far from being simply the victim of external social forces, the school plays a major role in determining the incidence of school crime and disruption.
Today only 8 percent of the elementary and secondary
schools in the country are still being seriously affected by crime, violence, and disruption, while crime
and vandalism rates in the community continue to grow.
This indicates that schools have been able to resist
external social trends and maintain their own social
controls.

We have suggested several organizational variables over which schools have control -- paramount
among them being the governance pattern -- that can
make major differences in providing an orderly climate
in which learning can occur.

Although many of these changes are within the
control of the school itself, nevertheless, it is important for the school to maintain appropriate relationships with the community and with other parts of
the educational system. Lacking such relationships,
schools become isolated from the help they need to
carry out their educating and socializing roles.

The results of such isolation are apparent in the
case of those large urban secondary schools which show
the highest incidence of crime and disruption. Principals in such schools more frequently report that
they receive little support from the central administration than do other principals.

A number of other factors relating to school
crime and disruption depend on resources outside the
school. The critical importance of the principal's

leadership style, for example, means that the training programs at universities and the selection and placement practices of school systems must be such as to locate, prepare, develop, and support suitable leadership personnel.

In making decisions that affect the number and location of schools, communities should examine the relationship of school size to the dysfunctional effects of overcrowding and anonymity. Similarly, we should reconsider the age-grade structure of schools which presents seventh graders with the problems of adjusting to a new and much less structured school environment at the age when they seem least able to adjust to it.

Schools should turn to appropriate juvenile as well as other community agencies for help when -- but only when -- it is necessary. Schools have traditionally been reluctant to call in the police for all except the most serious situations, and then often too late. Every major report on school crime and disruption points to an apparent tendency of schools to underreport crimes. Most serious attacks and fights are not reported to the police. Even of those involving weapons or injury, only one-sixth are reported.

Throughout our experience in looking at school crime and disruption, we found that emphasis on people rather than devices, on preventive discipline rather than presence of large numbers of security personnel, provided the most successful means of keeping schools safe.

Early identification of the youngsters in that small group most frequently associated with school violence and disorder also is important. Early identification should lead to adequate socialization for such students from early in their school careers, as well as to guidance programs and psychiatric care when necessary. Such measures should be characterized by a positive and preventive rather than a punitive style.

At present we are faced with a very real danger. Despite research indications to the contrary, the public continues to believe that school crime is escalating at an alarming rate. Until public opinion catches up with research, the schools may be tempted to turn increasingly to criminal justice instead of educational solutions.

Research on the social organization of schools indicates that there are structural changes and techniques of social control which do work in schools. Such changes in schools and in how they relate to their communities are within the school's own span of control and do not require major societal adjustments. They have the advantage that they have not been tried elsewhere and failed.

COMPETENCY-BASED APPROACH TO DISCIPLINE
--IT'S ASSERTIVE--

Lee Canter

Assertive discipline is a competency-based approach to discipline. It is designed to provide educators the competence and confidence necessary to assert their influence and deal effectively with the discipline problems in today's schools. This approach does not advocate teachers storming into their classrooms and "throttling" children who open their mouths. What it does advocate is that teachers must utilize a systematic approach to discipline which enables them to set firm, consistent limits for the students while at the same time remaining cognizant of the reality of the students' need for warmth and positive support.

What do we mean by <u>assertive</u>? Webster's Dictionary defines the verb "assert" as follows: "To state or affirm positively, assuredly, plainly or strongly." For our purposes we define <u>assertive teachers</u> as, "those who clearly and firmly express their wants and feelings and are prepared to back their words up with appropriate actions." In other words, they "say what they mean and mean what they say." Assertive teachers take the following stand in their classroom:

I will not tolerate any student stopping me from teaching.

I will not tolerate any student preventing another student from learning.

I will not tolerate any student engaging in any behavior that is not in his/her best interest and in the best interest of others.

And most important, whenever a student chooses to

Reprinted from THRUST, 8 (3): 11-13 (January 1979), by permission of author and publisher.

behave appropriately, I will immediately recognize and reinforce such behavior.

Finally, assertive teachers are the "boss" in their classroom. They have the skills and confidence necessary to "take charge" in their classroom.

In our research, we also focused on what types of teachers did not respond effectively to student behavior. We labeled such teachers non-assertive or hostile.

Non-assertive teachers do not clearly or firmly communicate their wants and needs to the students or if they do they are not prepared to back their words up with actions. They are passive and/or wishy washy with students. They lack the skills and/or confidence necessary to deal effectively with the behavior of disruptive students.

Hostile teachers get their needs met, but they violate the best interest of the students. They verbally and/or physically abuse their students. The following example illustrates how the three types of teachers would deal with a student's disruptive behavior.
The teacher wants the children to do their work without talking or disrupting each other. During a work period a boy put aside his work and began to talk loudly to the children around him.

Non-assertive teacher: Would typically walk up to the boy and ask him to get to work. When he doesn't she throws her hands in the air and states, "I don't know what to do with you!"

Hostile teacher: Would typically storm up to the boy and yell, "You have the biggest mouth I've seen. Shut it or you'll be sorry."

Assertive teacher: Would typically walk up to the boy, look him in the eye and firmly tell him, "Stop talking and get to work now! If you don't, you will have to finish your work during free time."

Now, here is an example to illustrate how the three types of teachers would respond when a student behaves appropriately.

A kindergarten teacher has a girl who would get

disruptive during the transition periods between activities. The girl would get very excited, fail to follow directions and would frequently run around the room yelling. The teacher assertively set firm limits, and one afternoon the girl cleaned up appropriately and came directly to the rug as instructed.

Non-assertive teacher: Would typically not verbally or non-verbally recognize or support the girl's appropriate behavior.

Hostile teacher: Would typically state to the girl, "It's about time I didn't have to chase you around the room to get you to clean up and sit down!"

Assertive teacher: Would typically say to the girl, "I liked the nice job you did cleaning up and following directions. You did so well you can sit on my lap and pick the story that I will now read to the class."

Assertive Discipline Competencies

As was mentioned, assertive discipline is a competency-based approach to discipline. The following are the competencies our research has indicated teachers <u>must</u> master to enable them to deal effectively with classroom behavior.

1. Teachers must know what specific behaviors they need the students to engage in. They must communicate these behaviors to the students. Typical behaviors teachers need from students:

--Follow directions
--Raise hand before speaking
--Stay in seat
--No cussing or teasing
--Keep hands, feet, objects to self
--Be to class on time
--Bring paper, pencil, books

2. Teachers must know how to systematically respond to the disruptive behavior of students. Teachers must provide a negative consequence <u>everytime</u> students disrupt. The consequences need to be included in a systematic Discipline Plan of Consequences. A hypothetical plan is as follows:

        1st Disruption -- name on board
        2nd Disruption -- one check (15 minutes of deten-
tion)
        3rd Disruption -- two checks (30 minutes of de-
tention)
        4th Disruption -- three checks (30 minutes of de-
tention and call parents)
        5th Disruption -- four checks (30 minutes of de-
tention, call parents, and go to principal's office)

        3.   Teachers must know how to systematically re-
spond to the appropriate behavior of students. Teachers must provide consistent praise or other meaningful
reinforcement when their students behave appropriately. For example, on an elementary level, teachers
need to praise every student each day for some appropriate behavior.

        4.   Teachers must know how to work cooperatively
with the principal and parents of problem students.
Teachers must establish and share their discipline
plan with both the principal and parents. They need
to also set down guidelines for what they expect from
both the principal and the parents.

Implementation of an Assertive Discipline Program

        What happens when a school utilizes assertive
discipline? This question can best be answered by
discussing what one school has accomplished.

        In September 1977, the faculty of Rice Elementary
School, along with their co-workers in Santa Maria
(California) Elementary Schools, were trained in assertive discipline. In the days following the training, the teachers set up assertive discipline plans in
each of their classrooms. The basic guidelines were
as follows:

        1.   All students were told disruptive behavior
would no longer be tolerated for any reason. Students
were expected to follow these general rules:
        -- Follow directions
        -- Raise hand before speaking
        -- Stay in seat
        -- No cussing or teasing
        -- Keep hands, feet, objects to self

        2.   All teachers set up systematic discipline

                            209

plans for their classrooms. The basic plan was as
follows:
        1st time a child broke a rule -- name on board
        2nd time -- one check, 15 minutes after school
        3rd time -- two checks, 30 minutes after school
        4th time -- three checks, 30 minutes and call
home
        5th time -- four checks, 30 minutes, call home,
and go to principal
        Severe disruption -- immediately go to princi-
pal's office

        Everytime any student broke any rule for any rea-
son they chose to get their name on the board, etc.
Each teacher consistently followed these guidelines.

        Each teacher's plan was approved by the principal
and a copy went home to each parent. If the initial
plan did not work with serious behavior problems, more
severe plans were developed.

        3.   All teachers balanced the negative conse-
quences with positive consequences when students be-
haved appropriately:
        They praised each student each day.
        They sent home positive notes to the parents.
        They set up classwide reward programs by which
the student's appropriate behavior could earn extra
P.E. time, etc.

        Teachers thus gave their students a clear choice.
Students who chose to behave chose to have the
teacher's positive attention, praise, etc. Students
who chose to disrupt chose immediate negative consequences from the teacher.

        Various reactions to the assertive discipline
program have been presented by the faculty, parents
and students of Rice Elementary School. Third grade
teacher, Barbara Zarling, presented a typical reaction
when she stated, "So far it works great. I haven't
raised my voice so far this year. With this system
you don't have to, it is so cut and dried. The children really learn to take responsibility for their own
actions."

        Parent reaction to the new discipline program was
voiced by Mrs. Nadine Pinales who stated, "Assertive
discipline is a good thing. They should have done it
a long time ago." Mrs. Robert Dort added, "I think

it's great. It's about time. It's also a good thing for parents because we have been slipping in the things we should be doing."

Gordon Herrmann, the principal, shared his views: "What assertive discipline does is make consistent what was haphazard before. Now the student knows what the consequence of his actions will be, and that's what makes discipline work. When his name goes on the board and a check is added to it, there's no question what will happen: the student will be staying 15 minutes after school. It was hard to keep discipline consistent from class to class before this system came along. We usually let the student off in the past whenever there was a question. But now it's, 'This is it -- this is the way it's going to be,' and the children benefit from this firm stand."

Herrmann concluded, "The teachers have taken more responsibility for discipline at this school. This year I probably have had one tenth of the kids come into this office that I used to have. Teachers are now laying down the law and students are keeping themselves in line."

Assertive discipline programs, such as the one utilized at Rice Elementary School, have been implemented in hundreds of schools, both elementary and secondary throughout the nation. Statistically, administrators and teachers report an 80 percent reduction in discipline problems the first year the program is utilized.

STRATEGIES IN CLASSROOM MANAGEMENT

Robert L. Shrigley

American schoolteachers could be an endangered species. Not that their vulnerability is due to some nesting or migration habit. Rather, forces within and outside the profession have made teachers vulnerable in dealing with disruptive student behavior in the instructional setting.

Teachers must therefore be prepared with planned strategies whereby they can confidently and rationally enter the classroom and keep the learning act afloat.

The following six strategies, some short, and others long-range, constitute a basic plan for coping with student behavior that interferes with learning in the classroom.

Coping Skills

Strategy 1. Deliberately designed coping skills curb surface, disruptive behavior of students. (1)

Most management strategies serve to prevent disruptive behavior. However, every successful teacher creates coping skills, some of them mild forms of punishment, deliberately designed to defuse crises, and thereby preserving the learning act.

As I counselled teachers trying their wings in my classroom, I was forced to operationalize coping skills that I have learned intuitively. Four coping skills are unique, and when used in sequence are particularly effective in curbing deviant behavior.

1. Ignore Behavior. Student behavior unrewarded

Reprinted from the NASSP BULLETIN, 63 (428): 1-9 (September 1979), by permission of author and publisher.

by the teacher (and other students) often subsides. Of course, behavior that directly interferes with learning can hardly be ignored.

2. Signals. A stare, uplifted eyebrow, or a flip of the lights may often short-circuit classroom turbulence.

3. Proximity Control. Standing near a trouble spot gives students the adult support needed to defuse disruptive behavior.

4. Touch. Although it must be used with discretion, a hand on the shoulder of a young student can serve to drain tension or anger.

Somehow as a young teacher I learned to click off these four coping skills quickly and quietly, seldom interfering with the teaching act of the moment. They also facilitated two other coping skills: "overlapping," the teacher's skill at attending simultaneously to two matters at one time; and "with-it-ness," the subtle, eyes-in-the-back-of-the-head skill used by the teacher to communicate nonverbally to students that "I am perceptive to behavior in all sectors of the classroom." (2)

There are other coping skills that facilitate the teaching act.

5. Remove Seductive Objects. A new baseball glove, a make-up mirror, or a motorcycle magazine are far too competitive for the teacher of junior high grammar. With the standing agreement that they would be returned no later than the day's end, I learned to casually collect the seductive objects without missing a beat in classroom teaching.

6. A Change in Pace. The wise teacher reads yawning mouths and out-the-window stares as signals to change the pace. On those warm, spring afternoons when our music teacher perceived the need to restructure the situation, she did what was ordinarily taboo. As she belted out "The Marine Hymn" on the piano, she invited all to keep time with their feet. Never did this maneuver fail to bring the wayward boys back into the mainstream although the racket probably brought a pause in conversation in the principal's office, located directly below.

7. **Logical Consequences.** Making a direct appeal to students based on logical consequences is a potent coping skill. The group that dawdles 10 extra minutes returning from gym today simply goes to the showers 10 minutes earlier tomorrow! This type of appeal, a subtle cause-and-effect consequence, is probably effective because the threat does not reside in the teacher's program, but the logic of the situation.

8. **Interest Boosting.** The student about to touch up a neighbor's unattended woodshop project can be diverted by the perceptive teacher who chooses that moment to show an interest in the student's own bookshelf.

9. **Non-Punitive Time Out.** The student who has encountered a hilariously funny, painfully frustrating or utterly fatiguing situation might be quietly invited to run an errand or get a drink.

10. **Punitive Time Out.** The student deserving isolation in my classroom was expected to remain behind the portable bulletin board and out of visual contact with others with the standing agreement that a decision to return meant the student was willing to conform to the expectations of the learning activity of the moment.

11. **Reinforcement, Direct or Adjacent.** Teachers can succeed at coping with some disruptions by reinforcing behaviors they wish to have repeated. Or, if desirable behavior seldom emerges from a student, reward adjacent peers with the anticipation that disruptive students will model peer behavior.

12. **V. Q.** Teachers must know their "vulnerability quotient." The beginning teacher (inexperienced) who plans a class discussion (a sophisticated teaching model) at 2:30 on Friday (fatigue) of the yearly rival football game (anxiety) has overlapped so many vulnerable conditions that the V. Q. is near disaster level. A written assignment, instead of class discussion, would lower the V. Q. considerably.

However, coping skills have their professional pitfalls. The teacher majoring in coping skills and minoring in excellent teaching will wind up constantly reacting, constantly putting out brushfires. Coping skills serve to rescue the teaching act, and they usually focus on the symptoms. They may do little to answer the deep-seated problems of disruptive individuals.

Expertise in Teaching

Strategy 2. Excellent teaching tends to prevent disruption, and central to excellent teaching is the teacher's capacity to make professional decisions confidently and rationally.

Which mode of teaching -- lecture, debate, or CAI -- would you use when confronting the issues of pollution, race, and overpopulation in senior social studies? Does a film on volcanos make more pedagogical sense in seventh grade earth science than building a volcano and simulating eruption? And how do you encourage students to make thoughtful and creative contributions to class discussion?

The teaching strategy model is suggested as a means to confident and rational decision making in the classroom.

For creative classroom discussions, wait-time, a technique accomplished by sandwiching a three-second pause between the verbal actions of the teacher and the students, is a sound strategy. Not only does wait-time increase verbal responses and thought on the part of students, it lowers the number of disciplinary moves needed by the teacher. (3)

Central to any profession must be a deliberate decision-making mode of operation, and there are sources of teaching strategies that could be generated to help teachers make decisions in the classroom. Teachers committed to open education have Barth's 29 assumptions (1971) as a basis for decision making. Alfke (1974) designed operational questioning for the teacher who expects students to successfully seek answers from science materials instead of a textbook. And Heimer and Trueblood (1977) offer 12 teaching strategies for teachers of mathematics.

Making classroom decisions based on teaching strategies professionalizes teaching; students sense direction and security. Although excellent teaching does not guarantee teachers smooth sailing in the classroom, there will be fewer rudderless moments, fewer opportunities for students to seek diversion.

Irritating But Normal Behavior

Strategy 3. We have the professional obligation to tolerate those normal, but sometimes irritating student behaviors documented as typical for the age group we teach.

The teacher who groups very young students, expecting them to work toward the accomplishment of a common goal, may read deviant behavior as willful disobedience. The teacher may be confronted with the egocentrism of all young children. The gym teacher soon learns that for one age, coed dancing is accepted with zest, but at age 10 many boys rebel against holding girls' hands. The teacher who presses the boys for compliance may be working against their normal social development patterns.

To be effective at managing a classroom the teacher must have a working knowledge of human development patterns for the age group taught.

Legal Implications

Strategy 4. Granting juveniles the adult rights of free expression and due process has forced teachers to be better informed in school law and to rely more heavily on preventive rather than coercive alternatives when dealing with deviant student behavior.

In 1969, the Supreme Court ruling on Tinker set into motion a series of court decisions directly affecting the expedience by which school officials can cope with disruptive behavior. This decision ruled that juveniles are "persons" under our Constitution, therefore granting students the right of free expression heretofore guaranteed only to adults.

For the American teacher who traditionally has considered the rights of free expression something to be earned, and if granted at all, only at high school graduation, today's student seems to have the best of both worlds. The student can assert adult rights when free expression, privacy, and due process are at stake; but that individual would hasten to claim legal concessions of juvenile status if found guilty of a criminal action on the school grounds. Juvenile rights are certainly not co-existent with adults as shown by a contrary point of view on voting rights, contracts, and criminal law (Nolte, 1976).

Furthermore, granting any group the right to free expression has to assume also some degree of maturity and self-discipline. For example, students making the school newspaper an instrument of criticism can be motivated by a student staff with a mature and genuine concern for a better school, or their effort can be the manifestation of adolescent rebellion. And when irresponsibility is obvious in the words of a student editor, teachers can easily feel they have been betrayed by the courts.

Therefore, today's teacher must be thoroughly briefed in the legal rights of students. Uninformed and weary school officials might fail to suspend or expel the incorrigible student who deserves no less just to play it safe or to avoid possible court action. As teachers and principals make judgments, they must have the security of knowing that legal counsel is available, not only to advise, but defend them, if students or parents involve them in a court action.

Over the long haul we must give students fewer reasons to be critical of the operation of the schools. Shifting from the coercive to preventive perspective of classroom management means that we must become more professional at teaching.

Punishment

Strategy 5. Considered with some constraints, punishment is one option teachers must consider in curbing and modifying deviant behavior that hampers the learning act.

It is wishful rather than rational thinking to believe teachers can be successful in a social situation as complex as the public school classroom without considering punishment as an intervention technique. However, the decision to punish necessitates the consideration of several professional constraints. (4) Punishment should be:

1. Legal. Suspension and corporal punishment, for example, are illegal if certain due process procedures are ignored.

2. Infrequent. Teachers who use coercion con-

217

stantly in the classroom can be modelling aggression as a way of life.

3. Prompt. There are obvious exceptions, but punishment should be prompt enough for the young student to relate it directly to the deviant behavior.

4. Appropriate. Expecting a student to sand graffiti from a desk top is far more appropriate than a double homework assignment in algebra.

5. Impersonal. The teacher viewing all deviant behavior as a personal threat, and punishing to vent frustration, can hardly be considered a confident and rational professional.

6. Private. Administering punishment privately serves to respect the dignity of the student.

7. Just. The teacher who administers a harsh punishment to an individual just to "make an example" is hardly just.

8. Mild. Critics of punishment assume it cannot have a positive effect on the disruptive student. However, evidence is mounting that mild forms of punishment can change behavior of the disruptive student in a positive direction. Whereas severe punishment can result in conforming behavior only as long as the teacher is present, punishment severe enough to curb the behavior, but not threaten the individual, can result in a behavior change in a positive direction. (5)

For example, the threat of detention provides more than enough reasons for a student to refrain from fighting -- as long as the teacher is nearby and ready to bring down the axe. However, if mild punishment, such as a frown, can curb the fighting but not provide adequate reason for conforming behavior the student is prone to rationalize or "invent" a reason for not fighting. Thus a positive and long-range change may have been accomplished.

Other Authority Bases

Coercion, the authority to punish, is remedial and after the fact. There are four other bases for authority, more positive in nature, that serve to prevent deviant behavior. (6) They are:

218

1. Reward. Positive verbal feedback and grades are examples of the authority to reward students.

2. Legitimate. The teacher's contract makes the teacher the adult in charge of classroom teaching.

3. Referent. Students who identify with the teacher as a person are extending to a teacher referent authority.

4. Expert. When we ask the beginning teacher to overprepare a teaching assignment, we are strengthening this authority base.

Therefore, the teacher striving to be a professional is prepared to use wisely all five bases for authority.

Ills of Society

Strategy 6. The classroom teacher cannot be expected to solve singlehandedly social evils of the community that spill from the street into the classroom.

This is more a plea than a strategy! Hazard (1976) claims we are naive to believe that the schools can somehow overcome such societal ills as violence, discrimination, and poverty. But Berger (1974) claims that the school is becoming the sole acculturalizing agency in our society.

How would the experts handle the societal ills evidenced in the schools by willful student violence? Here is a sample:

1. Amend compulsory education? We might have fewer trouble-makers in the school if our youth were excused from the 12-year lockstep march through school and instead given a certain number of school years to be spent anytime. And a student could postpone the latter years of school indefinitely.

2. Apply technology and the law? Unbreakable glass can curb the school vandal. To thwart the thief school officials can install floodlights and TV monitors. The court can handle the drug pusher in a student body as it does drug traffic on the streets. Stronger trespassing laws would better control assault and extortion on the playground. And parents could be

made legally responsible for their child's destruction of school property (Elam, 1978).

3. Provide students with structure? When the social ills were at their height at one ghetto school, a strong principal is credited with transforming a "snake pit" into a learning laboratory. To show that she cared for students, she tooled up the faculty so that all could learn. Strict school routines provided the structure, and rulebreakers were suspended without hesitation. (7) Are disruptive students searching for social limitations that should be set by teachers?

4. Provide students with moral training? Can we not all agree that theft, vandalism, and violence are alien to "the good life"? Then does the solution not reside in the moral training of our youth? And is not neutrality of the public schools toward moral training claimed by many American educators a myth? (McQuilkin, 1977)

5. Give students a stake in school? Glasser (1978) would give students a stake by (1) caring and (2) assuring them of success. Standards would not be lowered; rather resources would be brought to bear on the problems and students would succeed regardless of how long it took.

6. Give students a stake in society? The failure of our society to induct children into satisfying societal roles normally reserved for adults may contribute to anti-social student behavior. Tanner (1977) would encourage children to imitate the junior high schoolers who persuaded a town council that sewage lines should be extended to an underprivileged neighborhood.

Coping singlehandedly with school violence having its origin in society is expecting teachers to walk on water! The orchestration of all societal resources is necessary.

Postscript

The professional teacher, one capable of keeping student disruptions at a minimum, may have best been described by La Mancusa (1966) in her book aptly titled, WE DO NOT THROW ROCKS AT THE TEACHER! She claims that a teacher's finest hour is when the teacher can stand alone and strong without need for personal, emotional support from students. Students do not remember with fondness, she continues, the teacher whose sole aim was to please. Rather they remember teachers who expected the classroom to be a learning laboratory, ones who persisted in providing a climate favorable to study, work, and growth: "...they were fair and square, brave and honest, intelligent and talented, and even funny."

Footnotes

1. Several authors have assembled and analyzed similar coping skills including: F. Redl and D. Wineman, CONTROLS FROM WITHIN -- TECHNIQUES FOR THE TREATMENT OF THE AGGRESSIVE CHILD (New York: The Free Press 1952); N. Long and R Newman, "A Differential Approach to the Management of Surface Behavior of Children in School," (Bulletin of the School of Education, Indiana University, July 1961); and M. Hipple, "Classroom Discipline Problems? Fifteen Humane Solutions," CHILDHOOD EDUCATION, February 1978.

2. "Overlapping" and "withitness" have been researched by J. Kounin. DISCIPLINE AND GROUP MANAGEMENT IN CLASSROOMS (New York: Holt, Rinehart and Winston, 1970).

3. "Wait-time" has been researched by M. Rowe, "Wait, Wait, Wait...." SCHOOL SCIENCE AND MATHEMATICS, March 1978.

4. Several of the constraints were addressed by a group of teachers including J. Brown; A. Donaldson; J. Donaldson; S. Mort. GOOD CLASSROOM DISCIPLINE FOR INSTRUCTIONAL AIDES (Saxton, Pa.: Tussey Mountain Schools, n.d.).

5. Research on this constraint was conducted by E. Aronson, ed., "Cognitive Dissonance as It Affects Values and Behavior," in VOICES OF MODERN PSYCHOLOGY (Reading, Mass.: Addison-Wesley, 1969).

6. The five authority bases were designed by J. French and B. Raven, "The Bases of Social Power," in GROUP DYNAMICS: RESEARCH AND THEORY, eds. D. Cartwright and A. Zander (Evanston, Ill.: Row Peterson, 1960).

7. "And Finally a Success Story; How One School Changes from Snake Pit to Model," AMERICAN SCHOOL BOARD JOURNAL, January 1975.

References

Alfke, D. "Asking Operational Questions." SCIENCE AND CHILDREN, April 1974.

Barth, R. "So You Want to Change to an Open Classroom." PHI DELTA KAPPAN, October 1971.

Berger, M. VIOLENCE IN THE SCHOOLS: CAUSES AND REMEDIES. Bloomington, Ind.: The Phi Delta Kappa Educational Foundation, 1974.

Elam, S. "The Editor's Page." PHI DELTA KAPPAN, March 1978.

Glasser, W. "Disorders in Our Schools: Causes and Remedies." PHI DELTA KAPPAN, January 1978.

Hazard, W. "About This Issue." JOURNAL OF THE NATIONAL CENTER FOR LAW-FOCUSED EDUCATION, February 1976.

Heimer, R., and Trueblood, C. STRATEGIES FOR TEACHING CHILDREN MATHEMATICS. Reading, Mass.: Addison-Wesley, 1977.

La Mancusa, K. WE DO NOT THROW ROCKS AT THE TEACHER! Scranton, Pa.: International Book Co., 1966.

McQuilkin, J. "Public Schools: Equal Time for Evangelicals." CHRISTIANITY TODAY, December 1977.

Nolte, M. "Are Students 'Persons' Under the Constitution? Goss v. Lopez Implies as Much." JOURNAL OF THE NATIONAL CENTER FOR LAW-FOCUSED EDUCATION, February 1976.

Tanner, L. CLASSROOM DISCIPLINE FOR EFFECTIVE TEACHING AND LEARNING. New York: Holt, Rinehart and Winston, 1977.

DISCIPLINE: FOUR APPROACHES

J. Michael Palardy and James E. Mudrey

What approaches can teachers use in dealing with discipline -- one of their most demanding and most complex responsibilities? We begin with the knowledge that there are no easy answers to discipline problems. But we also begin convinced that, generally, there are right and wrong approaches to finding answers.

Discipline is defined in various ways. Our definition can be given best by asking three questions: What can teachers do to prevent behavior problems? What can teachers do when behavior problems occur? What can teachers do to prevent behavior problems from recurring? Discipline is what teachers do in response to these three questions.

Ours is not one of the more encompassing definitions. In fact, some object to the idea that discipline, as in our definition, deals only with behavior problems. We are aware of the limitation of our definition, but we make no apologies. Teachers are asking these questions. We think they deserve a response.

There are four basic approaches to discipline: the permissive, the authoritarian, the behavioristic, and the diagnostic.

The Permissive Approach

One school of thought has a simple answer to the discipline questions. The answer is, "Do nothing." What can teachers do to prevent behavior problems? Nothing. What can teachers do when behavior problems

Reprinted from THE ELEMENTARY SCHOOL JOURNAL, 73 (6): 297-305 (March 1973), by permission of the authors and The University of Chicago Press. Copyright 1973 by The University of Chicago Press.

occur? Nothing. What can teachers do to prevent behavior problems from recurring? Nothing.

Why do nothing? Some advocates of the permissive
approach believe that if pupils are involved meaning-
fully in a relevant curriculum they will not misbehave. This is to say that given the right conditions
all children will always behave. This is not so.
Others believe that pupils must feel free to do what
they want whenever they want. For pupils to feel otherwise, they say, inhibits their natural, God-given
pattern of development. This, too, is not so. Psychologists are convinced that all pupils, for the sake
of their mental health, need set limits for behavior.

Consequently, although permissiveness is one approach to discipline, it is not, in our opinion, a realistic, or an educational, or a responsible approach.
Pupils cannot do what they want whenever they want.

The Authoritarian Approach

If permissiveness is at one end of the discipline
continuum, authoritarianism is at the other. The authoritarian approach assumes that most pupils are going to misbehave as often as they can. Given this
assumption, what can teachers do to prevent behavior
problems? The answer given here is not all inclusive,
but it is representative enough to give the general
idea.

Since pupils are going to misbehave as often as
they can, teachers have to prepare for the worst. One
way of preparing is to have a multitude of classroom
rules, designed and communicated in such a way that
pupils know immediately that they have an inferior
status. The more rules, the better. Teachers must
let pupils know that deviations from rules will not be
tolerated. Teachers must be tough and must act tough.
They must demand respect and should not worry about
earning it. They must keep their distance from pupils
because friendliness, warmth, understanding, and interest breed problems. Teachers must let each pupil
know that they carry a big stick and will use it at
the slightest provocation.

Ridiculing pupils, embarrassing them, questioning
their integrity are other good authoritarian techniques. These, too, are going to help prevent behavior

problems. So the advocates of authoritarianism would have teachers believe!

But what can teachers do when misbehavior does occur? And what can teachers do to prevent it from recurring? The answer is obvious. Teachers must get tougher. They must become more rigid, more abrasive. They must impose more rules.

Effective teachers know that this approach does not work. Why should it? Human beings learn to act in the manner in which they are treated. If they are treated like criminals, they act like criminals.

But even if the authoritarian approach did work, should teachers use it? Our answer is no. Because the approach is inhumane to pupils. If schools can function only by being inhumane to pupils, we have to wonder about the legitimacy of having schools at all.

We have stated that permissiveness and authoritarianism are two approaches to discipline. We have stated also that in our opinion neither approach is legitimate. Since the score now reads two approaches down and two to go, we think it might be reassuring at this point to state that the remaining approaches, behavioristic and diagnostic, are legitimate -- not equally legitimate, in our estimation, but legitimate nonetheless.

The Behavioristic Approach

The psychology of behaviorism has been a key factor in American education for at least fifty years. But as it relates to discipline, behaviorism has only recently captured widespread attention. As is often true, attention has grown because of a new name. In this case, the new name is behavior modification.

The purpose of behavior modification is to change behavior -- for example, to change pupils' behavior patterns from undesirable to desirable. Supposedly, this change or reshaping is effected through four basic steps.

Before describing these four steps, we need to point out that the purpose and the techniques of behavior modification deal only with the last two questions on discipline. Behavior modification gives teachers no guidelines for preventing behavior problems. Behavior modification gives teachers guidelines only for dealing with behavior problems when they occur and for preventing their recurrence.

The first of the four steps in reshaping behavior is identification of the behavior problem. Teachers must identify the specific behavior they find undesirable. The key is to be specific. It is not sufficient for teachers to say that Johnny misbehaves. Rather, they must pinpoint the specific way he misbehaves. For example, he keeps getting out of his seat during reading class; he throws spitwads at Harry; he bullies Joe on the playground; he comes to class late three days a week. The more specifically the behavior is identified, the better.

The second step is identification of the appropriate behavior. Teachers must identify the specific way they want the pupil to act. In almost every case, such identification is the reverse of the undesired behavior. For example, Johnny remains seated during reading class; he refrains from throwing spitwads; he comes to class on time. This step may seem to be a duplication of effort, but for behavior modification the step is critically important.

The third step is the use of reward. When the pupil behaves in the way that was spelled out in the second step, teachers must reward him, they must pay him off. To return to our example, not even Johnny is out of his seat every minute of every reading class. When Johnny is seated, it is important for teachers to reward him.

The point is simple, but often missed. Good behavior is not necessarily its own reward. When teachers object to a pupil's behavior, they typically tell him "not to do it again." Then, when the pupil does what he has been told not to do teachers usually react, often by punishing. But when the pupil does what he is supposed to do, teachers tend to do nothing. Thinking that good behavior is its own reward, teachers fail to commend the pupil for his good conduct. According to the behavioristic approach, the omission is deadly. For only when teachers actively and consistently reward appropriate behavior will they succeed in eliminating misbehavior.

The fourth and last step is the use of extinction

procedures to help eliminate the inappropriate behavior identified in the first step. The key words are to help eliminate. Let's return to Johnny. He has two choices in reading class: to sit or not to sit. Even if teachers consistently reward Johnny when he chooses to sit, there will be occasions, particularly at first, when he will choose not to. When Johnny opts to leave his seat, teachers can do one of two things. They can either ignore his behavior or react to it. Each of these responses is what behaviorists refer to as an extinction procedure.

Critics often ask why teachers should ever ignore inappropriate behavior. As one example, suppose that Johnny gets out of his seat during reading class to attract attention. When teachers react to his behavior by saying, "Johnny, please sit down!" what have they done? They have given him exactly what he wants, attention. In essence, they have rewarded Johnny for behaving inappropriately. Even worse, they have reinforced his knowledge that whenever he wants attention, all he has to do to get it is to misbehave. There are times, then, when reacting to misbehavior has an effect entirely different from the one intended.

Some types of misbehavior, of course, demand that teachers react. They cannot simply stand by and watch a pupil destroy or deface school property. They have to stop him. Subsequently, they may even think it necessary to punish him. But it is important to note that reacting is not synonymous with punishing. Reminding Johnny that he is supposed to be seated during reading class is reacting. Keeping him in at recess because he needed reminding is punishing. To repeat, teachers can react to misbehavior without punishing.

The key to behavior modification is not the use of punishment, but the use of reward. Pupils can be conditioned to act in desirable ways if teachers will reward them for acting in these ways. Then, as pupils begin to be conditioned their need for reward lessens. At first, Johnny needs immediate and frequent payoffs for staying in his seat. Later, as he becomes conditioned to remaining seated, the payoffs can and should become less frequent. Finally, it is hoped, the conditioning process will work so well that payoffs will no longer be necessary.

Is this a legitimate hope? Does behavior modification work? We think it does, but not to the degree or with the frequency behaviorists predict. For the approach, in our opinion, has several serious flaws. The most significant is that only the symptoms of behavior problems are dealt with, not their causes.

Stated bluntly, but not unjustly, proponents of behavior modification argue that teachers are wasting time in trying to discover and treat the underlying causes of behavior. From the point of view of advocates of behavior modification, teachers can be effective if they deal only with the behavior itself. What does this mean when teachers observe Johnny sleeping in math class every other day? Primarily, it means that they should begin rewarding him for staying awake. It does not mean that they should try to find out why he sleeps. Whether he is bored, or malnourished, or fatigued, or on dope, or rebellious, or just plain lazy - each a possible cause of his sleepiness - is irrelevant for behaviorists. But for us, and for the pupil, the cause seems critically important. As long as the cause of the child's problem is undiagnosed and untreated, he is hurting and sooner or later symptoms of that hurt will emerge.

The Diagnostic Approach

To us, the most comprehensive and legitimate approach to discipline is what we call the diagnostic approach. Contrary to behavior modification, this approach assumes that there can be lasting effects on certain behavior problems only after their causes are ferreted out and treated. Unlike behavior modification, the diagnostic approach responds to the first question on discipline.

According to the diagnostic approach, what can teachers do to prevent behavior problems? What are some strategies of prevention? We have listed nine strategies which, in our opinion, are essential. But we need to emphasize that preventive strategies are not failure free. Even if all the preventive strategies described here are used, behavior problems may still emerge. But from the diagnostic point of view and our own, if the strategies described here are used the number of these problems will be reduced.

Prevention

Here are nine strategies to prevent discipline

problems:

1. Teachers must feel comfortable with themselves, their pupils, and their subject matter. The major reason, we think, that student teachers and first-year teachers often have difficulties with discipline is their uneasiness -- uneasiness with themselves because being on the other side of that desk, particularly at first, is no easy task; uneasiness with their pupils because they may be "so different" or "so little;" uneasiness with their subject matter because, in terms of the real world, college methods courses often leave much to be desired. But regardless of the cause, and regardless of the teachers' years of experience, teachers who are uneasy are going to communicate that uneasiness to their pupils. When this happens, the door to restlessness among pupils is wide open.

2. Teachers must believe in their pupils' capacity and propensity for appropriate classroom conduct. For according to sociologists, teachers' beliefs serve as "self-fulfilling prophecies." If teachers believe that pupils can and will act in socially acceptable ways, pupils will do so. But if teachers believe, for any number of reasons, that pupils neither can nor will behave appropriately, they will in fact misbehave. The principle of the self-fulfilling prophecy is profoundly, and often painfully, clear: the tendency of pupils, as of every other social group, is to live and act as others expect them to live and act.

3. Teachers must insure that their instructional activities are interesting and relevant. The words interesting and relevant may be overworked in educational literature, but there can be no mistaking their importance. Nor can there be any mistaking the fact that dreary classrooms, monotonous routines, irrelevant, antiquated content, and boring methods of presentation are more characteristic of more educational settings than most care to admit. There is little doubt that these characteristics are major causes of misbehavior. Some pupils, to be sure, become acculturated to drabness in school life, learn to play the game, and become model citizens in school. But just as certainly, and possibly even more expectedly, other pupils become indifferent, rebel, and become troublemakers.

4. Teachers must match their instruction with the

capabilities of pupils. Behavior problems are often the result of the teachers' failure to adapt their instruction to their pupils' capabilities. When pupils are handed materials that are too difficult, when pupils are required to complete assignments for which they lack readiness, when pupils are given directions they cannot possibly understand, is it any wonder that they lose interest and cause trouble? We think not. When other pupils are assigned tasks that insult their intelligence, is it any wonder that they lose interest and cause trouble? Again, we think not. Teachers must see to it that all pupils are challenged. Failing this teachers should at least lay the blame for misbehavior where the blame belongs.

5. Teachers must involve their pupils in setting up "the rules." There are two major reasons for following this practice, one long range and one short term. From the long-range perspective, a democracy requires that citizens have the skills to participate actively and intelligently in group decision-making. Schools, in our opinion, are potentially the single best medium through which children can practice and master these skills in a gradual, non-threatening way. From the short-term perspective, when groups of individuals help make the decisions that affect their lives, they are more likely to live within the framework of these decisions. Groups of pupils are no exception. Pupils who help set up the rules and regulations of the classroom better understand the necessity of having the rules and are more committed to following them than pupils who play no such role.

6. Teachers must make certain that their pupils know and understand "the routine." No two teachers hold the same set of expectations for pupils. No two teachers have the same classroom routine. Given differing expectations and differing routines, the problem confronting pupils is real. In this day of team teaching, departmentalization, open space, and hosts of grouping patterns, even the youngest pupils come daily into contact with two or more teachers. Pupils must remember not only what routine to follow, but also whose routine. This is no easy task, but one that teachers often take for granted. Too frequently, they make the mistake of assuming that their standards for proper behavior are the only standards for proper behavior. In fact, though, behavior is relative, and its appropriateness can be determined only in context. Given differing routines or contexts, what one teacher

perceives as proper behavior another teacher may perceive as misbehavior. And pupils are caught in the middle.

7. Teachers must identify their problem times. When do pupils tend to act up? When they first get to class? Or toward the end of the period? On the playground? In the lunchroom? In the halls? With the music teacher? In mathematics, or reading, or science? On Moday, or Wednesday, or Friday? The day before or after a big test? Knowing when the problem times are is an important step in planning to prevent them.

8. Teachers must remember that pupils are not little adults. Rather, in the elementary school, they are children ranging in age from five or six to twelve or thirteen. These children cannot be expected to display the same control over their behavior as adults. Yet, in too many instances, they are expected to display more. There is no doubt that teachers would save their pupils much frustration, and themselves many headaches, if they refrained from insisting on proper adult conduct from nonadults.

9. Teachers must give evidence that they genuinely respect their pupils. Teachers do not give such evidence when they complain about pupils in the halls and lounges; when they laugh at pupils behind their backs; when they tell pupils in hundreds of ways that their culture is deficient, that their homes are inadequate; when they do not take time to make a home visit or prepare an extra lesson that Johnny and Mary need. The list could go on, but the point is unmistakable. Teachers do not give evidence that they respect pupils by voicing platitudes. Teachers give evidence only through their actions, and only through these actions will they succeed in earning pupils' respect. To earn it is probably the most important preventive strategy of all.

These nine strategies are measures teachers can and must take to prevent behavior problems. But even with these measures, behavior problems will still emerge. When they do, what guidelines does the diagnostic approach give teachers? What can teachers do when behavior problems occur?

Intervention

According to the diagnostic approach, there is no

one method of dealing with behavior problems, just as there is no one method of preventing them. There is no single strategy of intervention that works every time. Rather, there are many intervention strategies, and only teachers themselves can assess which ones work best in various situations. There are, however, seven strategies that we believe should be in every teacher's repertory. Again, these seven strategies in no way constitute a comprehensive list, but they do provide teachers with as sound a point of departure as we think there is.

1. The use of nonverbal techniques, particularly at the beginning stages of misbehavior, can be an effective way of letting pupils know that one or all of them had better settle down. Eye contact, body posture, facial expression, and silence are probably the most noteworthy of these techniques. Verbal techniques can be effective also. But they are so overused that their impact is questionable. Witness the number of teachers who intersperse every other sentence with "sh."

2. When a pupil is misbehaving, merely walking up to him and standing beside him for five or ten seconds can frequently bring about the desired result. When this technique is used, few pupils fail to get the message, and even fewer are brazen enough to disregard it.

3. Removing the source of a disturbance can bring about the desired result. One form of removal is the "take-it-away type." The teacher may take away rubber bands, water pistols, food, and contraband reading materials. Most teachers are familiar with this form of removal. Another form of removal is the "let-it-run-its-course type." Teachers may be less familiar with this type. Almost daily, in the classroom and outside, there are phenomena that pupils are naturally interested in, that they naturally give their attention to. Hailstorms, ambulance sirens, Johnny's new shoes, Mary's coiffure, Mrs. Smith's student teacher are a few examples. When such attractions capture pupils' attention, the surest way of recapturing it is simply to let pupils have a few minutes of exploration.

4. Pointing out to pupils the consequence of misbehavior can be an effective method of intervention. The key is to find the right consequence. To tell

Johnny that he will have a terrible time with long division if he does not stop horsing around in second-grade addition is probably not a very meaningful consequence to him. But to tell him that he will not be able to sit next to Billy might be. Matching the pupil with the right consequence is no easy task. But making false matches yields no benefits whatsoever.

5. The use of behavior-modification techniques can be an effective method of intervention. These techniques, as well as some of their limitations, were described earlier.

6. Asking a pupil to leave the room can be an important intervention strategy. This technique has a single purpose: to give the pupil a chance to cool off. Asking him to run an errand, sending him to get a drink, telling him to walk around the playground are all legitimate tactics. Trying to deal with a pupil who is on the verge of losing self-control is almost inevitably a lost cause. In such situations teachers often become angry and lose their own self-control.

7. Punishing pupils can be a necessary and an effective strategy. But when punishment is being considered, five principles should be kept in mind:
First, punishment should be used sparingly. The more often punishment is used, the less effective it becomes. Teachers who frequently resort to punishment find that they have to punish more often and more severely just to maintain the status quo.
Second, punishment should never constitute retaliation. It is beneath the dignity of professionals to punish pupils to get back at them. Teachers who do so do not belong in education.
Third, subject matter should not be used as punishment. In most cases, requiring pupils to do another page of mathematics or to write an extra book report reduces the chances that they will develop favorable attitudes in these areas. In the long run, much more is lost than gained.
Fourth, mass punishment should not be used. The entire class should never be punished for the transgressions of a few members. Many teachers fall into this trap; few escape without some loss of respect.
Fifth, corporal punishment should not be used. We know that there are strong differences of opinion about whether corporal punishment is effective. We believe that it is generally ineffective. But this is not the key point. The key is that corporal punishment

is intended to be a last-ditch effort to change behavior. The implication is that if corporal punishment fails, nothing else can be done. This implication is anathema, both from the diagnostic point of view and from our own.

According to the diagnostic approach, then, if the strategies of prevention and intervention are used, most common forms of misbehavior can either be eliminated or be dealt with effectively. But some behavior problems cannot be. These are the problems that are symptoms of underlying causes and, consequently, continue to recur until the causes are diagnosed and treated.

Diagnosis

There is no quick, easy, or fail-proof formula for diagnosing the causes of pupils' behavior problems. But there is one absolutely essential step: to learn as much as possible about the pupils. To do so, teachers must draw on all possible sources of information. These include achievement and IQ tests, social and psychological inventories, attendance records, cumulative folders, previous teachers, clergymen, parents, relatives, siblings, peers, social workers, visiting teachers, medical personnel, employers, coaches, and, most important of all, the pupils themselves.

After the information from these sources has been gathered and analyzed, it is our contention that a reasonably reliable determination of the causes of most behavior problems can be made. It is also our contention that teachers can then take steps to help eliminate these causes and the resulting behavioral symptoms. But, as we said earlier, neither of these contentions is universally supported.

Most critics of this approach argue that the whole effort of diagnosis is a waste of time and energy because nothing can be done anyway. These critics are quick to assert that teachers cannot force parents to love their children or to feed them adequately, that teachers cannot mend broken homes, that teachers cannot keep Joe's father off the bottle or Mary's mother off the streets.

But we disagree with this argument. First, because it assumes that the causes of behavior problems are never school related or school induced. Like it

234

or not, many are.

Second, even if the diagnosis shows that the causes are not school related or school induced, much can still be done. Pupils' ego needs can be met in school, their self-respect enhanced, their enjoyment of life increased. In school, pupils can be given love and can learn to give it in return. Schools can provide food and clothing. They can make medical, dental, and psychological referrals. They can contact community action programs, welfare departments, civic organizations, churches, and even law-enforcement agencies. Schools can provide for adult education, sex education, and early education. We disagree that diagnosis is a waste of time because nothing can be done! This logic has long been refuted by schools and teachers who have done all these things and more.

We said that there are no easy answers to discipline problems. We know that we have proven ourselves right, but hope that in the process we have helped.

MOTIVATION MAXIMS:
WHY THEY FAIL TO MOTIVATE

Charles Dedrick and Len Froyen

Some say <u>you cannot teach an old dog new tricks</u>. If we believed this maxim, there would be no point in writing this article. While you must forgive the metaphor, we believe a reasonably bright and professionally trained teacher can learn new tricks. Most teachers, we believe, want to learn new ways of looking at and performing their job.

<u>Experience is the best teacher</u>. Experience may be a good teacher, but it is not always the best teacher. Many teachers keep repeating the same mistakes. Little wonder certain maxims persist, despite so much evidence to the contrary. Our experience tells us that theory may be the best teacher. At least theory applied to practice may be best for the teacher.

Finally, <u>you cannot judge a book by its cover</u>. There are those that would dispute this maxim, too. The covers on today's novels are provocative statements about the contents. We hope this is an article you can tell by its title. We intend to identify some educational maxims that we think are as refutable as those used to introduce this article. These are maxims that should be retired. They are obstacles to reality which stand between teachers and sound educational practice.

Beliefs That Mitigate Against Academic Motivation

1. <u>Schooling is a democratic process, children and young people are the equal of adults, and the goals of education are emergent rather than prescribed.</u>

Reprinted from THE EDUCATIONAL FORUM, 44 (3): 295-303 (March 1980), by permission of authors and publisher.

Motivation to learn would certainly be enhanced if this myth were true. People are generally more willing to invest their energies in an enterprise when they have something to say about what will be done and how it will be done. Being equal partners often stimulates cooperation and contributes to a concerted effort to achieve mutually agreed-upon ends. The individual's satisfaction of attaining one goal and the excitement of striving to achieve another does provoke persistence and resourcefulness. The myth captures the substance of a sound motivational principle, but none of the elements accurately reflects the situation in our schools.

Traditionally the school has been assigned the responsibility for socializing the child into the ways of the culture. Teachers are expected to be sensitive to the needs of society and to assist the family in the process of socialization. What is considered essential to perpetuating the culture is the inculcation of certain moral and ethical values and the corresponding behaviors. This process can only be achieved when the representatives of the culture insist upon adherence to societal norms of conduct. Ideally, there is a consensus among adults about standards and the behavior that exemplifies conformity to them. The consensus is the foundation for the consistent application of behavioral controls. The adult community exercises these controls in the interests of all its members. The ends are given. The means are restricted by the choice of ends. This is hardly a democratic process.

Schools are supposed to inculcate not negotiate the mores of society. Children and young people are to emulate their elders, not fault them. Adults are to exact certain behaviors from the young, not enter into compromises with them. Likewise, educators are advocates of goals that stretch the mind and spirit. The ultimate goals of the good life are immutable not disputable. They are the aims of humankind that transcend the centuries. They are preserved by the moral authority of those who are educated. Teachers, like parents, are not merely guardians who minister to the fleeting whims of children. Rather, they are representatives of the culture who, if necessary, are expected to coerce the young to behave in ways that are consonant with approved ethical and moral standards.

In this age of self-determination and self-interest, there are bound to be contests of will. It is inevitable that young people will try to break away from the standards of conduct that necessitate placing group welfare above self-interest. They will continue to seek their immediate ends at the expense of the more remote ends of school and society. Here the school and family must work together; the power of the peer group can be awesome and compelling.

The school is an extension of the family. The family is the nuclear group responsible for the preservation of the culture and the well-being of its members. As the American family restructures itself to deal with social, economic, and political realities, it is readily apparent that the school must recast its role and alter its responsibilities. During the past several decades, the school has increasingly absorbed more responsibility for nurturing the growth and developing the talents of the young. Children and their parents are spending less time together. Teachers often become the most significant adult in the lives of children. Elementary teachers are referred to, and often accepted, by children as surrogate parents. It is tempting for teachers to accept the myth that, as persons, children are the equal of adults. Similarly, it is tempting to believe that children are inherently good and, given the freedom to choose, will make choices that are right for them.

Teachers who abide by these myths are likely to interact with a child as a friend, a buddy, or another member of the child's peer group. Whereas teachers should have a genuine love for children, they should not assume that children have the humane purposes of adults nor the wisdom to make choices that will assure these ends. Children are all too conscious of the narrow aims and capricious nature of their peers. They recognize and appreciate the steady and reliable guidance of adults. It is the humane adult who understands a child's need for the consistent application of behavioral standards and realizes the self-assurance that accrues to the child in this process.

Our current motivation problem in schools stems from a lack of consensus among adults about the ends of education and the evidence we will accept that these ends have been achieved. The concomitant problem is our lack of insistence that young people address themselves to these ends and behave consistently with them. It is a crisis of values, one that manifests itself in a diminished tenacity among young people to do something and be somebody. It is a crisis that adults respond to by offering the young alternatives that appeal to their shortsightedness and accommodate their limited capacity to tolerate frustration. We allow them to choose the lines of least resistance and skirt the demands that require surmounting obstacles along the way.

Adults today must reassert their moral authority and responsibility to educate the young. They must reject the narcissistic attitude that everyone should be free to do their own thing. That is not freedom, but anarchy. Despite illusions to the contrary, young people do not really want this kind of choice. The young are confused when confronted with value neutrality, situational ethics, and moral ambiguity. They will continue to complain and engage in subtle diversionary tactics as long as they detect a lack of unity among parents and educators. Do not be misled or disillusioned. They are striving for clarity, not for their own way. They want adults to take the lead and provide them security in a world that is long on problems and short on solutions.

It takes courage and resoluteness to stand firm amidst the clamoring of the young to be free of adult constraints. We will at times be regarded as the enemy. There will be conflicts and confrontations. There should be reasoned dialogue, but the moral authority of adults should not be compromised. We must stand firm on those civic responsibilities and moral principles that are the thread and fabric of our society. When parents and educators act as a corporate body of informed and caring adults, young people will be inspired to assume those duties that will make them productive citizens and enlightened individuals.

2. <u>Learning is fun, and when it ceases to be fun, there is something wrong with our ends or our means.</u>

Teachers have been mesmerized by enterprising publishers and have capitulated to the palaver of educational critics. This unlikely partnership has promulgated a philosophy that learning should be fun. Schools have purchased all manner of paraphernalia and have consumed assorted advice from those who would take all the work out of learning. Motivation to learn has been transformed into technological gimmickry, so-called creative games, and assorted simulation materials and activities that seduce students to learn. Form has replaced substance. Perseverance is minimized; the payoff must surpass tenacity. In short, we try to make it possible to learn something without any significant expenditure of effort and with a minimum of cognitive strain. Education has become a form of subliminal wizardry. The teachable moment of which Jerome Bruner speaks has been replaced by the unsuspecting moment. The aim of education is to teach something before the pupil realizes it.

Some learning is fun. Things that students learn because they are naturally interested in are fun. Things we learn in our leisure pursuits are often fun. But schools were not created to teach the things that come naturally, nor are schools meant to be an outlet for one's leisure. It is precisely this that accounts for the many difficulties teachers encounter when students are required to learn those things that distinguish human beings from animals. It is when teachers begin to behave as though the things that one must learn in school are well-suited to intrinsic motives that we have a problem. The things one must learn in school often require more than a passing fancy and loose commitments. The aims of school focus on the future. The impatience and impertinence of youth mitigate against their adopting the long term perspective.

There is not a whole lot of fun in practicing the scales on the piano or in repeatedly serving a ball in tennis. Similarly, there is little excitement in practicing the computation of fractions or in repeating the spelling of a word. However, these are fundamentals one must master to attain the proficiency that brings enduring enjoyment and satisfaction. There are certainly ways to make these lessons lively, but there is no escaping the occasional drudgery and periodic hardships that underlie competence. Unfortunately, we have been spending a great deal of time trying to make competence easy and fun, only to learn that the activity is memorable but little of the content remains. Teachers are so busy collecting and collating interesting things to do, they have lost sight of the reason for doing them.

When the sole aim of the learner is focused upon escaping the diligence associated with achieving competence, there is bound to be a compromise in the ultimate outcome as well. All masterful performances are preceded by adversities that require endurance and fortitude. We now seem prepared to compromise excellence in the interests of avoiding adversity. Yet, even modest proficiency requires commitment and resoluteness that transcend creative exercises which do little more than entertain.

The teacher is not an entertainer, nor should the schools be modeled after the entertainment business. Yet many teachers are tempted to adopt the entertainment media model, a model which relies heavily upon visual stimulation. They try to emulate the slick appeal of "Seasame Street" and "The Electric Company," neglecting to note the very limited objectives of the programs. The learning tasks require little more than a series of conditioned responses. What passes for a process is little more than assimilation of information. Students may become mesmerized by the softsell and the cleverly constructed message, but there is little substance in the package.

It is this glib and deceptively simple solution that has contributed to the loss of confidence in education. Confidence has also been undermined by the marginal performance of pupils who are not well served by the philosophy that learning is fun. As Ebel (1) stated, "Learning is not a gift any school can give. It is the prize the learner himself must pursue. If a pupil is unwilling or unable to make the effort required, he will learn little in even the best school."

3. <u>The urge to know and the desire to learn can best be understood and regulated by attending to the inner life of students.</u>

When teachers have a motivation problem in class, they are likely to attribute the cause to things that go on inside students and to talk in terms of feelings that contribute to a pupil's behavior. The pupil is characterized as not caring about school, feeling alienated from his or her classmates and teachers, lacking interest in math, or lacking self-esteem. The solution to the problem is changing these feelings about school, subjects, and self. If the student can only be helped to feel differently, he or she will behave differently.

Many educators advocate values clarification exercises as the remedy for marginally motivated and low achieving students. They reason that a student's values and allied feelings direct that student's behavior. A shift in values will produce a corresponding shift in behavior. One learns to value oneself as a capable learner and then engages in those behaviors that substantiate the claim. This is at best a circuitous route to competence. A more enlightened view begins with behavior rather than values. Pupils will feel differently only when, and if, they behave differently. The emphasis must be on behavior, not on feelings. The pupil's feelings are only by-products of his or her behavior. Successful pupils, those who engage in success-producing behaviors, will _feel_ successful. What is essential is the positive feedback that accompanies a correct response. In some cases, the feedback is inherent in the completion of a designated task. In other cases, the feedback is informational in terms of the teacher's response. When we view problems from this perspective, motivation becomes a matter of getting students to act differently. They will eventually come to hold the values associated with those behaviors that make them feel good.

Inner states are an unreliable guide to understanding and helping people. We are unable to observe these states or use them as reference points for interpreting student behavior. The urge to know and the desire to learn must be nurtured as a consequence of successful experiences. The teacher's emphasis should not dwell on helping Johnny feel good but rather on helping Johnny behave in good ways. Teachers must make a concerted effort to engage pupils in those activities that have a high probability of eliciting desirable behaviors. The teachers should then selectively reward behaviors that are indicative of academic competence. When students experience successful outcomes, those experiences further increase the chances they will become actively involved in future academic tasks. In the absence of success-producing behaviors, there will be no corresponding internal condition. Motivation may be described and explained by internal states, but there is no substitute for action in producing this internal state of affairs.

4. _Look to the intentions of the child rather than to the student's deeds._

Teachers' grading practices best illustrate this

maxim. We like to recognize the earnest efforts and the engaging personalities of pupils when we assign an evaluation to their work. We are unable or unwilling to divorce attitude from achievement. We like pupils who perform as though they are motivated, even if the results fall short of our expectations. Here again, motivation becomes the end, regardless of outcomes served by it.

Students are quick to discern our pleasure with a "good effort." They become adept at producing the verbal and nonverbal ploys that are designed to influence our impressions of their desire to learn. "Psyching out" the teacher is largely ascertaining how to get the most for the least. The tactic is best executed by those students who can figure out how to get good grades without doing what the grade is supposed to signify.

There should be no substitute for good deeds. This stance presumes that we know what constitutes a good deed and that good deeds can be measured by overt student performances. Teachers should never reward a pupil's interpretations of the good deed. Students can disguise their real intentions by engaging in substitute behaviors that make the teacher feel they were well-meaning. Many teachers will object to the arbitrariness of this principle and insist that it does not allow for uniqueness or individual freedom. There are others who will want to disassociate themselves from the principle because of its authoritative connotations.

Once again the issue becomes: who should be in control, and what are the important outcomes for American education? If we reward good intentions or what passes as such, many will choose the path of least resistance. Even more crucial is the fact that students will leave the educational establishment without the continuous urge to know or the requisite skills for successful adulthood. In the marketplace they will do only what is necessary to get by. These kinds of attitudes and behaviors shortchange the culture and, worse yet, curtail the fulfillment of individual potential. It is never enough to act as if one is motivated. Motivation should sustain behaviors that produce quality results.

5. <u>Punishment can negate the errors of judgment</u>

<u>and practice.</u>

The use of punishment to influence or change behavior is well-entrenched in our society. It is frequently used because it is quick and <u>seems</u> to work. We generally experience and observe an immediate change in behavior when we punish. We also experience satisfaction for having terminated a state of affairs which is unpleasant to us. This successful termination of an aversive situation reinforces our continual reliance upon punishment. However, the encounter often only teaches the second party what not to do. The object of the lesson is what to avoid doing in the future, rather than providing the learner with information about what to do. Although the use of punishment is least recommended as a technique to control and manage academic and social behaviors, if employed, it should always contain a correctional element.

The unfortunate side effects of these encounters is the avoidance of the person and situations that have generated the unpleasant consequences. The teacher and his or her instructional objectives become objects to be avoided and ignored at all costs. It is a natural human inclination to avoid or escape situations which inflict personal harm. It is no wonder that expulsion and dropping out of school are welcome reliefs for some students rather than suitable consequences of inappropriate behaviors.

If teachers and schools are persistently associated with painful consequences, they cannot be a source of influence. The student will avoid those contacts that have the potential for influencing behavior in more appropriate ways. Rather than being motivated to see the school as a place where one has positive experiences and develops the tools and knowledge for successful adulthood, the student may avoid the school and fall under the control of less desirable influences. Under the worst circumstances, the school becomes a place to vent hostility for all the injustices that have been inflicted upon the student. Apathy and resistance toward learning escalate into more serious acts of retaliatory behavior such as vandalism, harassment, and physical acts of violence, even murder.

The best alternative to punishment is the effective and consistent use of positive reinforcement. However, teachers must have an accurate inventory of what reinforcers will influence appropriate academic and social behaviors. Grades and social displays of approval are among the most powerful social reinforcers, but they must be dispensed with caution. They will work for some students but have little appeal for others. If social praise is used, it is necessary that the teacher be judged as a valid reinforcer by the students. Social reinforcers may also become weakened if they are too freely and indiscriminately dispensed. When reinforcers are ineffective, teachers may use punishment as a means of controlling behavior. Teachers often resort to what works without asking why positive forms of behavior control are not working. The shift away from punishment as a form of control is not abdicating responsibility for controlling; it is merely substituting a form that produces the best results over the long haul.

Remote goals are, for many students, of little use in influencing day-to-day classroom behavior. What is most essential is that successful student performances be immediately reinforced. Immediate knowledge of results can be a powerful reinforcer. There is intrinsic satisfaction in knowing that one is right. Teachers should design instructional programs which insure immediate reinforcement for correct responses.

We can minimize the use of punishment as a motivator if we will institute the measures advocated in the discussion of the previous maxims. Punishment is often a last-ditch effort to offset the errors of our ways. Rather than nullifying our mistakes, however, punishment usually compounds them. In actuality, we have institutionalized a counterproductive means of controlling student behavior. The result is that many students develop a lifelong negative attitude toward school and academic learning, an attitude which undermines the basic purposes of American education and decreases the number of individuals who might otherwise live fruitful lives.

The authors have attempted to highlight some of the ways in which teacher belief systems can actually worsen existing problems in the area of academic motivation. These belief systems, which are faulty ways of conceptualizing the teaching/learning situation, have been nurtured by some schools of education and solidified and reinforced by the professional literature. The following suggestions are offered in the common goal of improving classroom instruction:

1.   It is the teacher's moral and professional responsibility to select educational goals and to prescribe acceptable behavior. Both of these activities will reduce the teacher's ability to rely solely on intrinsic motives for learning. However, if there is a reasoned consensus among parents and educators about the ends of education, children and young adults will expend the effort to do what is required. The opportunity to be free of such prescription is the ultimate reward of being educated.

2.   The teacher should not operate under the premise that all learning is fun. Real learning, learning which results in reorganization and refinement of ideas and skills, is often hard work. But hard work does produce results that engender self-respect and the admiration of others.

3.   Feelings are by-products of behavior. Success is the result of a completed project, an acceptable score on a history test, or the ability to play a musical instrument. People feel good about their accomplishments. In the absence of accomplishment, there is little to feel good about.

4.   Teachers should focus on overt behaviors rather than attempt to infer the nature of inner states. Influencing behaviors is direct and the results are observable. Trying to alter inner states is indirect and the results are unpredictable.

5.   Teachers should positively reinforce appropriate academic and social behaviors. Students should have ample opportunity to enjoy the fruits of their endeavors, the self-satisfaction that comes when a task is completed. Punishment and threat should be avoided at all costs. Punishment as a form of behavior control often results in unproductive side effects. Often these side effects diminish the will to learn and contribute to self-defeating behaviors.

Notes

1.   Robert L. Ebel, "What Are Schools For?" PHI DELTA KAPPAN, September 1972, p. 6.

MILESTONES IN MOTIVATION

Marlow Ediger

Motivating learners has indeed been a problem for numerous teachers throughout the history of education.

The Puritans in colonial America used corporal punishment to force pupil learning. If a pupuil did not achieve, he was slapped, spanked, or made to kneel on dry beans. "Licking and learning" went hand in hand.

With the introduction of the Monitorial System of Instruction into the United States in 1805, methods of embarrassment replaced, in part, the use of physical punishment.

Joseph Lancaster believed that embarrassing pupils was a more humane means of motivation. Thus, a pupil with an unwashed face could be asked to wash in front of the entire student body. Because, generally, there were no partitions among classes in a Lancastrian school, as many as 1,000 pupils could watch the embarrassed pupil wash his face.

Or, learners who had misbehaved might be yoked together to encircle the school arena. A boy who misbehaved could be suspended in a basket from the ceiling or wrapped in a blanket and left in the school building overnight. The misbehaving pupil could truly experience embarrassment in these situations!

There are, of course, a few teachers today who try to stimulate learning through use of threats of physical punishment -- a relic of Puritans in colonial America. More teachers today use embarrassment of pupils -- a relic of the Lancastrian Monitorial System

Reprinted from SCHOOL AND COMMUNITY, 66 (3): 12-13 (November 1979), by permission of author and publisher.

of Instruction.

B. F. Skinner, in a more modern approach, theorizes that individuals seek rewards and attempt to avoid punishment. Pupils achieve sequential progress in small steps, according to Skinner.

For example, in programmed learning, after reading one or more sentences, the pupil responds to a completion item and then checks his own response with that given by the programmer. If the response given by the learner is correct, the learner feels rewarded or reinforced. If the response given is incorrect, the learner now knows the right answer and also is ready for the next programmed item.

The same procedure may be followed again and again in programmed learning -- read, respond, and then check the response. Being successful reinforces learning. Success in on-going activities is vital to motivation, according to reinforcement theory.

Educators advocating reinforcement theory suggest extrinsic rewards, such as gold and silver stars next to a pupil's name on a chart, candy, gum and fruit, and free choices of learning activities be given those who achieve specific objectives.

Jerome Bruner has a different approach. He emphasizes the importance of mastering key, structural ideas in any given subject matter specialty.

Learning, according to Bruner, is its own reward. Extrinsic rewards, like prizes and free time for achieving, are not emphasized. In Jerome Bruner's thinking the achievement of structural ideas inductively (learning by discovery) motivates pupils. Motivation comes from within the learners and is intrinsic to the learning activity.

The teacher's responsibilities are: to choose relevant generalizations; to select methods of teaching which can stimulate learners to have an inward desire to learn; to appraise whether key content is being acquired and whether pupils are using desired methods of learning.

Bruner emphasizes a spiral curriculum. Generalizations are not learned in one lesson; rather, the spiral curriculum emphasizes the achievement of key ideas at succeeding levels of complexity throughout the school years of the learner.

A different approach is that of the humanists. Humanists say that pupils will be motivated when they have a voice in selecting objectives, learning experiences, and evaluation procedures. The teacher serves as a stimulator and guide.

The teacher's task in reflecting humanism as a psychology of learning might well include the following:

Establish a stimulating environment from which pupils may choose what to learn. Learning centers might be part of the school setting.

Determine means of involving pupils in deciding what to learn. (Dictating what pupils are to learn does not harmonize with humanist thinking.)

Plan activities with pupils. Encourage decision-making. See that the needs of the "whole child" are met so that pupils can develop into fully functioning individuals.

In summary, teachers, principals, and supervisors need to study all psychologies of learning. Ultimately we might improve our methods of motivating pupils.

Part 5

ORGANIZING STUDENTS

FOR INSTRUCTION

INVEST EARLY FOR LATER DIVIDENDS

Irving Lazar

In our fast-paced society the pendulum has swung in less than 15 years from a "war on poverty" to "Proposition-13 fever." As legislators come under increasing pressure to lower taxes and cut spending, the crucial question becomes: Which of many programs and services to fund? Preschool programs for children from low-income families deserve support. Indeed, they have the potential to reconcile opposing poles by both helping poor children improve their later school performances and saving tax dollars.

Intervention Programs

The nationwide Project Head Start epitomizes preschool intervention programs for most people. Since the summer of 1965 when it began as part of the 1964 Economic Opportunity Act, Head Start has provided a stimulating learning environment -- in group settings and in the home -- for children from low-income families. The purpose is to teach children concepts and encourage their curiosity, self-confidence and motivation to learn so that they will enter elementary school on a more equal footing with their middle-class peers. In addition, Head Start attempts to meet the health and nutrition needs of children from low-income families, to involve the parents and the community in helping foster children's development, and to provide new careers for low-income adults in the early-education field.

Early Evaluation Research

The high hopes for preschool were dashed in 1969

Reprinted from COMPACT, 13 (3): 12-13+ (Fall 1979) by permission of author and publisher.

with the release of the Westinghouse/Ohio Report. It concluded that any cognitive and affective gains from the Head Start experience had largely disappeared by the time children reached the second and third grades. The resulting pessimism about durable benefits of preschool lasted almost 10 years. Recent evaluations of preschool graduates, through examination of their actual school performances, have now caused critics to reconsider their negative judgments.

Evidence for Early Education

In 1975, concerned about attacks on Head Start and the effectiveness of early intervention, 12 investigators who had independently conducted experimental preschool studies agreed to pool their research efforts (1). Their model infant and preschool programs dated from the early and mid-1960s for the most part; consequently, the original participants (now ages 10 to 19) were well along in their school careers. It was a unique opportunity to assess the long-range effects of preschool programs for children from low-income families. Calling themselves the Consortium for Longitudinal Studies, they agreed to attempt to re-establish contact with the original participants for tests and interviews. All data would be analyzed by a neutral party who had not managed such a program (2).

Consortium members had operated their preschool programs at sites scattered throughout urban and rural areas of the Northeast, Southeast, and Midwest. Despite this dispersion, sample children were relatively similar across programs. Most were blacks (92 percent) from low-income families. The average parent had 10.2 years of education with an occupational status of semiskilled or unskilled labor. Most Consortium members designed their studies to include a group of children who attended preschool (treatment) and a comparison group who did not attend preschool. The two exceptions compared the relative effectiveness of different preschool curricula or treated the entire population of preschool children at risk of school failure.

Let me present the results of this unique collaborative effort in the form of questions directed to me over the past years by public officials and educators.

<u>1. Is there any evidence of long-term education benefits of preschool?</u> Yes, definitely. The longitudinal study permitted examination of children's actual school performances as opposed to scores on standardized tests or predictors of school performance, such as IQ scores. Specifically, we looked at children's progress through school: did they stay "on grade" with age mates or had they fallen behind by being assigned to special remedial classes or by being retained in grade (grade failure)?

We found that children who had preschool experience were significantly less likely to be assigned to special classes or retained in grade, compared to control children. Furthermore, on fourth-grade standardized achievement tests, preschool completors scored significantly higher than control children on mathematics achievement and tended to score higher on reading as well. It is important to emphasize the strength of these findings. Four of the investigators used an experimental research design, randomly assigning children to either preschool or control group status. The essential feature of such a design, of course, is that the preschool and control groups are equivalent on everything except the treatment itself; in this case, the preschool experience. For those projects, we can state with a good deal of confidence that the preschool experience caused the later school performance differences between treatment and control children.

<u>2. Can preschools help save tax dollars?</u> Economists conducted a detailed cost-benefit analysis of the Perry Preschool in Ypsilanti, Michigan, a Consortium member project and fairly representative in terms of costs and outcomes (3). The benefits of the program -- measured in reduced need for high-cost special education services and in increased projected lifetime earnings for the children -- outweighed the costs by 236 percent. In other words, the children cost less to educate and will produce more for themselves and for society.

<u>3. Are there specific program models that states should implement?</u> The preschool programs directed by members of the Consortium for Longitudinal Studies were quite varied in their approaches. One program began when children were 3 months old; others when children were 2, 3, or 4 years old. Some programs focused exclusively on visits to the children's homes; some combined home visits with daily group sessions

254

in a preschool center; others focused on the group program with no home visits. Some curricula were tightly structured and focused only on school-readiness skills; others emphasized a "discovery" approach and attempted to influence children's motivation and self-concepts as well as their cognitive development. With so much diversity among the programs, we expected to analyze data and be able to specify which program dimensions were superior. To date, however, we have failed to identify any dimensions of preschool that were more effective than others. Apparently, all these programs were equally able to help poor children avoid special remedial education placement.

It behooves us, then, to consider what all these successful programs had in common. All had low child-to-adult ratios -- on the average, five children per adult (this included paraprofessionals and volunteers as well as professionals with training in early childhood education). The staff members received regular inservice training. They had access to supervisors who both monitored their work and provided support for their efforts. A carefully specified curriculum provided the teaching staff with guidelines on how to arrange time blocks and which activities to emphasize. In other words, a particular curriculum per se does not appear to be crucial but it is probably very important to adequately train and support the teaching staff.

Let me say a word about involving parents in these programs. Our data were not suitable for addressing this issue, but others have demonstrated the feasibility and importance of involving parents in preschoolers' education. Despite their socioeconomic status, these parents generally have high aspirations for their children and recognize the role education can play in their children's futures. Involving parents in the actual process of teaching their children can build on those attitudes, reinforcing them and providing parents with concrete skills for achieving their aims. Additionally, congruence between the home and school settings should help the children by reinforcing their school experiences and supporting their motivation.

4. With Head Start already operating on a national level, why should state governments invest in preschool education? Many people are not aware that Head Start currently serves only about 20 percent of all

eligible children (401,983 out of about two million poor children currently ages 3 to 5 years). The proposed austerity budget at the national level would neither provide Head Start with funds to serve more children nor provide for increased costs due to inflation (4). State and local education agencies invest large amounts of money in elementary school compensatory and special education programs.

High quality preschool programs can reduce the needs for such services and would represent a good investment of state education funds.

5. How should preschools articulate with other educational programs? Of course, savings in remedial education -- and an increased probability of better life chances for poor children -- are not the only reasons to invest in early education. One of the outstanding demographic trends of our time is that over half the mothers of young children are now in the labor force. This, coupled with the evidence of preschool effectiveness, suggests that we should consider seriously funding alternatives that will meet both needs: preschool experiences and quality day care.

As for articulating preschool with elementary school, a mechanism already exists in the form of vacant space in school buildings constructed at the height of the baby boom. Some schools are already renting or donating empty classrooms to other community institutions for use as preschool and day-care facilities. Besides making good use of expensive space such collaboration has the potential to mesh children's early experiences with later school programs and perhaps improve public appreciation of the schools.

It is time to think creatively about how to meet the needs of young children, especially those from our most needy families. Preschool is no panacea, but neither is it merely "throwing money at a problem." Investment in preschool pays. In these inflationary times, it even can be considered a bargain.

Footnotes

1. They include: E. Kuno Beller, Temple University; Martin and Cynthia Deutsch, New York University; Susan Gray, George Peabody College; Ira Gordon (de-

ceased September, 1978), University of Florida; Merle Karnes, University of Illinois; Louise Miller, University of Louisville; Francis Palmer, Merrill-Palmer Institute; David Weikart, High/Scope Foundation; Phyllis Levenstein, Verbal Interaction Project; Myron Woolman, Institute for Educational Research; and Edward Zigler, Yale University.

2. Dr. Irving Lazar of Cornell University, joined in 1977 by Dr. Richard Darlington, also of Cornell University.

3. See Weber, Foster & Weikart. AN ECONOMIC ANALYSIS OF THE YPSILANTI PERRY PRESCHOOL PROJECT. Monograph of the High/Scope Educational Research Foundation. No. 5, 1978.

4. Testimony of the Children's Defense Fund on FY 1979 Supplemental and FY 1980 Appropriations for Project Head Start, March 28, 1979.

WHY OUR OPEN CLASSROOMS FAIL

Kenneth T. Henson

American education has experienced a decade of criticisms that have come mainly from within its own ranks. Indeed, a brief visit to the nearest bookstore or library will turn up many books (most written by American teachers) with such titles as CRISIS IN THE CLASSROOM (Silberman, 1970), DEATH AT AN EARLY AGE (Kozol, 1967), DESCHOOLING SOCIETY (Illich, 1970), HOW CHILDREN FAIL (Holt, 1964), THE UNDERACHIEVING SCHOOL (Holt, 1970), and THE WAY IT SPOZED TO BE (Herndon, 1975). Supportive evidence is beginning to emerge carrying the all-too-familiar note, "I told you so." Scholastic Achievement Test scores have declined for ten continuous years (Newsfront, 1979). A decade of testing by the National Assessment of Educational Progress (NAEP) reports that the achievement of our elementary pupils is down in four major areas (Neill, 1979). More than 70,000 teachers are assaulted physically each year in classrooms and hallways (Armstrong, 1978) and a staggering $600 million worth of school property is destroyed each year, an increase of 66 percent a year since 1977 (Kratcoski et al., 1978).

Whether our schools really are responsible for our national energy crisis, inflation, pollution, unemployment, poverty, and other societal problems is a philosophical question of little consequence. The fact remains: Americans are disenchanted with their schools and, according to a recent national survey, are no longer willing to support them (Gallup, 1978). Ironically, as public opinion of schools declines, the cost of educating each child rises 7 percent annually (Lublow, 1978).

These are the conditions that have caused U.S. educators to look beyond their own realms for answers.

Reprinted from EDUCATIONAL HORIZONS, 58 (2): 82–85 (Winter 1980), by permission of author and publisher.

But why the British schools? After all, if England's
schools were held accountable for that country's current state of economic, social, labor, and political
affairs, they would fare even less well. The sterling
pound has hit all-time lows repeatedly in the past
three years. In most areas that are used as indexes
of national welfare, Great Britain's problems are
equal to or greater than those of the United States.
Her airline, bread, and coal strikes have kept her unemployment rate considerably higher than the unemployment rate in America. Former Prime Minister James
Callaghan's rapport with the Queen had been so poor
that he even declined an invitation to attend a social
hosted by Her Majesty, an unprecedented gesture in a
country that has always prided itself in following
traditions and social graces. Englishmen are spending
numerous hours standing on a box in Hyde Park affirm-
ing that the country can no longer afford the two million dollar annual budget for a figurehead who has no
actual authority.

In the storm of national problems, as though to
announce the state of British affairs, on August 5,
1976, even the clock in Big Ben, a symbol of steadi-
ness and strength for the past 170 years, screeched,
clanged, screamed, and stopped. It is indeed strange
that with all of Britain's current national problems,
America is still looking at British schools to learn
how to improve its own schools. But the peculiarity
disappears as one closely examines the schools that
are revolutionizing our own schools. These are the
world renown British Infant Schools, which enroll
children from age five to age seven.

The British have different expectations for their
schools. Unlike Americans, the British do not hold
their schools responsible for their society's conditions. In fact, the British people rarely interfere
with their schools at all. Parents may offer to assist
but they almost never interfere. While many assist
daily with supervising the playgrounds and swimming
pools, and help children dress and undress for swimming, they do not become involved in planning the
school program. Members of the Parent Teacher Association provide service by raising money for the schools,
but even they do not get involved in decisions about
how the school is run.

Unlike American schools, which resemble large,
cold factories, the British Infant School carries the

259

personality of its headmaster or headmistress, who has complete autonomy to run the school as he or she sees fit. The respect for the head carries on into the school, where every teacher perceives the principal as a master teacher. Indeed, that is the true meaning of "head" or "head teacher." One can quickly see that this difference runs below the title surface, since the British heads continue to teach throughout their careers as heads of the schools. Of course, this affects their relationship with each child, since they know every child by name, a nearly impossible task for American principals of schools with enrollments numbering in the thousands.

The closeness of the British head with the pupils sets the stage for discipline in British schools. As one head recently explained, "I don't use corporal punishment because I don't need to." This contrasts sharply with the attitude toward corporal punishment in America. The 1979 Gallup Poll (Gallup, 1979) found that Americans still feel that lack of discipline is the number one problem in American schools. The head explained, "When a child is sent to me for discipline, by the time he reaches my office he has already been disciplined." (1) Because each child knows the head personally and vice versa, and because the head is respected, the child is humiliated by having to appear before the head for misbehavior. Usually, a brief talk between the two is all that is necessary to admonish the undesired behavior. In rare instances where the child has repeated an offense, the head will delay the meeting, leaving the child to sit alone and think about the misbehavior for some time before they begin their talk. This approach is called the "mellowing period."

The warmth between the British head and each pupil is passed on to the teacher-pupil relationship. Rarely does one see a British Infant teacher admonish a child. Even during conflicts among pupils, the teacher is reluctant to interfere. The teacher views misbehavior as a temporary and self-correcting thing that will soon pass by itself if left alone. In the meanwhile, others, including peers and teachers, must be willing to tolerate it. If the children do not correct their behavior in a reasonable length of time, the teacher will move over close and may even place a hand on a child's shoulder, offering comfort and security.

The prevailing attitude is that the British teacher's time is too valuable to be spent reprimanding pupils and could be better spent planning experiences for them. This concept is reflected throughout every British Infant School. Each classroom is different and unique. The walls are covered with school programs, each designed by the teacher in that room. One wall might have a "Sherlock Snoopy" theme with a picture of Snoopy the dog in his Sherlock Holmes cap searching with his magnifying glass for missing parts of speech. Another room may have pupils learning to cook or to keep house.

These roles and relationships are basic to the underlying philosophy in British education, which espouses the concept that school is not preparation for life. School is life. Therefore, the quality of life in school is all important. School faculty and staff share the responsibility of helping each child learn to enjoy school life. Family grouping (multi-age grouping) helps the younger and older children learn to cooperate and learn from each other. Groups of near equal ability, called "houses," compete for trophies, as opposed to our system, which often forces individuals to compete with others of infinitely more ability. The absence of tests and letter grades further increases the enjoyment of school life. Having no report cards with which to compare children with their peers is another positive factor, for it removes the fear of disappointing one's parents at reporting periods.

We Americans must remember that Silberman's comprehensive study of American schools, which led to his book CRISIS IN THE CLASSROOM, reported that the single variable that correlates highest with students' success in American schools is not the children's IQs or how seriously they apply themselves; it is the income level of each child's family. No wonder we parents insist on A's and B's. They don't reflect our children's success in school; they reflect our success in life.

The belief in quality of life is borne out of the experiences that make up the British Infant School day, experiences that are built around those activities that children naturally enjoy. A visit to any British Infant School reveals a flexible climate where children are allowed to pursue activities of their own choice. For example, all children like to play in water and sand, and all children love to play with animals. This manipulation of concrete objects is consistent with the world renown learning theorist Jean Piaget, who says that children are unable to deal with abstractions until about age twelve. Actually, "formal-stage thinking emerges in adolescence (and even then only) as a potentiality only partially attained by most and fully attained only by some" (Dulit, 1978). Some people actually never mature enough cognitively to deal with the abstractions that we demand of our children. In fact, 25 to 75 percent of all adults have not achieved formal operations (Good, 1979).

To provide their pupils with the necessary manipulative-type experiences, the British Infant Schools have a physical plant design called "indoor-outdoor planning." This physical environment is complemented by the attitude of the British teachers, who are willing to allow pupils the necessary freedom to pursue their own interests, either in groups or individually.

Unfortunately, the operation of British Infant classrooms appears deceptively simple to the casual observer, who may notice only the physical openness of the room itself. This is exemplified by the American open classroom, which has emerged as a modification of the British Infant School classroom. Many such schools house a traditional program in an open building. These classes are often accurately described as noisy, unruly, and chaotic. While the British Infant School may appear free and unstructured, a great deal of planning and structuring is necessary to make the system succeed. Some open classrooms in this country are highly successful. These, like their British counterparts, operate on the common beliefs that:

The child is an active agent in his own learning.

One child may learn differently from all others.

The teacher is responsible for helping each child discover how he learns best.

The function of the school is to encourage exploration.

The child has rights as well as obligations.

The teacher is a trained observer, diagnostician of individual needs, consultant, and facilitator (Rathbone, 1971).

American educators have learned much from the British Infant School, but only when seen in its total perspective does it offer much improvement for American schools. True improvements require willingness to adopt the basic philosophy that undergirds the British Infant School system. This philosophy must be accepted by the teachers and principal. Success with our open classrooms will be increased if parents, too, understand the underlying philosophy.

Letter grades are for parents; they are against children. Parents should become involved with every opportunity to work with the school. Quietness and stillness aren't always best. Whether the climate is traditional or modern, each child must know the goals he or she is pursuing. Parents should share the responsibility of helping their children learn to enjoy school and feel successful in school each day.

Some open schools in this country have succeeded in achieving these goals. Such success has followed sacrifices by teachers who are willing to invest a lot of hard work in planning and to risk a lot of their own security by yielding many responsibilities to students. The greatest success has come when parents have been willing to trust in the nature of experimentation, in the expertise of their children's teachers, and in the capabilities of their children.

Footnote

1. Taken from a personal interview with Mr. Alan Dixon, headmaster of St. Barnabas & St. Philip's School in Kensington, London, England, May 13, 1976.

References

Armstrong, O.K. "The Scandal in Our Public Schools." THE SATURDAY EVENING POST, May 1978, p. 40.
Dulit, E. "Adolescent Thinking a la Piaget: The Formal Stage." JOURNAL OF YOUTH AND ADOLESCENCE, 1972, 96. In R.E. Grinder, ADOLESCENCE. New York: John Wiley and Sons, 1979, p. 202.

Gallup, G.H. "The Eleventh Annual Gallup Poll of the Public's Attitude toward the Public Schools. PHI DELTA KAPPAN, 1979, 61, 33-45.

Good, R. et al. "Piaget's Work and Chemical Education." JOURNAL OF CHEMICAL EDUCATION, 1979, 56 (7), 426-430.

Herndon, J. THE WAY IT SPOZED TO BE. New York: Simon and Schuster, 1975.

Holt, J. HOW CHILDREN FAIL. New York: Pitman, 1964.

Holt, J. THE UNDERACHIEVING SCHOOL. New York: Pitman, 1970.

Illich, I. DESCHOOLING SOCIETY. New York: Harper and Row, 1970.

Kozol, J. DEATH AT AN EARLY AGE. Boston: Houghton Mifflin, 1967.

Kratcoski, P.C., Kratcoski, L.D. & Peterson, D. "The Crisis of Vandalism in Our Schools. USA TODAY, 1978, 107 (2398), 15-16.

Lublow, A. "Ohio's Troubled Schools." NEWSWEEK, September 25, 1978, p. 105.

Neill, G. "Washington Report." PHI DELTA KAPPAN, 1979, 61, 157.

Newsfront. "Oops! SAT Scores Still Falling." PHI DELTA KAPPAN, 1979, 61, 155.

Rathbone, C.H. "The Open Classroom: Underlying Premises." URBAN REVIEW , September 1971, pp. 4-10.

Seligman, J. "Empty Desk Blues." NEWSWEEK, April 24, 1978, p. 94.

Silberman, C.E. CRISIS IN THE CLASSROOM. New York: Random House, 1970.

DEVELOPMENTAL CHARACTERISTICS OF MIDDLE SCHOOLERS AND MIDDLE SCHOOL ORGANIZATION

Hershel D. Thornburg

The developmental and learning characteristics of early adolescents who find themselves in middle school is an aspect of this new school structure which has been consistently overlooked. The thesis of this article, therefore, focuses on the individual rather than the school itself. Within this unique middle school organization is an even more unique early adolescent.

There is one somewhat philosophical statement which underlies my persuasions about the middle school student and his/her relationship to the educational process. "The extent to which the middle school becomes a viable educational alternative to traditional school models is directly proportional to the ability of middle school educators and researchers to identify and investigate the developmental needs and learning capacities of the students which it serves (Thornburg, 1979b).

What are the characteristics of preadolescents and how do they interface with the school? There is no theory as to how these individuals are changing. They get "tacked on" to the end of childhood theories or to the beginning of adolescent theories, although this is inadequate. By viewing human development as a continuous process across the life span, it is easy to see that there are no clearly demarcated events which characterize entrance into and exit from this pre-adolescent developmental period. The elusiveness of such well-defined characteristics may become a source of challenge or discouragement. Early adolescents are a large, distinctive group. Clearly the task is a more demanding one than isolating the characteristics of

Reprinted from CONTEMPORARY EDUCATION, 52 (3): 134-138 (Spring 1981), by permission of author and publisher.

children or adolescents.

I should like to discuss some characteristics of early adolescents in light of the contemporary educational and social environments. These characteristics exist primarily because of the ways in which they developmentally unfold, although they are affected by the environment.

Social Characteristics of Early Adolescents

Developing Friendships with Others

An important aspect of development is developing friendships with others (Thornburg, 1970). In contrast to the eighth and ninth years of life where children typically have a low need for social interaction, the gradual emergence of peers is vitally important for 10- to 15-year-olds. Their curiosity and exploratory nature manifests itself socially as well. Peer group formations are usually initiated among friends of the same sex (Dunphy, 1963). Learning to accept and be acceptable to others is of vital importance. There is security in the same sex companionships at 10 to 12 compared to the opposite sex companionship in later development. They have learned over the years that friends are important and what were tentative friendships in the primary grades take on more solidarity by the middle school age.

Research is rather sketchy as to when and under what conditions early adolescents make the transition from the same sex to opposite sex companionship. The trend has been down from ages 14-15 to 12-13 within the past decade (Thornburg and Gould, 1980). This correlates with increased emphasis on physical maturation and social pressure to be involved in adolescent-like activities as a preadolescent. Studies on pre-teen drug use, sexual behavior, female pregnancy, runaways, and delinquents provide increasing insight into the behavioral world of the early adolescent, most of which is reciprocated by one's friends (Cottle, 1979; Diepold & Young, 1979; Levin & Kozak, 1979; Moore, Hofferth, & Wertheimer, 1979; Redican, et al., 1979).

Awareness of Increased Physical Changes

A second developmental characteristic is becoming

aware of increased physical changes (Thornburg, 1970).
Primarily as a result of better nutrition and general
health, the age of adolescent developmental maturity
has moved into the pre-teen years (Peterson, 1979).
Girls begin their growth spurt around age 10, boys
some 12 to 18 months later. Both are within the traditional elementary school years.

The female begins breast development in her tenth
year, experiences considerable genital growth in her
eleventh year, and begins to menstrate in her twelfth
year (12.8) (Hammer & Owens, 1973; Sommers, 1978).
Virtually all females by 15 are experiencing menarche
regardless of ethnicity or socioeconomic status (Mac-
Mahon, 1970).

Male height, genital growth, and involuntary
erections all begin around age 12. These growth processes continue for approximately three years during
which all secondary sex characteristics emerge. Thus,
while the male is less developed than his female coun-
terpart throughout the middle school years, his maturity is comparable by 16. Anxiety often accompanies
physical growth, especially given the opportunity to
compare personal growth with classmates and to compare
oneself to existing social stereotypes.

Many preadolescent behaviors seem to be heavily
attributed to stereotypy. Being stereotypical is a
13-letter word -- or is it? The pervasiveness of images in American society is something with which people of all ages must constantly contend. For middle
schoolers this stereotypy is a viable attachment since
these young girls and boys are changing in so many
ways and must use others and images as their criteria
for evaluating personal change. Research on physical
attractiveness indicates that early adolescents are
very concerned about their appearance (Adams, 1977;
Learner, Orlos, & Knapp, 1976). Boys identify strongly
with the masculine (mesomorphic) look which is characterized by their height, shoulder width, and body proportions. Girls express concern over the shape of
hips, legs, breast, and waist. The prevalence of athletic events, beauty contests, and media productions
which stress beauty, manliness, and "sexiness" help
our emerging adolescents plug into stereotypes. Recent
research (Thomsen, 1980) on television viewing habits
of middle schoolers indicates that stereotypes play an
important role in program selection. The external environment often capitalizes on the vulnerability of

267

early adolescents, sometimes to their betterment and sometimes to their detriment.

Learner Characteristics of Early Adolescents

Problem Solving Strategies

One important developmental aspect of the learner is the ability to organize knowledge and concepts into problem solving strategies (Thornburg, 1974). The preteen falls within Piaget's concrete and formal operations stages (Inhelder & Piaget, 1958). The concrete stage is a conceptual stage where the early adolescent organizes information around categories or concepts which are generalizable from one instance to another. The formal stage is not characterized only by abstract thought. In addition, it utilizes the components of logic and reasoning in making decisions. This process is the beginning of the type of thought process which exists in most adults.

The developmental aspects of these two stages can be enhanced within the middle school environment. Learning experiences can be structured for youth so that there is an easier transition into the advanced stages of thought. By grades five and six, information is ordered, organized, and structured within the mind. By grades seven and eight, deductive reasoning and reflective thinking are operating, thus lending greater flexibility to the earlier thought processes.

Self-Direction

Another important characteristic is that preteens show interest in planning many of their own learning experiences (Thornburg, 1979a), in being self-directive. They have inquiring minds which cause them to go beyond many ideas presented in class and into many personal interest areas. Teachers and the curriculum should have enough flexibility to let students explore personal academic interests at various times. This statement should not be interpreted to mean that the teacher should abdicate responsibility for directing learning in lieu of the student's rights to be self-directed. I should hope, however, that it comes to mean greater flexibility, greater awareness of the value of student input, and greater willingness to structure teaching-learning activities within the context of the learner's natural environment (Thornburg, 1979b).

Emerging Value System

The emerging value system of the pre-teen is the third learner characteristic I wish to discuss (Thornburg 1970). Throughout the first eight years of life a child's primary value source is his/her parents. Values are represented through moral teaching such as the concepts of right or wrong and good or bad. Even when the child begins school, parents remain more dominant than teachers in value teaching (Hoffman, 1980).

During early adolescence there is a shift from parents being the predominant influence on behavior to peers becoming this predominant influence (Thornburg & Gould, 1980). This sets in motion the likelihood that many parents, teachers, and other adults will be challenged in some of their moral and value teachings. Pre-teens will identify discrepancies between their parents and themselves. They may ask why a behavior, such as using profanity, is acceptable for the parent but not for the child. This generation is not as likely to accept the explanation "because parents are older," as did previous generations. They will wonder why teachers favor some students and pick on others. Then their friends will be their greatest sympathizers in the process of trying to unscramble the discrepancies. Indeed, this is the way in which moral development change occurs.

The impact of individuality within the society throughout the 1970s has been rendered literally by many pre-teens to mean "no one has the right to tell me what to do." This belief has been reinforced by older adolescents, some parents and teachers, and the media. The question is not whether individuals have rights but whether we can get them to explore those rights along with their accompanying individual responsibility. In a real sense, adults and society have done children and youth an injustice by failing to teach them the reciprocal elements of rights and responsibility. Thus, within contemporary society, we are faced with the harsh reality that pre-adolescents are being pressured, sometimes enticed, into behaviors prior to their social and emotional readiness for them. There are many opportunities for pre-adolescents to hear of and carry out the idea of individuality. The critical issue in the middle school is to teach both elements so that pre-teens have a complete basis for making value judgments and acting upon them.

The learning characteristics of the early adolescent, and the instructional effectiveness of the teacher have not yet come into functional synchronization. In effect, the school environment is still not conducive to positive growth for these youngsters. It is true that as educators we are more aware of the changing nature of these youngsters. It is also true that the middle school is a partial answer to past educational inadequacies. Still, it isn't enough. There are 23 different school organizational configurations which accommodate students in grades 5 through 9. We are not even close to determining which, if any, of these structures best meet the needs of students. In addition, teacher training programs and state licensing requirements for middle school and junior high teachers are dismal at best. We must do something about these limitations.

Teacher Effectiveness

As our information base on early adolescence continues to increase, it is essential for the effective teacher to keep abreast of what is happening. What this requires is involvement with pre-teens. If teachers dislike their jobs, are negative with students, or are too routine in their classroom teaching, the effect on students will be negative, thus impeding effective teacher/student interaction. With childhood stability breaking up, early adolescents need positive teachers who can guide them into new learning experiences.

The teacher must remember that learning must be functional to the student (Thornburg, 1979b). Student interest in academic learning is directly related to how useful the student thinks that learning is. Here I must underscore the concept of relevance. If the teacher presents things students already know, could care less about, or that are so far removed from the student's immediate life that they have no relevance, most students will disregard such teaching (Thornburg, 1979a, p. 78).

Noncompetitive Teachers

Teachers must not actively compete with students'
friends or with powerful external influences such as
the media. No matter what a teacher does, he/she will
never be as popular or as well-liked by any single
student as much as that student's friends. This is
neither demeaning nor uncomplimentary to the teacher.
Rather, it is the recognition that within the school
environment the perceptual worlds of teachers and students are significantly different. A student needs
both -- other students and teachers. The professional
role of the teacher can promote reciprocal respect.

The average middle school student spends six
hours a day watching television (Shin & Burpeau, 1980;
Srygley, 1978). Programs and advertisements are geared
to the interests and energies of pre-teens in a way so
powerful and influential that the critics are coming
out of the woodwork. Its effects are unknown, yet
speculation is that it not only promotes violence and
insolence in pre-teens but actually affects the ability of the child to think and be active (Stevenson,
1980). Some writers have asserted that extensive television may retard the development of problem-solving
skills and promote mediocrity of thought (Hartman,
1978; Hornik, 1978).

Understanding Social Contact and Responsibility

Learning must include understanding social contact and responsibility (Thornburg, 1979b). Teachers
should be aware of the importance of pre-adolescent
friendships. Perhaps some teachers perceive this as a
potential problem within the classroom rather than the
normal development of social skills. An aspect of effective instruction includes helping students learn
how to make friends and get along with others. Teachers should not see such companionship as a threat to
classroom order or management. It simply is not true
that kids always cause trouble or do unacceptable
things when they get together. Teachers should support groups of early adolescents as well as the individual person.

Teachers generally fail to take a contemporary
stance when ascertaining the needs of early adolescents. Social behaviors and the pressure to be involved in them is more intense now than ever before in

our society.   As professionals teachers can take
neither "the good old days" nor the "immoral, degener-
ate" stance. They must recognize that society is different and early adolescents have been socialized differently. The more teachers are aware of the multiple
decisions and dilemmas young adolescents have to encounter, the greater the likelihood that teachers can
help them make appropriate decisions.

Educational and Environmental Relevance

     Teachers must present educationally and environ-
mentally relevant issues. There is little question
but that most curricula are outdated. Contemporary
social issues must increasingly become a relevant part
of the school days. Learning to make socially correct
and responsible responses to situations encountered in
daily living is very important. Learning must be extended into the students' natural environment. Teachers cannot continue to take the chance of students
turning them off. The middle school must respond to
students' needs.

                    Conclusion

     The ideas I have discussed are vital if we are to
meet the needs of pre-teens within the school environment. The needs are not always evident, nor are the
strategies to resolve such needs. However, the emerging adolescent is so potentially dynamic that teachers' energies, without question, are warranted.   It
could be that the combined energies of the developing
adolescent set in motion behavioral tendencies which
are stimulated through physical growth, social awareness, and peer pressure. The instability fosters insecurity, thus the pre-teen acts to find security and
sameness, important components of the early adolescent's identity process. Early adolescents are growing up faster socially and psychologically.   Their
reference groups are changing (Gabarino et al., 1978);
they are moving from elementary to middle schools;
their self-concepts and self-esteem temporarily lower
(Blyth, Simmons, & Bush, 1978); they show much preoccupation with self (Elkind & Brown, 1979; Thornburg &
Thornburg, 1980; Thornburg & Gould, 1980); and their
behavioral range is great as manifested by the scope
of pro- and anti-social activities in which they are
involved. Indeed, the challenge to American educators

has been forcefully presented by the early adolescent.

References

Adams, G.R. Physical attractiveness research: Toward a developmental social psychology of beauty. Human Development, 1977, 20, 217-239.

Blyth, D., Simmons, R.G. & Bush, D.A. The transition into early adolescence: A longitudinal comparison of youth in two educational contexts. Sociology of Education, 1978, 51, 149-162.

Cottle, T.J. Children in jail. Crime and Delinquency, 1979, 25(3), 318-319.

Diepold, J. & Young, R.D. Empirical studies of adolescent sexual behavior; A critical review. Adolescence, 1979 14(53), 45-64.

Dunphy, D.C. The social structure of urban adolescent peer groups. Sociometry, 1963, 26, 230-246.

Elkind, D. & Bowen, R. Imaginary audience behavior in children and adolescents. Developmental Psychology, 1979, 15, 38-44.

Garbarino, J., Burston, N. Raber, S. Russell, R., & Crouter, A. The social maps of children approaching adolescence: Studying the ecology of youth development. Journal of Youth and Adolescence, 1978, 7(4), 417-428.

Gould, A. & Thornburg, H.D. The frequency of peer group involvement in middle school and junior high school students. Paper presented to the Rocky Mountain Psychological Association, 1980.

Hammer, S.I., & Owens, J.W.M. Adolescence. In D.W. Smith & F.I. Bierman (Eds.), The biological ages of man. Philadelphia: W.B. Saunders, 1973, pp. 139-153.

Hartman, H.D. TV in American culture. The Crisis, 1970, 05, 15 10.

Hoffman, M.L. Fostering moral development. In M. Johnson (Ed), Toward adolescence: The middle school years. Chicago: NSSE Yearbook, 1980, pp. 161-185.

Hornik. R.C. Television access and the slowing of cognitive growth. American educational research journal, 1978, 15(1), 1-15.

Inhelder, B. & Piaget, J. The growth of logical thinking from childhood to adolescence. New York: Basic Books, 1958.

Lerner, R.M., Orlos, J.B. & Knapp, J.R. Physical attractiveness, physical effectiveness, and self-concept in late adolescence. Adolescence, 1976, 11, 313-326.

MacMahon, B. Age at menarche. National Center for Health Statistics, Vital and Health Statistics. Series 11: Data from the National Health Survey, No. 133, 1970.

Moore, K.A., Hofferth, S.L., & Wertheimer, R. Teenage motherhood: Its social and economic costs. Children Today, 1979, 8(5), 12-16.

Peterson, A.C. Can puberty come any earlier? Psychology Today, 1979, 12(9), 45.

Redican, K.J., Olsen, L.K., Stone, D.B., & Wilson, R.W. Cigarette smoking attitudes of lower socioeconomic sixth grade students. Journal of Drug Education, 1979, 9(1), 55-65.

Shinn, J.M., & Burpeau, M.Y. The social characteristics of early adolescents. Paper presented to the Rocky Mountain Psychological Association, 1980.

Sommers, B.B. Puberty and adolescence. New York: Oxford University Press, 1978.

Srygley, S.K. Influence of mass media on today's young people. Educational Leadership, 1978, 35, 526-529.

Stevenson, H.G. The mass media and popular culture. In M. Johnson (Ed.), Toward adolescence: The middle school years, Chicago: NSSE Yearbook, 1980.

Thomsen, M. Early adolescents' perceptions of the role of television viewing in their lives. Paper presented to the Rocky Mountain Psychological Association, 1980.

Thornburg, H.D. Learning and maturation in middle school age youth. Clearing House, 1970, 45, 150-155.

Thornburg, H.D. Behaviors and values: Consistency or inconsistency. Adolescence, 1973, 8(32), 513-520.

Thornburg, H.D. Pre-adolescent development: Readings. Tuscon, The University of Arizona Press, 1974.

Thornburg, H.D. The bubblegum years: Sticking with kids from 9 to 13. Tuscon: H.E.L.P. Books, 1979a.

Thornburg, H.D. Can the middle school adapt to the needs of its students? Colorado Journal of Educational Research, 1979b, 19(1), 26-29.

Thornburg, H.D. Is the beginning of identity the end of innocence? Keynote address at the Western Regional Middle School Consortium Conference, 1980.

Thornburg, H.D. & Gould, A. The types of peer group involvement in middle school and junior high school students. Paper presented to the Rocky Mountain Pyschological Association, 1980.

Thornburg, H.D. & Thornburg, E.E. The extent of the imaginary audience in early adolescents. Paper presented to the American Educational Research Association, 1980.

THE MAKINGS OF THE MIDDLE SCHOOL:
21 KEY INGREDIENTS

William Tim Brown

As educators, we read about new research findings every day, but it's often difficult to digest those recommendations and incorporate them into working programs for our schools. I've read quite extensively from the growing body of research on early adolescence and the middle school. While I was doing my doctoral dissertation, I noted several curricular practices that kept turning up, and I decided to test their validity by asking fifteen experts in middle school education from eight states their opinion of these practices.

The final result of this communication was the list of twenty-one key characteristics of a middle school that appears below. Many of these characteristics follow William Alexander's recommendation that a middle school have a planned sequence of concepts in the general education areas; a major emphasis on interests and skills for continued learning; a balanced program of exploratory experiences and other activities and services for personal development; and appropriate attention to developing values.

1. Grade organization. The most easily identified feature of any school, of course, is its grade organization. The organization must carry out the objectives and goals of the educational program. Research studies recommend that there be at least three grades in the middle school. Two grades, which means that children must move quickly from one school to another, do not provide enough stability. Though a variety of organizations exist, the most common are grades

five through eight or six through eight.

2. <u>Team teaching.</u> Team teaching, practiced in a majority of the middle schools throughout the nation, capitalizes on the strengths of individual teachers; aids in grouping students; and makes efficient use of planning and instructional time. In team teaching, teachers have a chance to share and develop ideas.

3. <u>Instructional planning.</u> One of the keys to any effective instructional program is a school organization that allows cooperative and team planning with the school's teachers, instructional leaders, and administrative staff. The faculty work together as they assess, diagnose, prescribe, and plan an instructional program centered around the students.

4. <u>Student groupings.</u> The school organization should also allow a variety of student groupings; one-to-one, small groups, or large groups. No one group arrangement can serve every learning situation. The type of group depends on the objectives of the learning activity.

5. <u>Flexible scheduling.</u> Students' diverse physical characteristics and the changes in intellectual growth and social behavior they are undergoing demand flexibility in scheduling to allow teachers and students time to design a program around the needs of the students. Flexibility makes it possible to offer students more subjects by using instructional time effectively.

6. <u>Continuous progress.</u> Since adolescence is a time of pronounced individual differences, middle school programs need to promote continuous progress, focusing on individual needs: achievement level, abilities, interests, and rate and style of learning. Individual styles of learning are a particularly important consideration in the middle school.

7. <u>Individualized instruction.</u> A student is first and foremost an individual; different students respond differently to the same situation. Because individual differences peak during middle school years, recognizing those differences and planning your program accordingly will help you reach all students.

8. <u>Independent study.</u> Independent study may be an outgrowth of a basic program in individualized in-

struction, for example, or it may be completely out-side the school program, depending on the individual student's interest. Like individualized instruction, independent study provides an opportunity for students to pursue their increasingly varied interests.

9. <u>Instructional materials.</u> A good textbook is valuable, but because middle school students all re-spond differently, they need a variety of instruc-tional materials to match their different responses, backgrounds, ideas, and interests. Instructional ma-terials and classroom activities planned as a unit are better than a single textbook approach.

10. <u>Basic skills.</u> Not all middle school students have mastered the basic skills, but without those skills, students will be ill equipped for continued learning throughout their lives.

11. <u>Remedial programs.</u> The effective middle school offers remedial programs in reading and math to reinforce students' basic skills.

12. <u>The exploratory strand.</u> Elective short-term courses and activities based on student interests let students explore all types of subjects. Because young adolescents are beginning to think about their life careers, they will want to explore their interests in many areas. A balanced program of exploratory activi-ties will let students explore as many areas as possi-ble.

13. <u>Creative expression.</u> Activities such as stu-dent newspapers, literary magazines, dramatic produc-tions, music and art programs, and darkroom instruc-tion let students express themselves creatively. If they don't have these opportunities, many of their in-terests may fall by the wayside and never be fully developed.

14. <u>Social development.</u> Adolescence is a trau-matic time for many middle school students as they begin to develop more mature relationships with par-ents, peers, classmates, and teachers. They need ex-periences and guidance that will help them develop so-cial skills and self-confidence in social behavior.

15. <u>Intramural sports.</u> An intramural sports pro-gram supplements the regular physical education pro-gram and gives more students a chance to participate

in sports activities than does the high school style interscholastic sports program. A comprehensive intramural program provides an outlet for students to develop physically.

16. <u>Focus on growth and development.</u> The many physical and psychological changes that adolescents go through can leave them confused and in conflict. Middle school students need help in understanding the principles of human growth and development so that they can understand themselves and what is happening in their lives.

17. <u>Individualized guidance services.</u> Group guidance is important, but students have individual needs that they may want to share with only one person, either a guidance counselor or a classroom teacher. The classroom teacher can play an important guidance role, for often the teacher can relate to a child in a way that a guidance counselor cannot.

18. <u>Home base program.</u> An important part of the instructional guidance service is a home base group where the teacher provides personal and academic guidance for students. The use of an advisee-adviser program, in which each student is assigned an adviser -- a home base teacher, another classroom teacher, or anyone with whom the child can relate and discuss personal and academic problems -- is recommended.

19. <u>Values clarification.</u> As young adolescents grow in academic and social experience, they come into contact with a wide variety of values and beliefs, which often conflict with and call into question their own ideas. Sometimes adolescents act like children, sometimes like adults, which shows the wide range of values and identities with which they are experimenting. Students at this age need help in sorting out or clarifying their values. One successful program in South Carolina gives high school students academic credit for leading small-group discussions for sixth-grade students. The discussion sessions, held throughout the year, help the sixth graders see themselves more realistically, be more independent, take more responsibility for their own lives, and make intelligent choices for themselves.

20. <u>Student evaluation.</u> Often middle school evaluation systems don't reflect an individualized in-

struction program, but follow traditional letter systems. Evaluation should be positive and nonthreatening and should consider the students' work as personal and individual.

21. <u>Transition from elementary to high school.</u> Finally, one of the lasting effects a middle school can have on its students is how well it prepares them to make the transition from middle school to high school. Whatever the organization pattern may be, when students move from one school to another, they need to bridge the gap. A middle school should provide a gradual transition from the self-contained classroom of the elementary school to the complete departmentalization of the high school.

Students go through many changes in the middle school, but the proper framework, organization, and opportunities for students, as suggested in these twenty-one characteristics, can help them make the transition from elementary school to high school as easily and productively as possible.

ALTERNATIVES FOR THE EIGHTIES:
A SECOND DECADE OF DEVELOPMENT

Robert D. Barr

During the past decade the concept of alternative schools has emerged as the reform strategy with the greatest potential to improve public education. Consequently, it is now being used to address the most serious problems confronting public education.

Alternative schools have been successfully used to assist in the desegregation of urban schools. They have been used to reduce school violence, vandalism, and disruption. They have served as a way of increasing parent and community involvement in public education. Alternative schools have been adopted by back-to-basic advocates and have been used to explore the demand for effective learning and accountability. Most important, alternative schools have proven their effectiveness in meeting the distinctive instructional needs of a wide variety of students. Both gifted students and school dropouts have been shown to learn better in alternative schools than they did in conventional schools. No other idea has been used so effectively during the past decade to address so many disparate problems in education.

In addition, alternative schools have been used as experimental laboratories for field-testing and validating new educational concepts. It is here that public schools have experimented with written evaluations instead of letter grades and have perfected the concepts of peer tutoring and a variety of out-of-school learning programs. Alternatives have, in fact, been instrumental in moving education out of the classroom and into business, social agencies, museums, and government offices. The concepts of a school without walls, a school-within-a-school, the Walkabout,

Reprinted from PHI DELTA KAPPAN, 62 (8): 570-573 (April 1981), by permission of author and publisher.

and Challenge Education were all developed in alternative school settings. Alternative schools have been used to develop experimental curricula for gifted and talented students, pregnant students, disruptive students, students from different cultures, and students interested in a multitude of careers. Alternative schools have also experimented with the development of a number of different learning models: Summerhill education, open education, individualized continuous progress education, fundamental education, experiential education, and behavior modification. Not since the Eight-Year Study has so much experimentation, development, and documentation occurred in public education.

To the alternative movement goes the credit for making Montessori education available within the domain of public education. This alone has enriched the public schools. Already students can attend Montessori public schools in Cincinnati, Houston, Indianapolis, and several other urban school districts. Surely during the 1980s Montessori public schools will be a choice in almost every school district in the U.S.

It is also possible to view alternative schools as a competitive response to urban decline. As large numbers of city dwellers have abandoned the cities and their schools in favor of suburban public and private and parochial schools, there has been a competitive effort in most American cities to retard this migration. The tactic most frequently employed by urban school districts is the development of large numbers of alternative magnet schools that offer nearly everything that private academy or parochial schools have to offer and, more important, are supported by tax dollars. Magnet schools have become the "elite private academies" within public education. The hope, of course, is that these "elite" public schools will help to retain middle-class families -- black, white, brown -- in urban public schools.

Perhaps most remarkable of all, in spite of a decade of rampant inflation, taxpayer revolts, tax cuts, defeated bond elections, and decreasing enrollment, alternative schools have continued to grow in substance and in number throughout the U.S. During the past decade especially, alternative schools have been as carefully evaluated as any other idea in American education; important research projects have been conducted in alternative schools. (1)   Alternative schools have been mandated by legislation in a number of states, recognized and accredited by the North Central Association of Schools and Colleges, and supported by parents in every Gallup poll on the schools in recent years.

In 1968 there were only a dozen or so alternative schools in operation in the U.S. Today there are thousands, and the number continues to grow (2); some two dozen national associations are active in the area as well as a number of well-organized state associations.

In a little more than a decade, the concept of alternative schools has changed from a radical idea to a conservative response to local school problems. It has evolved from a grassroots movement generated simultaneously in a few scattered communities across the U.S. to a truly national movement. As recently as 15 years ago, there were no books on the topic; today there are hundreds of books and articles on the topic, dozens of doctoral dissertations, a growing number of major research reports, and hundreds of local school evaluations. During the 1970s nearly every major education journal devoted a special issue to alternative schools, and such diverse magazines as U.S. News & World Report and Better Homes and Gardens have explored the issue.

Unfortunately, the news is not all good. There is a darker, less optimistic side to the development of the alternative school movement. A large number of public school systems have not developed any alternative schools; outside urban areas, the vast majority of those that have done so provide only one or two small alternative programs for a few students. Despite the massive development of alternative schools during the last decade, fewer than 5% of U.S. schoolchildren have had the opportunity to enroll and participate in such programs. More surprising, the majority of teachers, administrators, parents, and even graduate students in education may never have heard of alternative schools. And those who are aware of alternatives may have an inaccurate understanding of the concept. Alternative schools have often been used -- misused, actually -- for unfortunate purposes. They have been used as dumping grounds for students labeled as disadvantaged, deprived, disruptive, or dull. Some alternative schools are little more than grim detention centers. Some states equate alternative schools with special education. In other school districts, alternatives for the gifted and talented have shunted the best and brightest of our students into special programs.

The ideal of diversifying the whole of public education into a system of optional alternative schools and programs serving all youth has simply not materialized. While many cities have an exciting range of alternatives, nowhere has the monolithic uniformity of public education truly given way to a diverse system of alternatives. At their best, alternative schools have functioned as an exciting laboratory where unique and often daring programs are conducted and evaluated. At their worst, alternative schools represent some of the most unfortunate tendencies toward social tracking, political manipulation, and educational hucksterism.

There has always been confusion over alternative schools, particularly the terminology used to describe alternatives. The term "alternative" has been used to describe nearly every type of school imaginable, and even that term is used interchangeably with "magnet schools," "schools of choice," "voucher schools," and "options." More than 150 different types of schools have been identified as "alternatives." But if the terminology is confusing, the concept of alternatives is based on a rather simple, straightforward set of assumptions. Different people learn in different ways. Different teachers teach in different ways. It is important not simply to match learners with teachers but to develop an educational system in which parents, students, and teachers can choose the type of program they believe to be in their best interests.

The impact of this "simple" idea on public education has been profound. American schools have traditionally permitted little choice among options. They have assigned teachers, students, and parents, often arbitrarily and on the basis of where they might happen to live, to uniform and monolithic educational programs. In such a system the development of alternative schools has led to a dramatic change in perspective. The impact of this change in perspective has yet to be determined. Alternative schools may well offer the most promising area of development in all of public education, but care must be taken to scrutinize and evaluate alternatives so that they are not misused -- either at the expense of those students enrolling in them or at the expense of the many effec-

283

tive conventional public schools.

Trends for the Eighties

The 1980s offer considerable cause for optimism in the area of alternative schools. As the decade begins, at least four areas seem to hold a great deal of promise.

Alternative Schools as a Strategy for School Reform -- What may well be the most important aspect of the alternative school movement is often overlooked: its effectiveness as an institutional change strategy. Seymour Sarason said it best when he wrote, "It's easier to start a new school than to change an existing one." (3) After a decade of frustration during the 1960s, during which public education, the federal government, and the major foundations tried almost every conceivable diffusion, dissemination, and change model, research in the 1970s indicated that public education had resisted all of those efforts and remained largely unchanged.

But in the 1970s the alternative school movement provided a new area for development. It now seems clear that public schools, by using the concept of alternatives, can achieve what proved so elusive during the 60s: namely, enduring, innovative educational programs based solidly on educational theory and research. These new, distinctly different types of schools can be developed within public education; they have defied many of the research conclusions of the 1960s. For example, the literature of educational change in the 1960s maintained that a dynamic principal was a key element in school reform; when the principal left a school, most of the gains accomplished would soon be lost. A number of alternative schools (e.g., Philadelphia's Parkway School, the St. Paul Open School, and Learning Unlimited in Indianapolis) have survived -- and prospered -- despite changes in school leadership. And researchers are being forced to reconsider their earlier findings.

But the development of new public alternative schools represents only a part of the anticipated impact on American education. Educators specializing in alternatives have long hoped that the development of these schools would have a dynamic effect on all other schools in a particular district, that alternatives could act as catalysts in comprehensive school reform. And while this is occurring in certain situations, some data suggest just the opposite, i.e., that alternative schools may in fact "bleed" other schools of teachers, students, and resources. (4) Of course, it is too soon for any final judgment. At the very least, though, public education now has a tried and tested technique for improving local schools. And the potential exists for an even greater impact in the coming decade.

Alternative Schools as Means of Reducing Violence, Vandalism, and Disruption -- Recent reports indicate an intriguing relationship between alternatives and declines in school violence, vandalism, and disruption. This relationship first gained national attention during the 1976 investigations by the U.S. Senate Subcommittee on Juvenile Delinquency. Many of the witnesses who appeared before the subcommittee recommended alternative public schools as a solution to violence and vandalism; the subcommittee's final report endorsed the strategy. (5) By the late 1970s alternative public schools were generally perceived as "the single most agreed upon recommendation of educators for the resolution of school vandalism and violence...." (6)

Research and evaluation data have revealed a surprising lack of physical violence and vandalism in alternative schools. This is even more surprising since many of the schools are serving students who have been labeled as "hard-core" offenders. The following five categories suggest some of the findings in this area.

1. School size. Research has consistently shown a high positive correlation between small school size and reduction of school crime. (7) Since many alternative schools have fewer than 200 students, they are better able to treat students individually. It is not surprising that one study found an "almost total lack of violence in alternative schools." (8)

2. Caring and competent teachers. Research on the importance of "significant others" in influencing behavior has verified the importance of positive, caring relationships between teachers and students. An impressive number of research projects and local school evaluations indicate that alternative school teachers are more caring and seem to be more student-centered. (9)

3. Student success in school. The relationship
between poor academic achievement (regardless of socioeconomic background) and disruptive or delinquent
behavior, both in school and out, is well documented.
Many alternative schools have been designed precisely
to provide academic success to youngsters who are far
below grade level in reading and who have rarely experienced success in school. Research indicates that
these efforts have been effective. (10)

4. Enhancement of self-concept. A survey of the
literature on juvenile delinquency, school discipline
problems, and dropouts indicates that many such students have feelings of low personal esteem and a negative self-concept. (11) One of the most promising approaches to remedying school vandalism and disruption
could well be to improve students' self-concepts. Most
alternative schools have attained impressive successes
in this effort. (12)

5. Student decision making. Student involvement
in decision making appears to have a positive effect
on reducing student discipline problems. Recent studies in the area of school political systems also support the importance of student decision making in reducing school crime. (13)

Perhaps the most promising development in this
area is a recent study at the University of Michigan
that suggests: "It is probably practical and possible
to implement some of the policies and practices of the
alternative school programs (that have been demonstrated so effective in dealing with violence and vandalism) in traditional, conventional high schools. To
do this, there need not be radical restructuring."(14)

Alternatives Schools' Contributions to School Desegregation -- During the last 15 years, when desegregation represented the most difficult challenge facing
public education, alternative schools have emerged as
one of the most promising remedies for correcting segregation in our schools. Usually referred to in this
context as magnet schools, alternatives have been specifically designed to attract students from different
racial backgrounds and have offered an attractive alternative to arbitrary forced busing.

Unfortunately, some critics believe that "magnet
schools have almost always been used to avoid or somehow deflect court-ordered desegregation efforts. In

286

the main the magnet school movement has emerged as a direct and sometimes creative response to court-ordered desegregation." (15) Nonetheless, all levels of the federal government have encouraged their development. And, although there has been considerable disagreement among various federal officials, magnet schools have become a major program in urban school districts.

The growing involvement of the federal courts in public education has led to considerable confusion regarding magnet schools. Federal judges have expressed opposing points of view on this subject. (16) In Minneapolis, the courts approved a voluntary magnet program as part of a larger desegregation plan. In other cases -- Los Angeles, Houston, Dallas, Milwaukee, and San Diego, for example -- federal judges have issued court orders requiring the creation of magnet schools. In cities such as Cincinnati, Seattle, Chicago, and Indianapolis, alternatives were developed in the midst of litigation and were clearly an effort to avoid additional court action. A few cities (including Cambridge and St. Paul) have developed magnet schools voluntarily. Still other magnet school plans -- in Dayton, Columbus, Cleveland, and Wilmington -- have been rejected by federal courts.

Research has begun to provide some insights into the effectiveness of magnet schools. A recent study by ABT Associates of magnet schools in 18 school districts concluded that magnet schools are an important component of urban desegregation plans. The report stated: "Only a limited amount of desegregation can be attributed to magnet schools. However, magnet schools can be an effective desegregation device when used as a component of a comprehensive, district-wide desegregation effort, and when used in districts with fewer difficulties for desegregation...." (17)

It has become evident that parents cannot be forced (at least for long) to bus their children to mediocre or poor schools. The availability of high-quality magnet schools seems to help retard "white flight" to suburban and private schools. There are, however, a number of thorny problems regarding magnet schools:

1. Magnet schools have been criticized for failing to assist the minority and poor youths who have been the focus of court desegregation orders. Too of-

287

ten magnet schools have been specifically designed to attract and hold middle-class youth. Such an idea, besides having serious legal implications, has angered minority leaders. As Charles McMillan has said, "If magnets are to prove their worth as a desegregation remedy, they must demonstrate, first and foremost, their ability to educate the minority child and the poor child whose rights have been denied." (18)

2. Many urban educators are concerned that magnet schools serve as a "brain drain" to skim away the best students and unnecessarily impair other schools. The greatest concern is that magnets "deny the minority community of its best students and thus "ghetto-ize" further the black community." (19)

3. Since most magnet schools have been created in the midst of court-ordered desegregation, the vast majority have been developed too rapidly, with little or no time for staff and parent training or curriculum development. As a result, many "special theme" magnets have failed to develop their unique curricular programs.

The crucial question is, Can magnet schools be developed that are different from one another and from the comprehensive programs available in their school districts? This distinctiveness is often missing in existing magnet schools. (20) Alternative schools have too often been built on the assumption that they provide better, higher-quality education than other schools in a district. This assumption is not always true.

Recent developments may generate an increased reliance on magnets as a means of achieving school desegregation. Following his landslide victory, President Ronald Reagan stated that "busing doesn't work"; Congress recently passed legislation directing the Justice Department not to initiate or intervene in school desegregation cases that involved busing as a remedy. Regardless of the outcome of the "forced busing" issue, magnet schools will continue to represent the most acceptable of the "three most promising" approaches currently being used to desegregate urban schools. (21)

Alternative Schools' Contributions to the Back-to-Basics Movement -- For 17 years scores on the Scholastic Aptitude Tests have been declining. The National Assessment of Educational Progress reported in 1975 that 12 of every 100 17-year-olds were function- ally illiterate and that only 10 of every 100 could calculate a simple taxi fare. In addition, schools are now reporting all-time highs in absenteeism, drug and alcohol use, and teenage suicide. These and other equally disturbing reports have given impetus to a re- turn to fundamental, back-to-basics education. In fact, Vernon Smith of Indiana University reports that these back-to-basics alternative schools are increas- ing at a faster rate than any other kind of alterna- tive. (22)

James J. Kilpatrick, the syndicated columnist, recently focused on the five "traditional" schools that have been developed in Louisville, Kentucky. "One of the most interesting experiments in American educa- tion went into its fifth year this month in Louis- ville," he reported. "With every passing semester, the city is demonstrating to a skeptical world that old-fashioned education is still in demand." (23) The five fundamental schools in Louisville include three elementary schools, each with a student body of ap- proximately 600. Some 1,125 students attend a funda- mental middle school, and the fundamental high school enrolls approximately 1,400 sophomores, juniors, and seniors. Each school concentrates on a rigorous core curriculum including reading, writing, arithmetic, science, history, language, and social studies. Two years of a foreign language -- including one year of Latin -- are also required. Like other back-to-basics schools, there is daily homework and a firm policy on behavior.

Many other alternative schools, while not charac- terized as back-to-basics alternatives, have nonethe- less been influenced by today's emphasis on cognitive proficiency. A 1974 report on alternative schools, funded by the Ford Foundation, found that alternative school students did as well as or better in cognitive development than students in conventional programs. (24)

Finally, two recent publications have attempted to analyze and summarize evaluations of optional al- ternative schools. One report examined the evalua- tions of six schools, generally recognized as exem- plary alternatives, that had been in operation for at least three years. The report concluded:

Each of the evaluations that measured cognitive achievement found most students to be learning at a rate consistent with or higher than the district norm. Higher grade-point averages, increased Scholastic Aptitude Test scores, and student gains in reading and math levels characterized the findings. In short, it appears that, in each of the schools that were analyzed, one could be assured that most students would achieve at least as well, if not better, than in the comprehensive school available to them. (25)

A similar conclusion was reached in a report by the Educational Research Service, which synthesized evaluation data from more than 25 alternative schools representing a wide variety of options. The report concluded: "In most cases, the academic achievement of students improved or remained stable...." (26)

These evaluations suggest that alternative educational settings seem to have many of the same academic goals as traditional schools but are pursuing these goals in very different ways.

Conclusion

Alternatives have come a long way during the past 12 years. When the concept was first developed and tried in public schools by groups of parents, teachers, and students who were willing to experiment, there was little or no research and evaluation to support their ideas. Yet these pioneers were willing to take the risk.

Now a decade of documentation, research, and evaluation has proven them right. We now know that people learn in different ways; when schools are able to develop programs designed to meet individual needs, impressive gains occur. We now know that all children do not need 50-minute classes and standard textbooks; some do not even need teachers. Some students learn best in individualized learning carrels; others learn best outside of school. Some students need a desk, visual aids, dictionaries, and libraries; others do not. Some students need rigorous structure to learn; others demand maximum flexibility.

We know that student attitudes can be enriched

and self-concepts improved. Not only do we know that it happens, but we have better insights into why it happens. We know that students who do not meet the usual requirements for college entrance can go on to college and succeed. We know that students can study in programs that differ dramatically, yet they can still compete equally with students in traditional programs. Parents can now enroll their students in a wide variety of different educational programs and feel comfortable about their decisions.

The coming decade offers considerable promise for experimentation, development, and research in the area of alternative schooling. It is quite likely that public education will continue to move away from a single educational program for all students and toward a diverse system of educational alternatives both in the schools and in the community. The Eighties may well fulfill the vast promise of the alternative school movement and become the decade of diversification for public education. The time is certainly right. Alternative schools have come of age.

Notes

1. For the best summary of research on alternative schools, see William Hays Parrett, "An Investigation of Teachers' and Students' Perceptions of Instructional Practices in Nationally Recognized Alternative Schools" (Doctoral dissertation, Indiana University, 1979), Chap. 2.
2. National School Board Association, RESEARCH REPORT: ALTERNATIVE SCHOOLS (Washington, D.C.: NSBA, 1976).
3. Seymour Sarason, THE CULTURE OF THE SCHOOL AND THE PROBLEM OF CHANGE (Boston: Allyn & Bacon, 1971).
4. There is conflicting information on this point. The Lilly Endowment has recently funded the Institute for Development of Educational Activities (I/D/E/A) for a project to use what has been learned in one of the nation's best alternative schools, Learning Unlimited of Indianapolis. The findings will be applied to an effort to improve secondary schooling in the Midwest. For evidence that alternative schools contribute to a decline in public education, see ABT Associates, Inc., FINAL REPORT: STUDY OF THE EMERGENCY SCHOOL AID ACT MAGNET SCHOOL PROGRAMS (Washington, D.C.: U.S. Office of Education, 1979), p. 11.
5. Sen Birch Bayh, REPORT OF THE SUBCOMMITTEE TO

INVESTIGATE JUVENILE DELINQUENCY (Washington, D.C.: U.S. Government Printing Office, 1977).

6. National School Public Relations Association, VIOLENCE AND VANDALISM: SPECIAL REPORT (Arlington, Va.: NSPRA, 1975). For a comprehensive summary of research regarding the relationship between alternative schools and violence, vandalism, and delinquency, see PROGRAM ANNOUNCEMENT: PREVENTION OF DELINQUENCY THROUGH ALTERNATIVE EDUCATION (Arlington, Va.: Office of Juvenile Justice and Delinquency Programs, Department of Justice, 1980).

7. Roger G. Barker et al., BIG SCHOOL, SMALL SCHOOL: HIGH SCHOOL SIZE AND MISBEHAVIOR (Stanford, Calif.: Stanford University Press, 1964).

8. Michael Burger, VIOLENCE IN THE SCHOOLS: CAUSES AND REMEDIES (Bloomington, Ind.: Phi Delta Kappa Educational Foundation, 1974).

9. Parret, op.cit., Chap. 5.

10. Robert Fizzell, THE TRUANTS' ALTERNATIVE PROGRAMS: AN EVALUATION REPORT TO THE STATE BOARD OF EDUCATION (Macomb: Western Illinois University, 1979).

11. Martin Gold, "Scholastic Experiences, Self-Esteem, and Delinquent Behavior: A Theory for Alternative Schools," CRIME AND DELINQUENCY, vol. 24, no. 3, pp. 290-308.

12. Robert D. Barr, "Curriculum in Optional Alternative Schools," paper presented at the National Institute of Education Conference on Public Issues in Educational Options, Chicago, 29 June - 1 July 1976.

13. Robert Barr and Devon Metzger, "The Impact of School Political Systems on Student Attitudes," THEORY AND RESEARCH, June 1978, pp. 48-79.

14. David W. Mann, "Disruptive Students or Provocative Schools? School Differences and Student Behavior," paper presented at the annual meeting of the American Psychological Association, Montreal, 1980.

15. Charles B. McMillan, MAGNET SCHOOLS: AN APPROACH TO VOLUNTARY DESEGREGATION (Bloomington, Ind.: Phi Delta Kappa Education Foundation, 1980), p. 18.

16. Nolan Estes and Donald R. Waldrip, eds., MAGNET: LEGAL AND PRACTICAL IMPLICATIONS (Piscataway, N.J.: New Century Education Corp., 1978), p. 112.

17. ABT Assoc., op.cit., p. 1.

18. Charles B. McMillan, "Magnet Education in Boston," PHI DELTA KAPPAN, November 1977, pp. 158-63.

19. ABT Associates., op. cit., p. 8.

20. McMillan, op. cit., p. 24.

21. Martha McCarthy and L. Dean Webb, "Intra-District Desegregation Remedies," NOLPE SCHOOL LAW JOURNAL, vol. 8, no. 2, pp. 127-44.

22. Vernon Smith in a speech delivered at the Wingspread Conference Center, Racine, Wis., 29 January 1981.

23. James J. Kilpatrick, in the Louisville Courier Journal, 13 September 1980, p. A-5.

24. Ford Foundation, MATTERS OF CHOICE: A FORD FOUNDATION REPORT ON ALTERNATIVE SCHOOLS (New York: Ford Foundation, 1974), p. 6.

25. Robert Barr et al., "An Analysis of Six School Evaluations: The Effectiveness of Alternative Public Schools," VIEWPOINTS IN TEACHING AND LEARNING, July 1977, pp. 1-30.

26. Heather Sidor Doob, EVALUATIONS OF ALTERNATIVE SCHOOLS (Arlington, Va.: Educational Research Services, 1977), p. 44.

ABILITY GROUPING: SEPARATE AND UNEQUAL?

Bill Waltman

The rhetoric goes on. Does homogeneous grouping make it easier for students to learn? Does it provide a less stressful environment for slower students? Does it permit brighter students to proceed at a faster rate? Does it make the teaching task easier? These and other benefits have been claimed by the proponents of grouping by ability. Just as adamant in rejecting these alleged benefits are those who oppose grouping practices. Many opponents of ability grouping add a dimension to the controversy: they believe that social class is a factor in ability grouping.

This paper will attempt to examine some of the above questions. Because of the tendency of some writers to lump together such diverse practices as tracking, ability grouping, and grouping for special purposes within a heterogeneous class, a definition of terms would appear to be in order.

Tracking refers to a career oriented practice in which students are assigned to curricular "tracks." The tracks are designed to prepare students for particular kinds of jobs (1). Curricular tracks usually include, but are not necessarily limited to, the following designations: (1) college prep, (2) general, and (3) vocational. Of all the types of grouping for instruction, tracking is perhaps the most insidious, because once a student is placed in a particular track it is difficult for him to transfer to another. If, for example, a student assigned to the vocational track decides in his junior year that he would like to prepare for college, he may not have had the courses necessary to prepare him for that alternative.

Grouping for special purposes within a hetero-

Reprinted from JOURNAL OF THOUGHT, 14 (3): 215-220 (July 1979), by permission of author and publisher.

geneous class is a practice best exemplified in the elementary school when teachers group for reading or other instruction. Much of this grouping is based on ability or achievement, but it may be based on such factors as the student's special interest in a particular study.

Homogeneous grouping is defined in THE DICTIONARY OF EDUCATION as, "the classification of pupils for the purpose of forming instructional groups having a high degree of similarity in regard to certain factors that affect learning." Many different instructional arrangements fit this definition, and a variety of practices has emerged, each designed to improve either teaching effectiveness or learning. Almost all of the schemes, however, involve the variable of student ability. So pervasive is the practice that the terms homogeneous grouping and ability grouping are used interchangeably by many educators. Ability grouping has been defined as, "the classifying of pupils with reference to intelligence, mental maturity ratings, levels of achievement, and teacher judgment for the purposes of instruction" (2). We will concern ourselves with this latter practice.

It is interesting that each generation of educators seems to believe that it has discovered an educational innovation in the practice of ability grouping. In point of fact, the practice is almost as old as public education in this country. One of the first attempts at homogeneous grouping occurred at St. Louis in 1867, where bright students were grouped on the basis of achievement and promoted rapidly through the elementary grades (3). Other attempts followed, and by the 1920's and 1930's, the practice was well established (4).

Research, apparently, has lagged behind the implementation of ability grouping practices even to this day. It was not until 1916, when Whipple studied a gifted class of thirteen boys and seventeen girls in the fifth and sixth grades at Urbana, Illinois, that any serious attempt was made to study homogeneous grouping under controlled conditions (5). Numerous other studies followed, and in 1929 R.T. Rock, in analyzing the research, concluded:
> The experimental studies of grouping which have
> been considered fail to show consistent, statis-
> tically or educationally significant differences
> between the achievement of pupils in homogeneous

groups and pupils of equal ability in heterogeneous groups (6).

An equally significant finding of the same analysis was that there was practically unanimous agreement
among the teachers involved in the studies that the
teaching situation was improved by homogeneous
grouping (7).

The debate, sometimes bitter, has continued over
the years. Those who favor ability grouping have managed to cite those research studies which support
their position, while opponents have done much the
same. In terms of sheer numbers of studies, both sides
have found support for their positions; however, on
balance, the best conclusion is that the results are
inconclusive. An experiment reported by the Horace
Mann-Lincoln Institute of School Experimentation
states: "Ability grouping of itself has no important
effect on the academic achievement of students" (8).

Despite the evidence (or lack of it) concerning
ability grouping and student achievement, teachers, in
the main, continue their unflinching support of the
practice. Wilson and Schmidt, reporting a recent
study of ability grouping, stated that two-thirds of
the teachers they surveyed were not familiar with the
research on ability grouping, yet 92 percent of them
felt it was instructionally effective, and 74 percent
of them practiced it (9).

There is, of course, no such thing as a homogeneous group. In any group there will exist wide ranges
of differences, and those differences, as we all know,
will exist in the very areas we have sought to homogenize. The best we can hope for in any grouping scheme
is to reduce the range of heterogeneity. If the range
of differences can be reduced, and the teacher is able
to ignore the remainder of differences, the teaching
task will, undoubtedly, be made easier. The key is
ignoring the remaining differences: for if the teacher
recognizes the differences, he is back at square one.
As Sykes expresses it:
> The teacher is able under conditions of ability
> grouping to aim for some hypothetical midpoint of
> instructional intensity. In short, he has to
> worry less about academic individual differences
> and more about patterns of identical homework as-
> signments and class presentations (10).

Could it be, then, that teachers have justified ability grouping on the grounds that it is good for students, when in reality they favor it because it makes the teaching task easier? It is a cruel question, but one which needs to be asked.

Given the evidence related to student achievement and ability grouping, as well as that dealing with teacher effectiveness, another question needs to be asked: are there important social factors which need to be dealt with before the decision to group is made? Many practitioners believe so, and the evidence would seem to agree. The now famous Rosenthal study, which dealt with teachers and students in a San Francisco elementary school, concluded that "teachers' expectations of their pupils' performance may serve as self-fulfilling prophesies (11). In other words, students performed as teachers expected them to perform. If we can generalize, the effect of "labeling" students is to cause teachers to view them in a particular way.

If you ask teachers in any school to describe students in a particular group, the description will be stereotypical of all students in that group. The results of such teacher behaviors are long term and prejudicial to the student.

In an article published by CLEARING HOUSE (12), Lefkowitz raises the question of whether or not we are deliberately creating a class system in education. An examination of grouping practices in this country will cause reasonable men and women to answer the question in the affirmative. It is, perhaps, purely coincidental that the highest groups contain mostly the children of the middle and upper-middle classes, while the lower groups are made up almost exclusively of lower class children.

Ours is not the only country to become concerned that education has become segregated along social class lines. A study conducted by the National Foundation for Educational Research, dealing with British junior high school students, concluded that there is a positive correlation between children's academic ability and their sociometric status (13). The study by Wilson and Schmidt (14) also concluded that ability grouping reinforces and perpetuates segregation along socioeconomic lines.

Educators have long believed that students learn

from their peers as well as from their teachers. If this is so, ability grouping systematically denies to certain children the opportunity to interact with the most talented of their peers, and is, therefore, a denial of equal educational opportunity.

A golfing friend once illustrated the importance of peer influence in describing a certain golfer. "If he is playing with another hacker," he said, "he justs hacks around, too, and shoots his usual 90; but if he is playing with a really fine golfer, he shoots 'way over his head'; he starts shooting 'lights out.'"

There is reason to believe that performance in the classroom may be affected in the same way. That is to say, highly talented students sometimes bring out the very best in others. If so, all children should have the opportunity to interact with the best talent available.

References

1. E. Edmond Reuter and Robert R. Hamilton, THE LAW OF PUBLIC EDUCATION (Mineola, NY: The Foundation Press, Inc., 1970), pp. 119-20.
2. Marsha A. Ream, ABILITY GROUPING (Washington, D.C.: National Education Association, 1968), p. 6.
3. Miriam L. Goldberg, A. Harry Passow, and Joseph Justman, THE EFFECTS OF ABILITY GROUPING (New York: Teachers College Press, 1966), p. 3.
4. Ibid., p. 2.
5. Ibid., p. 3.
6. Ibid.
7. Ibid.
8. Ibid., p. V.
9. Barry J. Wilson and Donald W. Schmidt, "What's New in Ability Grouping?" PHI DELTA KAPPAN, April, 1978, pp. 535-536.
10. Robert Rosenthal and Lenore Jacobson, PYGMALION IN THE CLASSROOM (New York: Holt, Rinehart and Winston, 1968), p. 186.
11. Dudley E. Sykes, "Defacto Dehumanization," NASSP BULLETIN, February, 1974, pp. 29-34.
12. Leon J. Lefkowitz, "DeFacto Segregation in the Classroom," THE CLEARING HOUSE, January, 1972, pp. 293-297.
13. Earl Ogletree, "Research Verifies Ill Effects of Ability Grouping, PHI DELTA KAPPAN, December, 1968, p. 223.
14. Wilson and Schmidt, pp. 535-536.

QUESTIONS TEACHERS ASK
ABOUT TEAM TEACHING

William L. Rutherford

Team teaching, an educational idea from the late 1950s and 60s, has been pushed out of the limelight by a persistent crowd of other innovations. Despite the lack of attention in journals and forums, team teaching, or "teaming" continues to flourish.

The number of teachers engaged in teaming probably has increased in part because of other new educational approaches, such as individually guided instruction, open concept schools, multiage grouping, continuous progress learning, and individualized instruction. Each of these seems to foster team teaching and to function better when it is used.

Accompanying its quiet growth are questions and concerns raised by team teachers. The University of Texas Research and Development Center's Procedures for Adopting Educational Innovations Project conducted two years of research on team teaching. Project staff interviewed 1,200 teachers in school districts where teaming is used. The questions and concerns of these teachers fall into four categories: variety of teaming patterns, difficulties of managing preparation time, possible dangers of sacrificing personal instruction, and problems and conflicts inherent in team processes. This article discusses those questions and concerns and provides information that may help answer them.

Patterns of Team Teaching

Many of the teachers interviewed seemed unable to define team teaching. Often they were uncertain whether their processes of sharing and cooperating

Reprinted from JOURNAL OF TEACHER EDUCATION, 30 (4): 29-30 (July 1979), by permission of author and publisher.

constituted teaming, and they were curious about alternative patterns and approaches.

Team teaching occurs when two or more teachers work together regularly to enhance instruction. Patterns of cooperation can include planning and designing materials or instructional processes, sharing groups of children and/or sharing instruction, or any combination of those activities.

The teachers surveyed described widely varying approaches to teaming within the three patterns. For example, one teacher would develop all the math worksheets, while another developed reading activities; all team members would use the materials in their separate classes. Other teachers met only to plan administrative structures, rules for discipline, and the like. Still others shared groups of students, who moved regularly from one classroom to the next, and met to plan not only activities but also classroom rules and structures, and to discuss individual student problems. Rarely, did two or more teachers instruct a particular group of students in the same room.

Each pattern of teaming seemed to offer its own difficulties and benefits for both teachers and pupils. The interviews provided no information to suggest that one approach was more effective than another in terms of pupil outcomes. No schools were found where alternative patterns were being compared.

Time Management

Most of the teachers were concerned about time. As teaming efforts became more extensive and the sizes of teams (sometimes called units or satellites) increased, the time required for cooperative planning also increased. In addition, teaming often meant that each teacher saw more pupils each day, which in turn required more planning and preparation.

The interviews revealed that, to some extent, problems of time are inherent in team teaching. Teachers can reduce planning time by reducing the number of activities shared or the size of the team, but such actions can reduce the effectiveness of teaming.

One positive action that can be taken is to de-

velop a clear, careful structure for using cooperative
planning time. Few of the teams surveyed had adopted
any systematic process for carrying out their team effort. They established specific meeting times, but
did not set agendas, set time limits on topics to be
discussed, or assign responsibilities in advance. If
such steps are taken, planning sessions should be
shorter and more productive.

Loss of Personal Contact with Students

Teachers who, by teaming, shared groups of students expressed concern about a loss of personal contact with their students. Many teachers no longer were
teaching one group of 30 students for five periods
daily, but 30 different students each period for a
total of 150 students daily. Although they had to
plan for fewer subjects, the teachers had overall more
work, more planning and preparation time, and less
contact with students.

This loss is in many ways inevitable with team
teaching. What is lost is the development of closer
interpersonal relationships between teachers and students. But what is gained is individualized instruction, the pacing and pattern of teaching aimed at each
child's level of need and ability.

Options are available for maintaining a stable,
personalized environment for students who can benefit
most from it. An alternative is to maintain one self-
contained classroom within the teaming unit; the
teacher for that classroom shares in cooperative planning, but his/her students do not shift from class to
class. Another alternative is to form groups of students who do move from class to class, but move as
single, intact groups. These alternatives enhance a
team approach by adding ways to meet individual student's needs.

Conflicts within Teams

Although resolution of conflicts among team members was their fourth major concern, most teachers
seemed to lack techniques for resolving problems if
working relationships became strained. The only alternative they identified was to request a transfer to
another building or team. Their concern about per-

sonal conflict was perhaps the most serious of the four; even teams that had never experienced such conflict considered it a potential threat to their effectiveness.

The teams that had weathered personal conflicts among team members had done so by working out specific problem-solving processes. They identified the problem as clearly and specifically as possible, and patiently explored ways to solve it. These teams recognized that solutions might be slow in coming, and that all team members might have to adjust to achieve solutions. For example, if one teacher disliked and resisted teaming, the other team members might have to change their plans and activities so that the one teacher would be less involved in the process.

Other techniques used to reduce conflict included development of closer personal relationships among team members through social activities and use of an outside agent, such as school counselor, to mediate.

Strengths of Teaming

Although they expressed concerns, an overwhelming majority of teachers responded emphatically that they would continue team teaching. Their reasons varied, but most often they cited the value of sharing ideas and the support from team members.

Other advantages they mentioned were: You can teach in areas where you have the greatest strength and interest. More minds result in more and better teaching ideas and materials. Personality conflicts between students and teachers can be minimized. You can develop a greater variety and enriched quality of instructional options. When you are absent or not feeling well, team members can take over, and the instructional program continues without interruption.

Despite their concerns, teachers support and are enthusiastic about team teaching and its effectiveness for them and their students. Teachers have been able to adapt the concept to meet their individual needs, a flexibility that, perhaps, is the major reason why team teaching continues its quiet growth.

Part 6

KEEPING CURRENT

EFFECTIVE SCHOOLS:
ACCUMULATING RESEARCH FINDINGS

Michael Cohen

Since the mid-1960s public concerns over how to use educational resources effectively and to open up educational opportunities for poor and minority children has led to a concentrated effort by educational researchers and other social scientists to identify characteristics of schools and classrooms that help improve learning and achievement. This 15-year effort, largely supported by federal research funds, has led to a body of research findings that the practicing teacher or school administrator should find useful. It also has improved the ability of researchers to ask the appropriate questions, thereby increasing the prospects for further progress.

The landmark study in this area is the EQUALITY OF EDUCATIONAL OPPORTUNITY REPORT done in 1966 by James Coleman and his colleagues. (1) Based on a national survey of principals, teachers, and students in some 4,000 public elementary and secondary schools, the study examined characteristics of schools (e.g., physical facilities, curriculums, and instructional materials), their staffs (e.g., teacher training, experience, ability, and attitudes), and their students (e.g., socioeconomic and racial or ethnic background). The most frequently cited finding from this study has been that, when compared to the ifluence of family background, these different school characteristics have relatively little influence on measured pupil achievement.

The data actually showed that, first, there was an association between family background and pupil performance -- that is, middle and upper class students did better in school than their peers from less

Reprinted from AMERICAN EDUCATION, 18 (1): 13-16 (January 1982), by permission of author and publisher.

304

well-off backgrounds. Second, students' achievement test scores depended more on their family background than on whether they attended a school with more or less of the kinds of characteristics and resources measured in the study.

This finding was widely misinterpreted as meaning that "schools don't make a difference" -- that there is nothing that schools can do to overcome the educational disadvantages produced by minority group status and poverty. And this misinterpretation ran counter to the prevailing beliefs of educators, researchers, and the public, for it directly challenged the belief that schools could serve as a vehicle for social mobility, by providing the necessary skills to enable the disadvantaged to achieve success in the labor market.

Paradoxically the Coleman Report's findings and their popular misinterpretation were themselves a direct result of another set of prevailing beliefs. This belief was that the educationally relevant characteristics of schools could be described by reference to such characteristics as the number of books in the school library, the age of the building and its facilities, the availability of science laboratories, the presence of certain types of specialists such as school nurses and psychologists, and, at the secondary level, the availability of a range of curricular offerings. While library books, specialists, and curricular offerings are important features of schools, we have learned from subsequent research that other aspects of the schooling process make powerful contributions to student learning.

At the time, however, the research caused considerable controversy and resulted in a number of attempts by researchers to re-analyze the study data, and to replicate (or refute) the findings in other studies. (2) While it is unnecessary to go into the details of the scholarly debate in this article, it is useful to understand how the criticisms raised in the ensuing debate helped point to more productive directions for subsequent research.

What About Schools Is Important?

Specifically, two major problems were identified in the Coleman Report and other similar studies. (3)

First, the types of school factors measured in these studies refer primarily to the types and levels of resources present or available in the school -- human resources (specialists, teacher ability, experience, and training), instructional resources (textbooks, library books, science equipment, etc.), and financial resources (per pupil expenditures). In reality, comparing schools on the resources available to them is not as meaningful as comparing schools on how well they organize and use their available resources -- on how well teachers and specialists coordinate their work together, how well teachers and students make use of the time available to them for instructional activities, and on how well teachers motivate their students and reinforce their efforts.

Second, the Coleman Report and other studies made comparisons among schools on their average achievement level. Overlooked was the fact that within a typical school there is a wide range of achievement levels. At elementary schools, for example, some fourth graders might be reading at the sixth grade level or above, while other fourth graders read at the first grade level. Additionally, by attempting to explain differences among schools in their average level of student achievement, researchers assumed that all school resources were equally available to, and utilized by, each of the students in the school. Yet we know that within a school, a student does not experience the "average teacher," but, rather a particular set of teachers, who differ from one another in regard to teaching styles, competence, and effectiveness. Similarly, some students benefit from contact with particular specialists, courses, or library books, while other pupils in the same school may never come into contact with these resources. Also, students are often grouped into classes, tracks, or ability groups, and thus are exposed to varying teacher skills, curriculum materials, and social environments. (5)

Consequently, the combined result of these problems was that much of the early research was not sufficiently sensitive to important things that happened to individual students within the school. Therefore, the research was only partially effective at identifying and describing things that really mattered for improving the instructional effectiveness of schools. Nonetheless, these early studies and the debates surrounding them were useful in sharpening the strategies employed in subsequent studies to learn what about schools may make a difference. More recent inquiry differs from, and improves upon, previous research in a number of respects.

First, in addition to comparing different schools and their influence on student learning, the differences among classrooms within a school have been studied. (6) By making the classroom the unit of analysis, researchers were able to get closer to the educational environment actually experienced by a student.

Second, rather than studying relatively static characteristics of educational environments (e.g., the level of training and certification of a particular teacher), researchers began to examine much more complex and dynamic processes in schools and classrooms (e.g., what a teacher actually does in the classroom over a period of time). So, for example, studies were conducted which examined how teachers organized and managed their classrooms, and the ways in which they managed and minimized disruptions in their classrooms. (7) Other inquiry focused directly on the nature of teacher-student interactions and communications, examining the ways in which teachers presented information, asked questions, and communicated goals, expectations, and rules to their students. (8) And, importantly, investigators began to conceive of time as an important school resource, and studied how time was used in classrooms. (9) For example, researchers have learned that some teachers may allow 45 minutes of classroom time each day to teach reading, while others may allocate as much as 75 minutes. Further, some teachers will be more efficient in their use of time, so that their students will spend 80 percent of the time for reading actually reading. Other teachers, however, are less efficient at managing the classroom so that students are actually engaged in appropriate learning activities only 50-60 percent of the time.

Third, the focus of this recent research has increasingly been on identifying and describing practices, at both the classroom and the school level, which are particularly effective at improving the achievement levels of students from poor and minority backgrounds. (10) Doing so involved identifying teachers or schools which, over a period of years, consistently produced students who scored well on achievement tests. These teachers or schools then were carefully matched with other teachers or schools also serving students from predominantly poor and minority backgrounds, with less success at realizing high levels of student achievement. Through contrasting instructional approaches, learning environments, and the behaviors of teachers and administrators, it was possible to identify those educational practices that contribute to instructional effectiveness.

Research in the Schools

Fourth, as a result of adopting the strategies described above, researchers have come to rely increasingly on first-hand observation and concrete descriptions of educational practices. They are more likely to conduct indepth interviews with teachers, principals, and students, rather than to rely exclusively on survey questionnaires typically administered in large groups or through the mails. A corresponding change was a general shift to studies with smaller samples -- studies of fewer schools or classrooms, but with the advantage of being able to provide richer and more thorough descriptions and analyses of the complexities of daily life in these settings.

Finally, researchers increasingly are collaborating with practicing educators in conducting their research. In many studies teachers and other practitioners play a significant role in framing research questions, shaping useful research designs, and interpreting research results. For example, a team of teachers, staff developers, and researchers in a California school district jointly planned, designed, and conducted a study to identify strategies and techniques classroom teachers could use to cope effectively with distractions from instruction. (11)

The Picture Now

Especially since 1972, when the Congress created the National Institute of Education, the Education Department's principal educational research agency, these strategies have increasingly characterized studies conducted to identify characteristics of schools and classrooms which contribute to instructional effectiveness. By now, enough research has been conducted, and enough findings have been successfully replicated, to permit a synthesis. A number of Effective Schools studies suggest that differences in effectiveness among schools, defined in terms of student performance on tests of basic skills, can be accounted for by the following five factors: (12)

'Strong administrative leadership by the school principal, especially in regard to instructional matters;

'A school climate conducive to learning; i.e., a safe and orderly school free of discipline and vandalism problems;

'School-wide emphasis on basic skills instruction, which entails agreement among the professional staff that instruction in the basic skills is the primary goal of the school;

'Teacher expectations that students can reach high levels of achievement, regardless of pupil background; and

'A system for monitoring and assessing pupil performance which is tied to instructional objectives.

While this is not an exhaustive list of the practices that promote school effectiveness, they seem quite sensible. They imply that a school in which the instructional staff and the principal agree on what they're doing, believe they can do it, provide an environment conducive to accomplishing the task, and monitor their effectiveness and adjust performance based on such feedback, is likely to be an effective one. Confidence in these factors is strengthened further by the similarities between these school level factors and several features of effective practice identified by research focusing specifically at the classroom level. (13) More specifically, research at both the classroom and the school level highlight the importance of commitment to basic skills as instructional goals. This research stresses the need for an orderly, businesslike environment which permits teachers and students to devote their time and energy to teaching and learning academic content. The need for mechanisms for systematically and frequently assessing student performance in the basic skills, which provides feedback to both teachers and pupils regarding their success, is identified in both sets of studies. And finally, the notion that successful instruction is, in part, a function of teachers' beliefs that such success is possible for themselves and their students, is supported by both lines of inquiry.

The Current State of Knowledge

Of necessity, the preceding paragraphs have pro-

vided only a brief outline of the major research findings. Any one of the factors described above is the
result of a large number of research studies, and is
simply a shorthand device indicating a highly con-
densed version of a much larger and more detailed
story about effective educational practices.

Though much has been learned from recent research, our understanding of what constitutes effective practice, and of what conditions are necessary in
order for practices identified as effective to work in
particular school settings, is incomplete. Additionally, there is still work to be done in identifying
the most useful applications of research findings for
educators. The challenge now will be to find the most
effective ways of enabling schools to take advantage
of new knowledge. Just as the early studies of school
effectiveness provided the groundwork for generating
our current research findings, so too will the existing knowledge base provide a helpful point of departure for addressing these additional research questions.

Notes

1. James S. Coleman et al., EQUALITY OF EDUCA-
TIONAL OPPORTUNITY (Washington, D.C.: U.S. Government
Printing Office, 1966).
2. For example, see Frederick Mosteller and Dan-
iel P. Moynihan, eds., ON EQUALITY OF EDUCATIONAL OP-
PORTUNITY (New York: Vintage Books, 1972), and Chris-
topher Jencks et al., INEQUALITY: A REASSESSMENT OF
FAMILY AND SCHOOLING IN AMERICA (New York: Basic
Books, 1972).
3. Michael Cohen, "Recent Advances in Our Understanding of School Effects Research," invited address
presented at Annual Meeting of American Association of
Colleges of Teacher Education, Chicago, Illinois,
March 1, 1979.
4. For example, see Phyllis Levenstein et al.,
SUMMARY REPORT: LASTING EFFECTS AFTER PRESCHOOL (Wash-
ington, D.C.: U.S. Government Printing Office, 1979);
National Institute of Education, THE EFFECTS OF SER-
VICES ON STUDENT DEVELOPMENT (Washington, D.C.: Na-
tional Institute of Education, 1977).
5. For example, see Richard A. Rehberg and Evelyn
R. Rosenthal, CLASS AND MERIT IN THE AMERICAN HIGH
SCHOOL (New York: Longman, 1978); James E. Rosenbaum,
MAKING INEQUALITY: THE HIDDEN CURRICULUM OF HIGH

SCHOOL TRACKING (New York: Wiley, 1976); and Aage B. Sorenson, "Organizational Differentiation of Students and Educational Opportunity," SOCIOLOGY OF EDUCATION 43: 355-376, 1970.

6. For example, see Thomas Good, Bruce Biddle and Jere Brophy, TEACHERS MAKE A DIFFERENCE (New York: Holt, Rinehart and Winston, 1975); Richard J. Murnane, THE IMPACT OF SCHOOL RESOURCES ON THE LEARNING OF INNER CITY CHILDREN (Cambridge: Ballinger Publishing Co., 1975); and Anita Summers and Barbara Wolfe, "Equality of Educational Opportunity Qualified: A Production Function Approach," PHILADELPHIA FEDERAL RESERVE BANK PAPERS, 1974.

7. For example, see Edmund T. Emmer, Carolyn M. Evertson and Linda M. Anderson, "Effective Classroom Management at the Beginning of the School Year," ELEMENTARY SCHOOL JOURNAL 80: 219-231, 1980; and Carolyn M. Evertson et al., ORGANIZING AND MANAGING THE ELEMENTARY SCHOOL CLASSROOM (Research and Development Center for Teacher Education: The University of Texas at Austin, 1981).

8. For example, see Jere Brophy and Thomas Good, TEACHER-STUDENT RELATIONSHIPS: CAUSES AND CONSEQUENCES (New York: Holt, Rinehart and Winston, 1974); Jere Brophy, "Teacher Praise: A Functional Analysis," Occasional Paper No. 28, Institute for Research on Teaching, Michigan State University, East Lansing, 1979; and Jere Brophy and Carolyn M. Evertson, STUDENT CHARACTERISTICS AND TEACHING (New York: Longman, 1981).

9. For example, see Carolyn Denham and Ann Lieberman, eds. TIME TO LEARN (Washington, D.C.: National Institute of Education, 1980); and David E. Wiley and Annegret Harnischfeger, "Explosion of a Myth: Quantity of Schooling and Exposure to Instruction, Major Educational Vehicles." EDUCATIONAL RESEARCHER 314, 7-12, 1974.

10. For example, see Wilbur Brookover et al., SCHOOLS CAN MAKE A DIFFERENCE, College of Urban Development, Michigan State University, 1977; and George Weber, INNER CITY CHILDREN CAN BE TAUGHT TO READ: FOUR SUCCESSFUL SCHOOLS. Occasional Paper No. 18 (Washington, D.C.: Council for Basic Education, 1971).

11. William J. Tikunoff, Beatrice A. Ward, and Gary A. Griffin, INTERACTIVE RESEARCH AND DEVELOPMENT ON TEACHING STUDY FINAL REPORT (San Francisco: Far West Laboratory for Research and Development, 1979); Grant Behnke et al., "Coping with Classroom Distractions," ELEMENTARY SCHOOL JOURNAL 81:3, 135-155, 1981.

12. For example, see R. Edmonds, "Some Schools

Work and More Can," SOCIAL POLICY, March/April 1979; and Michael Cohen, "Effective Schools: What the Research Says," TODAY'S EDUCATION 70:2, 46-49, 1980.

13. Jere Brophy, "Advances in Teacher Effectiveness Research," JOURNAL OF CLASSROOM INTERACTION 15: 1-7, 1979.

JOHNNY AND MARY
<u>ARE</u> READING BETTER

Wayne Martin

Contrary to public fears, Johnny and Mary are
reading better today -- in the elementary classroom --
than their peers at the beginning of the seventies.
And their older brothers and sisters in the junior and
senior high classrooms are generally reading as well
as their counterparts. Moreover, groups traditionally
viewed as "disadvantaged" have made substantial gains
at the elementary level.

The National Assessment of Educational Progress
(NAEP) first surveyed the reading skills of 9-, 13-,
and 17-year-olds during the 1970-71 school year. NAEP
repeated the survey -- using the same set of items --
during the 1974-75 school year. The results of the
second reading assessment revealed that, nationally,
9-year-olds had improved their overall performance by
1.3 percentage points, with black elementary students
and black 9-year-olds from the Southeast and Central
regions of the country posting the largest gains (4.8,
7.6 and 5.8 percentage points, respectively). At ages
13 and 17, the overall reading performance of students
remained the same between 1970-71 and 1974-75. However, performance of junior high students had declined
by 1.7 percentage points on items measuring reference
skills. Similarly, high school level students exhibited a downward trend on inferential comprehension
items.

Questions Raised

The second reading assessment results raised many
questions, which could be answered only by the results
of the third reading survey. Would the decline in the

Reprinted from COMPACT, 15 (2): 24-26 (Summer 1981),
by permission of author and publisher.

313

area of reference skills at age 13 continue, be reversed or stabilize? Would the downward trend among
17-year-olds in the area of inferential comprehension
become a significant decline or would the performance
of high school students improve in this area? Would
black students at age 9 continue to show large gains
in performance? Would the significant improvement of
1975's 9-year-olds manifest itself as similar gains
among the present 13-year-olds? Or would the public
feeling that students' reading abilities were seriously declining be borne out? To answer these questions, NAEP surveyed reading with the same set of
items for a third time during the 1979-80 school year.
What did the results reveal about students' reading
skills?

Overall, National Assessment found that the reading skills of 9-year-olds improved steadily over the
decade, increasing by 3.9 percentage points between
1971 and 1980. Reading skills of 13- and 17-year-olds
remained stable during the same period.

Black 9-year-olds made a dramatic improvement
over the decade. Their average performance rose by
9.9 percentage points -- one of the largest gains ever
found by NAEP -- while white 9-year-olds improved by
2.8 percentage points. Although still performing
below the national level, black elementary students
narrowed the gap between themselves and the nation by
6 percentage points.

Other groups of 9-year-olds posting sizable improvement include:
  `Those living in the Southeast (7.5 percentage
points)
  `Those living in the rural areas (6 percentage
points)
  `Those from economically disadvantaged urban
areas (5.2 percentage points)
  `Those whose parents have not graduated from high
school (4 percentage points)

At the junior high level, black 13-year-olds were
the only group whose performance on the entire set of
reading questions improved significantly during the
seventies. On the average, 4.2 percent more black
junior high students correctly answered the typical
reading item in 1979 than in 1970. Nationally, this
means about 19,000 more black students would have responded correctly in 1979. While still performing 11

314

percentage points below the nation, black 13-year-olds narrowed the gap between themselves and the nation by 3.4 percentage points.

For 17-year-olds, most groups followed the national pattern of stability over the decade. Some indications of decline occurred for groups typically considered more "advantaged" with regard to academic performance -- those whose parents have either graduated from high school or have schooling beyond high school and those from economically advantaged urban areas.

Disadvantaged Improving

To explore further the trends among the "advantaged" and "disadvantaged," NAEP performed special analyses of the data in terms of achievement for each of the three reading assessments. In essence, students were partitioned into four ranges of performance -- low achievers through high achievers -- based on assessment results. Thus, it was possible to determine if a change in performance occurred uniformly or differentially across achievement classes. These analyses revealed that the lowest achievers improved significantly over the decade at ages 9 and 13 (8.8 and 3.6 percentage points respectively) and exhibited an upward trend at age 17. On the other hand, high achievers declined by 2.4 percentage points at age 13 and 2.3 percentage points at age 17 and remained stable at age 9.

Changes in the distribution of the reporting groups within high and low achievement groups were also observed. The percent of students from the Southeast included among low achievers decreased with each reading assessment at all three ages; the percent of black students and those from rural areas included among low achievers also decreased over the decade at ages 9 and 13. Conversely, the percent of students from the Southeast included among high achievers increased with each assessment at all three ages. Similarly, the percent of black students included among the highest achievers at ages 9 and 13 increased over the decade, as did the percent of students from rural areas at age 13.

For the assessment, students responded to questions in the areas of literal and inferential compre-

hension and reference skills. Literal comprehension
items require students to identify a single fact, in-
cident or idea given in a reading passage. Questions
requiring inferential comprehension measure students'
ability to infer from a passage an idea or concept
that is not explicitly stated. Reference skill items
ask students to demonstrate specialized skills -- such
as using an index, encyclopedia or library catalog
card -- to solve a problem. How did the students perform in terms of these three areas of reading?

Nine-year-olds improved on all three types of
items. Performance on literal comprehension, the most
"basic" of reading skills, increased by 3.9 percentage
points. More elementary students responded correctly
to the typical inferential comprehension item (3.5
percentage points) and their reference abilities also
went up (4.8 percentage points) between 1971 and 1980.
Black 9-year-olds and those living in the Southeast
evidenced significant improvement in all three areas.

For 13-year-olds, the picture was not as clear.
Performance on literal comprehension improved (1.6
percentage points) but remained stable for inferential
skills across the three assessments. The reference
abilities of junior high students declined between the
first and second assessments (1.7 percentage points)
and then improved between the second and third assessments (2.6 percentage points), leaving students at a
slightly higher achievement level at the end of the
decade than at the beginning. Black 13-year-olds
posted gains on each of three types of reading items,
with the larger portion of the gains being made between the second and third assessments.

While 17-year-olds' performance nationally remained unchanged in the areas of literal comprehension
and reference skills, it declined significantly on the
inferential comprehension items -- dropping by 2.1
percentage points between 1971 and 1980. Most groups
of 17-year-olds exhibited declines in the area of inferential comprehension. Losses were most marked for
those living in the Northeast (3.7 percentage points),
females (2.6 percentage points), and those whose parents had either graduated from high school (4 percentage points) or had some education beyond high school
(3.1 percentage points).

Why Is It Better?

National Assessment convened a panel of English
and reading experts, including teachers at the elementary and secondary levels as well as those involved in
teacher education and research, to comment on the results of the reading assessments.

Discussing the gains made by 9-year-olds, panelists cited a number of specific activities during the
past decade that may have affected results. Among
these were:
'Increased federal funding for reading instruction during the early elementary years
'Changes in curricular materials and approaches
to the teaching of reading
'Increased access to print and electronic media
for teaching and training both teachers and students

The group also expressed concern about the loss
of momentum seen from age 9 to ages 13 and 17, raising
as possible explanations increases in class size as
resources are becoming limited, increased student participation in the work force and the rise in both the
number and attractiveness of recreational alternatives
and distractions.

Noting that the reading gains made by 9-year-olds
are larger than those seen in other learning areas
surveyed by National Assessment, the panel observed
that:
'Increased attention to language and reading development has had positive effects on the performance
of younger students.
'There is a need for continued support of reading
instruction at the secondary level, focusing on inferential and critical thinking skills.
'Reading instruction must accommodate the shift
between the reading needs of the early elementary
years and the middle and the higher years of secondary
schools.

Panelists agreed that improvements noted in students at ages 9 and 12 among Blacks, students who attend schools in disadvantaged urban areas and rural
communities are very likely the result of federal and
local compensatory programs over the past decade. However, panelists also concurred that educators and policy makers should not allow the progress of the nation's most talented students to be impeded by the

emphasis on programs for only the lowest achievers. Continued funding of reading programs should be directed toward providing support to youngsters at all achievement levels.

National Assessment's third survey of reading answered many of the questions raised by the results of the second: the decline in reference skills at age 13 was reversed, with junior high students performing slightly higher in this area at the end of the decade than at the beginning; the downward trend among 17-year-olds on inferential comprehension has become a significant decline; black 9-year-olds continued to make large gains over the decade, narrowing the gap between themselves and the nation; and the gains made by 1975's 9-year-olds were manifested as improvements by 1979's 13-year-olds only in the area of literal comprehension -- with the exception of black junior high students, who posted gains in all three areas of reading.

Questions for the Future

The results of the third reading assessment also raise questions for the future. Will the decline among high school students on inferential skills continue into the eighties? Will the gains made by 1979's black 13-year-olds be manifested as improvements by 1984's black 17-year-olds? Will the increases among 9-year-olds for the third assessment yield increases for 13-year-olds in the fourth survey? Will black 9- and 13-year-olds continue to narrow the gap between themselves and the nation? And what effect will the proposed decreases in Title I funding have on future measures of students' reading skills?

Work will commence on the materials for the fourth assessment of reading -- currently scheduled for the 1983-84 school year -- toward the end of 1981. In addition, National Assessment will continue to examine the results of the third reading assessment to answer other questions, such as the performance patterns of Hispanic students and students enrolled in public and private schools.

HOW TO EVALUATE THEE, TEACHER --
LET ME COUNT THE WAYS

Donald L. Haefele

The apparent decline in student scholastic performance, combined with a teacher surplus, has
prompted school administrators to establish more rigorous procedures for the evaluation of teachers. Many
school systems are developing or operating evaluation
programs without a clear understanding of the problems
associated with the more popular approaches.

This article is a critique of the most common
methods of and approaches to teacher evaluation. (Some
of the approaches included in this article are drawn
from TEACHER APPRAISAL FOR IMPROVEMENT, published in
1976 by Phi Delta Kappa.)

Approach 1: Teacher competence is measured by
performance of the teacher's classes on standardized
tests given at the end of the year. Year-end performance is compared with established norms.

Analysis of test data from schools located in diverse socioeconomic neighborhoods discloses a fallacy
in this approach. For example, standardized test data
from two Columbus, Ohio, elementary schools (call them
A and B) with predominantly white populations reveal
dramatic differences in the percent of students scoring above grade level. The average percent of sixth-
grade children achieving above grade level in reading
and mathematics at School A (91% white) is 93. At
School B (99% white) 28% of the sixth-graders scored
above grade level. School A is located in an upper-
middle-income area where the average home value is
$60,000 to $70,000, whereas School B is situated in a
low-income neighborhood where the price of homes averages $10,000 to $15,000. The environment (e.g. travel,

Reprinted from PHI DELTA KAPPAN, 61 (5): 349-352
(January 1980), by permission of author and publisher.

books, parental education) provided by the families of children in School A is likely to be more amenable to successful performance in school.

This differential in test performance is probably related, in part, to the mobility or turnover rate of each school. School A's mobility rate is 3%; School B's is 24% per year, eight times as high. School B's revolving population presents serious instructional problems for the teachers. And incidentally, the ADC (Aid to Dependent Children) rates are 0% and 40% for Schools A and B respectively. Thus, even if we assume that standardized test scores are sensitive to instructional variation, no informed administrator would recommend dismissal of teachers in School B on the basis of this test score differential.

Approach 2: Standardized tests are administered to students to determine how much they increase their learning over time. The amount of desired gain is established in advance by school personnel, teachers, and an independent evaluator.

In this approach the average gain in performance of Ms. Smith's ninth-grade students for previous years might furnish a gain norm. Comparisons with other schools would not occur. To establish appropriate gain norms, however, gains (autumn to spring) on standardized tests from prior years must be available and must be averaged to furnish a norm. Use of this approach involves comparisons of the gain in achievement test scores of this year's students with the baseline scores of previous years. If at the beginning of this school year the average entering ability and achievement levels of Ms. Smith's class are significantly superior (or inferior) to the norms of earlier years, the actual year's gain could surpass (or fail to match) the expected gain. Either situation could be explained as fortuitous, or the result of unusual events during the most recent year. Pronounced fluctuations in mobility rate and class composition from year to year could upset this proposed method of evaluation. Although this approach may appear superior to Approach 1, it presents serious problems.

Approach 3: Students in each grade or subject are tested at the beginning and end of each semester or school year. Gain scores are computed to contrast class performance (gain or loss) with classes of comparable ability. Teacher effectiveness is measured by proportion of "gainers" to "losers."

Instead of comparing test results of Ms. Smith's class with previous performance, her class is matched with other classes on important variables such as aptitude, past standardized test performance, subject matter, socioeconomic status, and school environment. Assuming that a sufficient number of classes match Ms. Smith's class, most of these influential extraneous variables would appear to be controlled and allow a valid comparison of year-end gains to losses. In this quasi-experimental situation, the teacher's performance is the independent variable -- the only critical one allowed to vary.

This technique of matching individuals or groups for comparison purposes has been increasingly criticized in recent years. (1) Daniel Klepak's research has disclosed diverse standardized test performance between seemingly matched or comparable schools. (2) Although student body composition, socioeconomic status, physical facilities, and other typical matching characteristics were similar, Klepak's study warns of the potential for serious error in this approach to the assessment of teacher effectiveness.

These three initial approaches to the determination of teacher effectiveness focused on performance of students on standardized tests. A court case, Scheelhaase v. Woodbury Central Community School District, considered this application of standardized tests:

> School boards are likely to rely on this
> method in the future, particularly since
> the Court of Appeals for the Eighth Circuit
> has held that a school board has the power
> to dismiss a teacher whose students performed
> less well on tests than did other students in
> the school. (3)

Standardized tests tend to inhibit curriculum innovation. Curricula (content and methods) are frequently fashioned to fit the tests. Achievement tests measure a limited range of objectives. (4) Educational objectives not measured by such tests include: joy and confidence in the use of the mind, a lively interest in the subject matter, pleasure in using skills, reading with zest and enjoyment, learning to learn, learning to cope with rapid change, gaining emotional un-

321

derstanding, and developing interpersonal and social competence.

A firm grasp of the relevant literature, a clear understanding of the shortcomings associated with standardized tests, and the foresight to perceive the pernicious effects these testing approaches can inflict on the instructional milieu are potent reasons for seeking alternatives to the use of standardized testing as an index of teacher effectiveness.

Approach 4: Informal observations and ratings of the teacher are conducted by the principal and/or other supervisory personnel. Comments by students, parents, and colleagues are incorporated in the final evaluation.

Informal observation suggests absence of a structured format including empirically based characteristics of "good teaching." Research demonstrates that criteria may fluctuate with the personal biases of the observer and yield invalid and inconsistent results even when highly structured observation instruments are used. (6) A teacher may have a disorganized room that upsets or negatively biases some observers, yet communicates effectively with students.

Comments by students, peers, and colleagues, particularly those who have observed or benefited from the teacher's instruction, usually amount to limited and often biased data regarding the teacher's effectiveness. Although it characterizes many currently employed teacher evaluation procedures, this approach is shot through with validity and reliability problems. For example, teaching behaviors, if rated, are usually undefined and lack evidence of relationship to student outcomes.

Approach 5: Systematic observation of the teacher is conducted by the principal and/or supervisor, using a rating form that lists characteristics of good teachers. The teacher's evaluation score is compared to a school or district standard.

"Systematic" observation suggests that all teachers are rated on the same characteristics or criteria a specific number of times under similar conditions. As noted earlier, systematic observation does not guarantee reliable observation; rater bias is a constant problem. Ratings by at least two observers on different occasions, if consistent, can be useful. Where lack of agreement exists, the utility of this approach is weakened.

Although a review of research by Barak Rosenshine and Norma Furst (7) and more recent studies (8) on teacher effects suggest teacher characteristics that may be effective in producing certain student outcomes, we lack sufficient evidence to define and establish validity for them operationally. Robert Heath and Mark Neilson's review of research on teacher characteristics disclosed by the Rosenshine and Furst analyses (e.g., clarity, enthusiasm, variability) produced two strong conclusions:

> First, the research literature on the relation between teacher behavior and student achievement does not offer an empirical basis for the prescription of teacher training objectives. Second, this literature fails to provide such a basis, not because of minor flaws in the statistical analyses, but because of sterile operational definitions of both teaching and achievement, and because of fundamentally weak research designs. (9)

Recent studies of teacher effects and reviews of several promising studies point to the existence of several teacher characteristics (behaviors) that display promise. (10) If this teacher evaluation approach is to be used, an observation system that includes those recurring and potent behaviors will reflect the greatest validity.

Establishment of a school or district standard of comparison not only implies a knowledge of characteristics of effective teachers but, in addition, a level of attainment that discriminates between more effective and less effective teachers. Insufficient data to establish such normative scales precludes construction of a valid standard. Experience suggests that such standards are arbitrarily fixed.

Approach 6: The teacher is systematically observed and rated by peers on the extent to which he exhibits important characteristics of good teaching. A predetermined school or district standard is the criterion.

This variation of Approach 5, ratings by peers,

does not significantly improve the worth of this approach over Approaches 4 or 5. Subjectivity and the propensity for bias remain potential problems. Peer teachers are, however, more apt to take into account day-to-day classroom demands and circumstances than are principals. Most principals assume managerial roles and become less aware of changes in curricula and innovations in classroom teaching. Thus many principals may feel inadequate and even uncomfortable in evaluating those teachers who employ more novel teaching arrangements. "Because they are rewarded for maintaining the system, administrators are not likely either to challenge it or reward subordinates who do." (11)

Teachers I have interviewed strongly oppose peer evaluation. Negative peer reports, they state, could create disharmony and alienation among faculty. Their perceptions of teachers and administrators as distinct groups with different functions and roles prompt them to assign teacher evaluation responsibility to administrators.

Approach 7: The teacher's students use a rating form to judge the extent to which the teacher exhibits important characteristics of good teaching. The teacher must meet a predetermined school or district standard of effectiveness.

An investigation of the relationship of student achievement and student ratings of the teacher indicated a significant, albeit modest, correlation between these two variables. (12) Student aptitude emerged as a more potent predictor of achievement than student ratings of the teachers. Another study concluded that teachers who seek approval from students in an ingratiating manner will be less effective in producing achievement in children than teachers who do not strive to be liked. (13)

Student ratings of teachers have, therefore, not been clearly linked with positive student outcomes. It may be that many students rate teachers on a popularity continuum and disassociate this rating from their performance in school.

As noted above, characteristics of good teaching lack solid empirical bases (validity). For example, teacher "clarity" has emerged in some studies as a characteristic of good teaching. (14) Recent research on teacher clarity disclosed that more than 3,700 junior high school students could significantly differentiate characteristics of clear and unclear teachers. (15) To confirm the validity of teacher clarity (or any other teacher trait) as a characteristic of good teaching, however, research must demonstrate that clear teachers produce superior learning and/or better attitudes toward learning than do unclear teachers. To date, the research has been promising yet inconclusive.

Approach 8: Teachers are required to take the National Teacher Examination (NTE) and achieve a predetermined standard composite score.

On 16 January 1978, in the case U.S. v. State of South Carolina, the U.S. Supreme Court ruled 5-2 that a state may hire and pay teachers on the basis of a standardized test -- in particular, the NTE. (16) The court ruled that NTE scores are related to teachers' performance. The implication is that teachers with high NTE scores will perform more effectively in classrooms than teachers who receive low scores. As Thomas McDaniel notes, a nagging question persists: "How much of a rational relationship actually exists between a test of cognitive knowledge and teaching performance?" (17) In this case, a content validation study conducted by the state of South Carolina and the Educational Testing Service met the court requirement for a validated test. Several hundred professors of education made content validity judgments on each question contained in the NTE tests, deciding how many minimally qualified individuals should be able to answer a given question.

Content validity does not indicate how well a teacher who surpasses or fails to meet the standard will perform in the classroom. To determine this, the degree of predictive validity for the NTE must be ascertained. There are, no doubt, "poor" teachers who can surpass the minimum score and "good" teachers who cannot attain the minimum standard. The dissenting justices said:

> The authors of the test themselves advise against using it for determining the pay for experienced teachers and believe that the NTE should not be the sole criterion for initial certification.

The NTE is an achievement test. As the Coleman report (19) and other studies (20) indicate, variation in levels of teacher knowledge of content in education is not clearly associated with successful teaching. Until research appears showing stronger relationships with practice, the practical utility of the National Teacher Examination is questionable. (21)

Approach 9: Periodically, the teacher is provided with an instructional objective, a sample test item measuring that objective, and information about the content it covers. A small group of students is assigned to that teacher randomly (to balance abilities) and is instructed by the teacher on the objective for one to 10 lessons. After instruction, the students are tested on the objective. Teacher effectiveness is determined on the basis of how well the students achieved the objective.

James Popham has advanced this approach as the preferred technique of teacher evaluation. (22) There are several problems associated with it, however. First, the objective must be related to the subject area of the teacher. If not, the teacher must spend time in preparation. Ability to prepare for instruction would then be measured as an additional variable that is associated with performance.

Second, random assignment of students the teacher knows little or nothing about could initially affect instructional effectiveness. At the start of the school year, teachers often use student records to determine readiness for specific instruction. Lack of this resource could pose a problem.

Third, we must assume that these students reflect levels of motivation, boredom, and judgment typical of students the teacher interacts with in class.

Fourth, the ability level of the assigned group could make a difference. Some teachers are particularly effective with more able students and not very effective with low-ability students.

Fifth, as Gene V. Glass notes, the technique embodied in this approach "would have to be repeated across 10 different instructional topics with 10 different pupil groups before the average score for a single teacher attained a reliability above .80." (23)

326

The costs of such a program in time and money would be staggering. Arvil Barr's study of teacher behaviors concluded that instability of teacher behavior from one lesson to another is the dominant source of unreliability in the effect of teachers' actions on student learning. (24)

This approach, although superficially attractive, encompasses complex features and arrangements that militate against its use as a measure of teacher effectiveness.

Approach 10: The Teacher Perceiver Interview is administered to teachers. Teacher effectiveness is based on how well the teacher meets a predetermined criterion or norm-referenced score.

The Teacher Perceiver Interview (TPI) and the NTE are similar in that right and wrong answers are presumed to exist. Whereas the NTE measures cognitive knowledge, the TPI purportedly assesses noncognitive traits such as empathy for others, goal or mission strength, responsiveness to students, satisfaction through others' achievements, ability to stimulate students, innovative ideas, and inner drive toward completeness. (25) According to a technical report, scores on the TPI predict teacher performance in the classroom. However, no studies relating TPI performance and teacher performance in the classroom are available in the manual or in journal publications.

The above list of traits includes personality characteristics. Attempts to select or evaluate personnel through personality measures have not been successful. As Robert Menges says,

> Paper-and-pencil instruments and situational tests have long been used in personnel selection. If such instruments are shown to discriminate effective from ineffective practitioners, their use in assessing readiness would be recommended. Such investigations have consumed large sums of money and enlisted many of the finest social science researchers.... These studies, unfortunately, offer little encouragement for the use of personality assessment in identifying readiness for professional practice. (26)

Those school systems using or considering the use

327

of the TPI should heed this caveat. A recent review
of the TPI process cites the subjective rating of oral
responses (rater bias) as a salient problem. (27) Many
teachers have decried the impersonal atmosphere established by some rater-interviewers. Interviewers are
not permitted to discuss responses. In most situations interviewers are only permitted to read the
questions and rate or tape the responses.

The TPI has not been established as a valid instrument for the selection or evaluation of teachers
and probably should be excluded from such use until
hard evidence (not testimonial) becomes available.
Many of the TPI questions establish simulated situations, calling upon the ratee to choose or develop the
best response. Not only is the response rated but, as
noted above, a facet of personality is purportedly assessed. Discussion of simulations in the evaluation
of teacher effectiveness (furnished below) has direct
implications for the validity of the TPI as a selection or evaluation device. Some school administrators
perceive the TPI as convenient, because it relieves
them from decision making. At times they have selected
new teachers simply on the basis of a high TPI score.
The error of equating a test score (and the TPI is a
test) with the performance of a teacher in a classroom
full of students must be avoided.

Approach 11:   The teacher is given written descriptions and/or shown films of typical classroom
problems. The teacher's effectiveness is judged on
the basis of answer quality.

The TPI contains many simulated problem situations or critical teaching incidents, as they are often labeled. An example of a simulated problem might
be the following: Two boys accuse another boy of
stealing in front of you (the teacher). You are required to describe what action you would take and to
furnish a rationale for your response to this problem.
According to one TPI workshop trainer, Gale Muller,
for each question on the TPI "there are, indeed, an
infinite number of potentially acceptable or unacceptable responses." (28)   Muller unwittingly highlights
one of the major problems associated with the use of
TPI and simulated data -- a multiplicity of acceptable
and unacceptable responses. The essential qualities
of reliability and rater agreement in the scoring of
teacher responses impose an exceedingly complex, actually an impossible, task on busy school administra-

tors. This complexity jeopardizes the utility and
validity of the instrument.

Donald Cruickshank, a noted expert in the area of
two widely used teacher problem simulations, attests
to the "high subjectivity" associated with ratings of
simulation responses. (29) He also asserts that performance on simulated incidents, whether presented
orally (as in the TPI), on film, or in written form,
cannot be presumed to indicate actual classroom performance.

Approach 12: The teacher, together with the
principal and/or curriculum supervisor, establishes
mutually agreed-upon (negotiated) instructional goals
and objectives for the year. Observation data and
other sources of information gathered at regular in-
tervals during the year are used to monitor and evaluate the attainment of goals.

When information from observations and evaluation
is used as feedback to aid in the teacher's self-de-
velopment, research suggests that teachers favor evaluation. (30) When this information is used exclusively for administrative decision making (e.g., re-
hiring, dismissal, assignments, salary increments),
teachers do not favor evaluation. This approach to
teacher evaluation, where data are employed to promote
teacher growth, is a positive approach. It affirms
the desire of all teachers to improve, to apply their
skills and energy to accepted instructional goals in a
nonthreatening environment. Each approach to teacher
evaluation and instructional improvement described
above suggests a monolithic model of teaching. This
negotiated approach asserts that each teacher is different; each possesses different strengths, styles,
and competencies. Instructional objectives are worked
out through teacher and principal agreement, with recognition of individual differences among teachers. A
plan of accomplishment and criteria of success are
also negotiated. Administrative support throughout
the year helps teachers achieve their objectives.

My optimism about this negotiated approach is not
unbounded. Working out objectives and an implementation plan demands both time and energy. Criteria of
success are not always agreeable to both parties, particularly when administrators press for standardized
test gains as indicators of success. One of my students described an experience wherein negotiations

disintegrated at the level of establishing objectives. The teacher told the principal of her objectives in reading for the coming year. The principal rejected the objectives, admonishing the teacher for failing to maximize reading achievement already. Obviously, this posture is inimical to negotiation. Teachers and administrators must realize that, for various reasons, all established targets may not be met. And at times target levels may be exceeded. The notable features are that (1) teachers and administrators work <u>together</u> for the benefit of students, (2) the goal is improvement, and (3) teacher self-evaluation is an important feature of this system.

I have attempted to point out the serious disadvantages embodied in a variety of teacher evaluation techniques. It appears to me that the goal-setting approach is a preferable though demanding route to instructional improvement. It is the only approach based on mutual trust. The other techniques may isolate teachers and administrators and establish adversary rather than cooperative relationships.

Notes

1. Stephen Isaac and William Michael, HANDBOOK IN RESEARCH AND EVALUATION (San Diego: Robert R. Knapp, 1971).
2. "New York Finds Schools Count in Reading Achievement," PHI DELTA KAPPAN, June 1974, p. 721.
3. Paul Tractenberg, "Legal Issues in the Testing of School Personnel," PHI DELTA KAPPAN, May 1976, pp. 602-605.
4. Murray Levine, "The Academic Achievement Test," AMERICAN PSYCHOLOGIST, March 1976, pp. 228-38.
5. Ibid.
6. Donald Medley, Robert Soar, and Ruth Soar, ASSESSMENT AND RESEARCH IN TEACHER EDUCATION: FOCUS ON PBTE (Washington, D.C.: American Association of Colleges for Teacher Education, 1975).
7. Barak Rosenshine and Norma Furst, "Research on Teacher Performance Criteria," in B. Othaniel Smith, RESEARCH IN TEACHER EDUCATION: A SYMPOSIUM (Englewood Cliffs, N.J.: Prentice-Hall, 1971).
8. American Association of Colleges for Teacher Education, "Research on Teacher Effects," JOURNAL OF TEACHER EDUCATION, Spring 1976, pp. 24-66.
9. Robert Heath and Mark Neilson, "The Research Basis for Performance-Based Teacher Education," REVIEW OF

EDUCATIONAL RESEARCH, Fall 1974, pp. 463-84.

10. Donald Cruickshank, "Synthesis of Selected Recent Research on Teacher Effects," JOURNAL OF TEACHER EDUCATION, Spring 1976, pp. 57-60.

11. John Goodlad, "The Schools and Education," SATURDAY REVIEW, 19 April 1969, p. 60.

12. David Potter, Paul Nalin, and Ann Lewandowski, THE RELATION OF STUDENT ACHIEVEMENT AND STUDENT RATINGS OF TEACHERS (Princeton, N.J.: Educational Testing Service, 1973).

13. David Berliner and William Tikunoff, "The California Beginning Teacher Evaluation Study: Overview of the Ethnographic Study," JOURNAL OF TEACHER EDUCATION, Spring 1976, pp. 24-30.

14. Rosenshine and Furst, op. cit.

15. John Kennedy, Andrew Bush, Donald Cruickshank, and Donald Haefele, "Additional Investigations in the Nature of Teacher Clarity," paper presented at annual meeting of American Educational Research Association, Toronto, Canada, March 1978.

16. "Court Backs Teacher Pay, Hiring Tests," COLUMBUS (Ohio) CITIZEN JOURNAL, 17 January 1978.

17. Thomas McDaniel, "The NTE and Teacher Certification," PHI DELTA KAPPAN, November 1977, pp. 186-88.

18. COLUMBUS CITIZEN JOURNAL, op. cit., p. 24.

19. James Coleman, EQUALITY OF EDUCATIONAL OPPORTUNITY (Washington, D.C.: U.S. Government Printing Office, 1966).

20. James Guthrie, "Survey of School Effectiveness Studies," in A.M. Mood, ed., DO TEACHERS MAKE A DIFFERENCE? (Washington, D.C.: U.S. Government Printing Office, 1970).

21. Robert Menges, "Assessing Readiness for Professional Practice," REVIEW OF EDUCATIONAL RESEARCH, Spring 1975, pp. 173-207.

22. James Popham, "Performance Tests of Teaching Proficiency: Rationale, Development, and Validation," AMERICAN EDUCATIONAL RESEARCH JOURNAL, January 1971, pp. 105-17.

23. Gene V. Glass, "Teacher Effectiveness," in Herbert Walberg, EVALUATING EDUCATIONAL PERFORMANCE (Berkeley, Calif.: McCutchan, 1974), p. 25.

24. Arvil Barr, WISCONSIN STUDIES OF THE MEASUREMENT AND PREDICTION OF TEACHER EFFECTIVENESS (Madison, Wisc.: Dembar Publications, Inc., 1961).

25. Selection Research, Incorporated, TEACHER PERCEIVER INTERVIEW: TECHNICAL REPORT (Lincoln, Nebr.: SRI, 1977).

26. Menges, op. cit., p. 181.

27. Donald Haefele, "The Teacher Perceiver Interview:

How Valid?" PHI DELTA KAPPAN, June 1978, pp. 683-84.
28. Gale Muller, "In Defense of the Teacher Perceiver Interview," PHI DELTA KAPPAN, June 1978, pp. 684-85.
29. Personal communication from Donald Cruickshank, 9 October 1978.
30. Mel Zelenak and Bill Snider, "Teachers Don't Resent Evaluation -- If It's for the Improvement of Instruction," PHI DELTA KAPPAN, April 1974, pp. 570-71.

THE DE-PROFESSIONALIZATION OF TEACHERS

Thomas R. McDaniel

It is characteristic of occupational groups in American society to claim - or aspire - to be professions. Thus, for example, it is not unusual to hear beauticians, airplane pilots, electricians, athletes, or house painters call themselves "professionals." Indeed, the well-recognized and established professions of medicine, law, and ministry appear to have been joined by a host of professions and would-be professions in unprecedented number. Traditional definitions and criteria are often strained beyond belief by some groups in their zeal to attain recognition as professions. Other occupations - college professors and engineers, for example - no doubt have achieved professional status. But what status can be claimed by the three-million public school teachers in the United States and what is the future status of this significant occupational group?

The answer to such a question depends in large measure on one's concept of, definition of, and criteria for "professionalism" and the evaluation of an occupation in terms of these concepts, definitions, and criteria. Professional status, then, is a matter of interpretation; to a certain extent an "eye of the beholder" phenomenon. Many educationists argue that teaching is already a profession (at least in most respects), is becoming one rapidly, or is a semi-profession. I want to develop the argument that teaching is a semi-profession in the process of becoming a craft.

This view will offend some teachers, I am sure. However, my intention is not to defame a large segment of our society (some of my best friends are elementary and secondary school teachers), but to de-mythologize a misconception about teachers and their occupational

Reprinted from THE EDUCATIONAL FORUM, 43 (2): 229-237 (January 1979), by permission of author and publisher.

status. It is not necessarily desirable or advantageous for teachers to be "professionals." It may not even be possible.

In identifying teaching as a semi-profession, not a profession, Etzioni says of teachers that "...their training is shorter, their status is less legitimated, their right of privileged communication less established, there is less of a specialized body of knowledge, and they have less autonomy from supervision and societal control of the profession." (1)

Few teachers, looking at the well-established professions (like law and medicine), would disagree with Etzioni's observations here. Teaching has some of the characteristics of a profession, but only enough to warrant the label of "semi-profession." To illustrate this contention, I want to move directly to a useful set of eight criteria for judging professional status developed by Ryan and Cooper. These criteria incorporate most of the basic concepts and definitions of professionalism used by such writers as Broudy (2), Lieberman (3), Vollmer (4), and Greenwood (5). The Ryan-Cooper criteria (6) will be the vehicle for my assessment of education as an occupation.

First, a profession renders a unique, definite, and essential social service. Only the people in the particular profession render the service. For example, only lawyers practice law. The service rendered must be considered so important that it is available to all the people in a society.

Public schools do render a definite and essential social service, and education has moved from its earlier status as a privilege or a luxury to its current recognition as a right, essential to the welfare of American society. However, it can hardly be the case that only teachers render the service of education. As Cremin says in describing Plato's enduring analysis of education and his vision of the good life, "it is the community that educates, by which he means all the influences that mold the mind and character of youth: music, architecture, drama, painting, poetry, laws, and athletics." (7)

Recent research by Coleman and by Jencks indicates that the educational influence of schools (and, therefore, teachers) is minor in comparison with the influences of family and peers. Since most all adults have themselves been through a long schooling process, they often see nothing unique in the service rendered by the teacher. In point of fact, many parents do teach their children all manner of skills, values, and content; and when a teacher must be absent from school most administrators call in untrained substitutes to provide the essential service of education. While only lawyers practice law, we would not be able to say that only teachers teach.

Second, a profession relies upon intellectual skills in the performance of its service. This does not mean that physical actions and skills are not needed, but rather that the emphasis in carrying on the work is on intellectual skills and techniques.

One of the greatest barriers to professional status for teachers is the apparent lack of coherent theoretical and empirical knowledge underlying pedagogical practices. This is not to imply that there has been a shortage of research studies on teaching, but only to suggest that there has emerged to date no clearly accepted discipline of education. There have been some efforts in this direction, however. (8) As Goode suggests,

> The crucial matter here is the interaction of the public and occupation. Even in the area of teaching techniques, the teacher is not thought to be the final arbiter. Most Americans with a college education believe they understand such techniques about as well as the average teacher. (9)

In part the issue is not whether such a presumption by the citizenry is true - I would argue it is not - but whether or not the public thinks it is. The intellectual skills, body of knowledge, and theoretical base for the professional's service puts him into an honored and superior relationship to the recipient of his service. As Broudy says, "We ask the professional to diagnose difficulties, appraise solutions, and to choose among them. We ask him to take total responsibility for both strategy and tactics."(10) But at this time neither the intellectual framework and skills of public school teachers nor the public's acceptance of superior knowledge by teachers exists to justify professional status.

Griffiths goes so far as to contend that "education has had a definite anti-intellect line since its

birth" and that "what passes for a professional literature, the speeches at educational conventions, the
dialogue among practitioners and in many cases the
quality of teaching in classrooms, can hardly hold up
as intellectual." (11) The lack of a genuine discipline of education, the unwillingness of the public to
recognize the superior knowledge and intellectual
skill of teachers, and a pervasive anti-intellectual-
ism at all levels of the enterprise pose serious hur-
dles to the professionalization of teachers.

Third, a profession has a long period of specialized training. Because professional work requires special intellectual skills, specialized intellectual
training is needed. General education, such as that
represented by a bachelor's degree, is valued, but not
considered adequate. The specialized training must
cover a substantial period of time and not be obtained
in cram courses or correspondence schools.

Few would argue that the professional preparation
of teachers is "long" when compared to prototype professions like medicine and law. The bachelor's degree
is considered adequate, and most teachers begin teaching with no more than a baccalaureate degree. The history of teacher education in the United States is less
than impressive in this respect. As Tyack says, "before the 20th century a majority of teachers probably
had no more than elementary schooling (if indeed they
had graduated from the eighth grade); in 1931 only
about 10 percent of all elementary teachers had a
bachelor's degree; and as late as 1952 not even a majority of elementary teachers had graduated from college." (12) Real progress has been made in terms of
formal education of teachers in the last two decades,
but the specialized training of teachers still represents a relatively small proportion of a four-year un-
dergraduate program - typically one or two semesters
of professional preparation.

Fourth, both individual members of the profession
and the professional group enjoy a considerable degree
of autonomy and decision making authority. Whereas
factory workers have very limited decision making powers and are closely supervised in the performance of
their work, professionals are expected to make most of
their own decisions and be free of close supervision
by supervisors. Also, professional groups regulate
their own activities rather than having outsiders set
policies and enforce adherence to standards.

Teachers do have a certain amount of autonomy in decision making, particularly in terms of teaching methods and evaluation of student progress. This autonomy varies a good deal from district to district and from school to school, however. Often autonomy is a matter of default rather than recognition of professional status; richer school districts tend to provide many supervisory personnel, administrators, and curriculum specialists who, by their very function, limit the decision making autonomy of teachers. The nature of mass education has evolved from the factory model and the assembly line, a powerful controlling metaphor in our national experience. Bureaucratic organization with its chain-of-command structure and superior-subordinate role relationships typifies a great many public school "systems" with a resulting lack of individual autonomy for the classroom teacher.

Furthermore, policies regulating curriculum, employment, and adherence to standards are determined to great degree by the public rather than by professional groups. Both the NEA and the AFT have been more assertive in this respect in recent years, yet it is lay boards of education, state departments of education, and state legislatures which have ultimate authority for educational policies. It is highly unlikely that the public will in the foreseeable future relinquish its well-established control of public education. Under the Tenth Amendment of the Constitution, education has been defined as a responsibility of state government; the control mechanisms of state law, state departments of education, intermediate and local boards of education, case law, and public financing of education have been a long and stable tradition in American society; bureaucratic organization has not been successfully challenged by reformers from Goodman to Illich in terms of increased autonomy for teachers.

Fifth, a profession requires that its members accept personal responsibility for their actions and decisions. Along with having a high degree of freedom and autonomy, the professional must shoulder a large measure of responsibility for his performance. Since the professional's service is usually related to the human welfare of individuals, this responsibility is an especially serious one.

One of the strongest movements in education today is the call for greater teacher accountability. Many states have enacted some form of legislation as a

337

response to that concern in public. Perhaps the point to consider here is the symptomatic nature of the movement: the public perceives teachers as unwilling to accept personal responsibility for their actions and, as a result, denies on this criterion the professional status of teachers.

More recently, there has been a related attempt to legislate teacher accountability through mandated competency examinations for students. As McClung points out,

> The competency testing movement in this country is gaining considerable momentum, spurred by legislators trying to be responsive to a public call for increased accountability of elementary and secondary schools....Educators in particular have a special interest in making sure that any competency testing programs in their states and school districts are equitable for all concerned. (13)

That educators will be allowed to have much control over such concerns is questionable, given the raison d' être of the movement. What is at issue is a public insistence on educational accountability to the public for results. But that insistence highlights the nonprofessional status of teachers more clearly than anything could. As Darland argues, "One characteristic of a charlatan, posing as a professional, is to personally guarantee outcomes. A real professional...rather indicates anticipated results which in turn are dependent on a whole series of conditions." (14)

Sixth, a profession emphasizes the services rendered by its practitioners more than their financial rewards. While the personal motives of any indivdual professional are not necessarily any higher than any other worker's, the professional group's public emphasis is on service.

Service has long been a prime motivation for young men and women to enter teaching. A 1972 NEA research report indicates that from a nationwide survey of 1,553 teachers 71.8 percent said "desire to work with young people" was one of their three main reasons for teaching. The second highest response was "value of education to society" with a 37 percent rating.(15) These responses point to the service motivation of teachers, and it must be concluded that teaching qualifies on this criterion of professionalism.

Of course, it should be noted that the financial rewards of teaching historically have been meagre. Both the NEA and AFT have taken stronger, more militant positions recently to dramatize teacher dissatisfaction with pay and working conditions. The growing ranks of the aggressive AFT - 50,000 in 1960, 500,000 in 1975, and an estimated 900,000 in 1980 - may serve as a warning that the service motivation will be rivaled by the struggle for economic respectability.

Among his arguments on behalf of the union is AFT President Albert Shanker's economic platform:

> Other workers are teachers' natural allies because they share patterns of organization, tactics, strategies, and goals. If teachers want higher salaries and better pensions...so do factory workers, airplane pilots, and the musicians of the New York Philharmonic. The taxes of these other workers help pay teachers' salaries and help make educational improvements possible. Over the past decade teachers have won as much as they can on their own; they cannot make further gains without the active support of the American workers. (16)

With both the NEA and the AFT engaging in the economic struggle - through sanctions, strikes, and collective bargaining - teachers are increasingly viewed by the public as skilled workers. And while there have been justified improvements in teachers' economic status, much of the taxpayers' revolt reflected in rejected bond issues and the accountability movement must be interpreted as the public's demand that teachers improve their "productivity." Still, teachers are probably as motivated by "service" as doctors or lawyers are.

Seventh, a profession is self-governing and responsible for policing its own ranks. This means there are professional groups who perform a number of activities aimed at keeping the quality of their services high and looking out for the social and economic well-being of the professional members. Also, these self-governing organizations set standards of admission and exclusion to the profession.

Teaching falls short of this standard, although both the NEA and the AFT look out for the social and economic well-being of their members. In terms of self-governing, policing, and admission to the profession, educational organizations have little influence. This is so - in contrast to the well-established professions - because education has been essentially public from the time of the common school movement in the nineteenth century to the present. It is state departments of education which certify teachers and boards of education which hire and dismiss teachers. While such developments as teacher centers are designed to give more control to teachers themselves in the preparation and selection of practitioners, there has been no widespread public acceptance of the notion that teachers should be self-regulating and self-screening professionals.

Eighth, a profession has a code of ethics which sets out the acceptable standards of conduct of its members. In order for a professional group to regulate the quality and standards of service, it needs a code of ethics to aid in enforcing these high standards.

The NEA has a code of ethics that is periodically revised. Although the code was first designed in 1929, there was no interpretation of the code until 1955 when the NEA's Committee on Professional Ethics printed a booklet with its first thirty-two opinions. Enforcement has been rare. The NEA took action against only one person between 1928 and 1955. (17) Certainly, in comparison with law and medicine, the NEA code has been of little consequence. Indeed, teacher preparation in most institutions neglects the issue of professional ethics, relegating the subject to a single lecture, if that. It would be surprising to learn that as many as 10 percent of NEA members could name a single principle from the revised code.

Perhaps, given teachers' lack of control over admission to the ranks and their lack of self-regulation it should not be surprising to find educational codes of ethics of little consequence in the practical governance of teachers. State laws have been enacted to protect the public from incompetent, unprofessional, or immoral teachers - and ethical actions against teachers are located in the legal-political structure of boards of education and court systems. Educational codes of ethics have been little more than professional trappings, devoid of any significant impact on the vast numbers of teachers in American public education.

Teaching has made great advancements in the 20th century. Salaries are better, formal education is longer, theory is developing, professional organizations are stronger, the importance of education as an essential service is gaining recognition, and the motivation of practitioners to render a public service continues to characterize a high percentage of public school teachers. There _are_ codes of ethics (although of limited significance), and teachers _are_ assuming greater responsibility for their actions and decisions in the performance of their service (although not always willingly or in a self-regulating manner).

It would seem fair - if the Ryan-Cooper criteria are sufficiently comprehensive as measures of professionalism - to say that teaching is a semi-profession. Because it falls short in degree (if not absolutely) on most criteria, because in particular it lacks the autonomy and self-regulating powers of professions, and because the public itself seems unready to accord professional status to teachers, the occupation resides in a limbo between craft and profession - having elements of each and (paradoxically, perhaps) momentum in both directions. It is difficult to tell what the future will bring, but I want to conclude this discussion by suggesting that elementary and secondary teachers increasingly will be viewed by the public, by their own organizations, by the institutions which prepare them, and by themselves as skilled craftsmen rendering an important social service.

In the first place, the constraints upon education imposed by tradition militate against professional status for teachers, as our previous discussion suggests. The public demand for an accountability of results measured in part (at least) by the quality of the product sharpens the public image of the teacher as a craftsman. That the public itself controls education via legislature and lay boards and that parents tend not to accede to claims of superior knowledge of teachers reinforces this image.

In the second place, advances by the AFT in membership and in power tend to support the "craftsman concept" of public school teachers. The NEA has modified its own image, as well as its posture on many issues, to conform to the craft union model. Members of both organizations are increasingly supporting the confrontationist approach - with a widening split between labor and management (i.e., between teachers and administrators) - which has accompanied the advent of collective bargaining. Since 1962 over half of the states have accorded teachers the legal right to bargain collectively.

In the third place, the technology of education and the prevalence in schools of education of increasingly sophisticated behavioral models of teacher training tend to promote the teacher-as-craftsman concept. Whether one considers the contemporary emphasis on competency-based programs of teacher education or the behavioral objectives approach to instruction or the renewed emphasis on longer periods of apprenticeships (on-the-job training under supervision), it is clear that performance, skills, specialized techniques and practical application of teaching methodology are being emphasized by teachers of teachers.

As Broudy has pointed out in his excellent analysis of teaching,

> A craftsman is guided by knowledge, but it is likely to be the kind of knowledge that has been gleaned from long trial-and-error experience.... Training for crafts tends to be the apprentice type that emphasizes practice of a skill under a master....Now, there is something, perhaps a lot, to be said for the notion that schoolroom craftsmen are precisely what we need these days. This argument is rarely advanced in public.

Broudy's major contention is that a profession is differentiated from a craft by the amount of theory which underlies the practice and that, furthermore, in a profession, the sound theoretical component must be in the practitioner. But even if there is a sufficiently strong theoretical base for educational practice, it does not necessarily follow that teachers have to master the theory itself. Much of what passes for professional preparation of teachers is in fact a process for giving teachers the skills and techniques which derive from theory rather than the theory itself.

Finally, it has been my experience that teachers on the whole see themselves as craftsmen. Generalizations are dangerous, of course, but it seems to me that teachers have little interest in educational theory or philosophy - which may say as much about the state of educational theory (19) as about teachers. The most dedicated and able teachers in the field do want to become more effective in the classroom, but this concern tends to be manifested in a desire for practical skills in such areas as discipline, individualizing instruction, evaluating learning, and techniques of instruction. It is exceedingly rare to find a teacher who feels in need of a stronger theoretical preparation for the role he or she fills in society.

None of this discussion is meant to denigrate teachers, but rather is intended to clarify the present and future status of teaching as an occupation. I find myself in agreement with Covert when he says, "we should become less paranoid about the prestige and status accorded to our occupation and get on with the business of establishing an optimal learning climate for all students." (20) While I tend to believe that teachers better fit a craftsman role model than a professional role model, I am convinced that the importance of the occupation is growing rapidly. Certainly, the efforts by scholars like John Walton, Marc Belth, and Bruce Joyce to develop the theoretical dimensions of a discipline of education must continue to be a high-priority interest in educational research. The significant question for most of us, however, is how we can best educate teachers to perform the increasingly difficult and complex task of educating youth for tomorrow's world. To this end, I suggest that we concentrate less on the professional status of teachers and more on improving the teaching skills of schoolroom craftsmen.

Notes

1. Amitai Etzioni, THE SEMI-PROFESSIONS AND THEIR ORGANIZATION (New York: The Free Press, 1969), p. v.
2. Myron Lieberman, EDUCATION AS A PROFESSION (Englewood Cliffs, N.J.: Prentice-Hall 1956), pp. 1-7.
3. Harry Broudy, "Teaching - Craft or Profession" THE EDUCATIONAL FORUM 20 (Jan. 1956): 175-84.
4. Howard Vollmer and Donald L. Mills, PROFESSIONALIZATION (Englewood Cliffs: Prentice-Hall, Inc., 1966) p. 2.
5. Ernest Greenwood, "Attributes of a Profession" SOCIAL WORK 2 (July 1957): 44-55.
6. Kevin Ryan and James Cooper, THOSE WHO CAN, TEACH (Boston: Houghton Mifflin, 1975) pp. 300-01.
7. Lawrence Cremin, THE GENIUS OF AMERICAN EDUCATION (Pittsburgh: University Press, 1965), p. 2.

8. See, for example, John Walton and James Kuethe, eds., THE DISCIPLINE OF EDUCATION (Madison: University Press, 1963; and see also Walton's INTRODUCTION TO EDUCATION (Waltham, Ma.: Xerox College Publishing, 1971). Also see Marc Belth, EDUCATION AS A DISCIPLINE (Boston: Allyn and Bacon, 1965) and THE NEW WORLD OF EDUCATION (Boston: Allyn and Bacon, 1970).

9. William Goode in THE SEMI-PROFESSIONS AND THEIR ORGANIZATION by Amitai Etzioni, p. 266.

10. Broudy, "Teaching," p. 429.

11. D. Griffiths, "Intellectualism and Profesionalism," New York University Education Quarterly 5 (1973): 1.

12. David Tyack, ed. TURNING POINTS IN AMERICAN EDUCATIONAL HISTORY (Waltham, Ma.: Blaisdell Pub. Co., 1967), p. 412.

13. Merle Steven McClung, "Are Competency Testing Programs Fair? Legal?" PHI DELTA KAPPAN, February 1978, p. 400.

14. Dave Darland, "Some Complexities of Accountability," TODAY'S EDUCATION, January-February 1975, p. 21.

15. As reported in Allan C. Ornstein, AN INTRODUCTION TO THE FOUNDATIONS OF EDUCATION (Chicago: Rand McNally Pub. Co., 1977), pp. 5-6.

16. Albert Shanker, NEW YORK TEACHER, Nov. 4, 1973.

17. Lieberman, EDUCATION, p. 447.

18. Broudy, "Teaching," pp. 424-28.

19. See Harold E. Mitzell, "Increasing the Impact of Theory and Research on Programs of Instruction," JOURNAL OF TEACHER EDUCATION, November-December 1977, pp. 15-20.

20. James R. Covert, "Second Thoughts about the Professionalization of Teachers," THE EDUCATIONAL FORUM 39 (January 1975): 153.

MERIT PAY -- YES!
VOUCHERS -- NO!

Jack Frymier

Let's face it. As a profession, we made a mistake. We argued for and worked for better pay for all teachers -- higher salaries for everyone who works in schools. We thought we could push the idea of the single salary schedule and raise every teacher's salary to a decent level. Our argument was that better salaries would enable us to attract and keep competent people in the teaching profession.

It has not worked. It will not work. We need to change our tactics and change our minds. Not to get more money for teachers' salaries -- although that will happen -- but to improve the quality of schooling: to ensure that young people will learn more, better, faster, and more effectively than they do today. At the same time, we need to fight the voucher system in every way we can. Not to save our jobs -- although that may happen, too -- but to guarantee the advantages of better schooling and a pluralistic society for the young people of this great land.

These are terribly difficult times. Educators have been under attack before, of course, but this time it is different. This time it is the public school as an institution that is under the gun. The attackers are out to do away with the public school. The immediate proposal is to provide public funds for the support of private schools. The long term consequences would surely be the disappearance of the public school as an institution dedicated to serving the common good.

Our task -- as a profession and as a people -- is twofold: we absolutely must improve the quality of

Reprinted from THE EDUCATION FORUM, 46 (1): 4-8 (Fall 1981), by permission of author and publisher.

345

schooling immediately, and we must lead the charge against every effort to allocate public funds for private schools. Suppose we consider two proposals that relate to the economics of schooling as a way of exploring the implications and complications of this twofold task with which we are confronted.

Merit pay has often been suggested as a way of rewarding effective teachers. If we had a way of deliberately differentiating salaries so that outstanding teachers could be recognized, the argument goes, then we would be able -- over time -- to attract and keep the very best people in the profession. That would mean that students would learn more.

As a profession, however, we have fought the merit pay idea like the plague. When state legislatures mandated it, we pushed to get the laws repealed. When school boards adopted policies supporting merit pay, we sabatoged those policies in a thousand different ways. And we won those battles. There is hardly a school district in America that employs the idea of differentiated salaries as a way of recognizing excellence in teaching or motivating staff. We have always won.

But what have we accomplished with those victories? We have achieved uniform salary schedules, but everybody's salary is low. The American people simply will not pay all teachers at a uniformly high level. They never have and they never will.

The American people know -- as those of us in the profession know -- that some teachers are incompetent. Some teachers are ignorant. Some teachers simply do not care -- about young people, about ideas, or about learning as a way of coping with human problems or as a way of bettering the human condition. There are not many people in those categories, of course, but there are some. Those few people are holding down the general level of support for all teachers.

There are at least two things that we might do. First, we could take steps as a profession to purge our group of those few persons who are incompetent or ineffective. We could "police our own ranks," as the saying goes, and demonstrate to society at large that we are seriously concerned about the quality of educational service that we provide to the young people with whom we work day after day. Taking deliberate steps to move toward truly professional status -- including admission to and expulsion from the profession according to the quality of service provided -- would probably do a lot to convince other people that we are seriously concerned about the learning and development of those young people that society has assigned to us.

Second, we could take steps to guarantee that the best among us receive recognition and reward. We could work toward some form of differentiated salary system that would assure the most effective teachers of better salaries -- much better. We all know that some teachers work harder, some are more creative, and some are more effective than others. We know full well that some teachers are more devoted to learners and learning than others. No reasonable person who knows anything at all about our profession would argue any other way. Even so, our history -- as a profession -- has been to stand firm against differentiated salaries.

Why have we fought the idea and the reality of more pay for better teaching? There have been at least three reasons, I think. We have been reluctant to allow administrators to "rate" teachers. We have been reluctant to define or describe effective teaching, and we have been reluctant to consider the concept of rank as a rational basis for differentiating salaries. However, "merit pay" can be made workable.

Consider the university as an illustration. Institutions of higher learning are all educational institutions. Many are public. All have teachers and students and administrators. Further, almost every college or university in America uses some type of differentiated salary policy as a basis for acknowledging excellence and rewarding outstanding accomplishment by staff members within the institution. Those outside the institutions joke about the "publish or perish" talk that is sometimes associated with the reality of differentiated salaries, but that talk is exaggerated. The fact is, the idea of differentiated salaries is now and has been a reasonably effective mechanism for motivating staff and acknowledging excellence in higher education. The idea works. Not perfectly, of course, but the system works.

Two things make differentiated salaries in colleges and universities function effectively: the concept of rank, and the concept of accomplishment. By positing the notion of rank (i.e., instructor, assistant professor, associate professor, and professor), institutions have been able to subsume concepts such as experience and responsibility, for example, and, in a meaningful way, build into the salary system the possibility of advancement. There is something for a young professor to look forward to: promotion.

Secondly, people are employed by colleges or universities on the basis of promise, but they are promoted on the basis of accomplishment. Evaluations are performed by faculty and administrators jointly, according to criteria that have been developed by staff in cooperative ways. "Rating" can be done by teachers and administrators together more effectively than by either group alone. Who knows more about teaching than teachers? We can and must describe effective teaching in practical ways.

By way of contrast, teachers in public schools can look forward to the same salary increments as every other teacher -- whether they do an outstanding job or just slide by. The basic assumptions inherent in the single salary schedule reward all teachers on the basis of promise rather than accomplishment. Without the concept of rank, the only advancement possible within the profession is to move out of teaching into administration.

To state the issue flatly: there are no motivational elements in the single salary schedule at all. The profession has opted for a salary system which presumes that, if students learn more, an increase in teachers' satisfactions will be sufficient to excite teachers to work harder and more creatively and more effectively. For a few teachers, that is enough. For most teachers, though, the lack of any kind of opportunity for advancement or promotion or exceptional salary increments means that there is no major motivational element in their work at all. They may enjoy teaching or not; be effective or not; work hard or not; try to do better or not. Whatever they do, it is completely unrelated to any systematic procedure or rational policy to encourage them to be more effective in their teaching role.

Most teachers are wonderful people, and they are dedicated to those with whom they work and what they do. However, that does not negate the fact that, as a profession, we have argued for, worked toward, and actually achieved a system of policies about salary that lacks any real consideration of motivational factors. All of us live in a larger culture, though, in which the prevailing system provides opportunities for most people to advance in their chosen field of work and to expect extra financial remuneration if they are especially effective. Even preachers who do a better job get a bigger church and make more money.

To argue that teachers should adopt a system of differentiated salaries as a way of improving the educational endeavor, however, is not to say that vouchers for schooling are an idea whose time has come. The voucher system presumes that each institution -- each school building -- should compete within the economic system in order to survive. Parents would receive vouchers from the state or federal government for their youngster's schooling, and those parents would then "spend" those vouchers at any school they chose. Schools would be forced to compete for the vouchers in order to exist. Choice for parents would bring vitality to schooling, the argument goes, since schools would have to satisfy parents' expectations or go out of business.

The idea of choice is an attractive and compelling argument in America -- land of the free. Personally, I feel that compulsory education laws, compulsory attendance, and assignment to particular teachers are grating practices in our schools. Expanding options -- between schools and within schools -- is an important idea and ought to be instituted in more ways than we have traditionally done in the typical public school setting.

To support the idea of expanding opportunities for personal choice in education is one thing. To create a system of education that would require schools to compete with one another -- to make a profit, if you please -- is something of a very different order. By definition, schools in America are nonprofit institutions. By definition, their purpose is to provide a service rather than to make a profit. The American people would be offended -- and rightly so -- if public schools (or colleges or universities) were forced to adopt a stance that made them function according to the principles of economic gain.

Hospitals, armies, post offices, and schools -- all such institutions are expected to be dedicated to the welfare of those they serve. Public servants are just that -- they serve the public. To employ the principle of economic incentive with individuals to encourage them to be more effective in their service roles makes a lot of sense. To employ the principle of economic incentive to public institutions (or to private nonprofit institutions) violates the sensibilities of people everywhere.

Would school boards (as the board of directors) be expected to "show a profit" for the operation of the schools? The idea is utter nonsense.

We need to tap the energies of people within the profession by devising salary systems that will encourage them to be more productive and more effective in what they do. We dare not adopt systems that force public institutions to compete with one another in order to make a profit. Economic incentive for individuals should be employed by the teaching profession as a means to a better educational end. Economic incentives in the form of vouchers to institutions will destroy the integrity of the educational effort in a thousand ways.

Private school and private enterprise are not the same. It takes money to make schools go, but the basic purpose of schools is to help young people develop and learn and grow. It would be a perversion of the worst order to force schools -- in the name of economic efficiency and effectiveness -- to try to make a profit, to serve an economic rather than educational end. That kind of tragedy we can and must avoid.

TEACHER SALARIES:
PAST, PRESENT, FUTURE

Allan C. Ornstein

In a period marked by inflation, reduced student enrollment, an over-supply of teachers, and research which purports to show that extra expenditures to improve school quality have little effect on academic achievement, the budget squeeze has come to American schools. Legislators are trying to avoid deficit spending by cutting funds for education. In 1979 voters thwarted more than 50% of all attempts to increase property taxes, a primary source of school support. Because salaries of instructional staff accounted for nearly 65% of total public school costs in 1979-80, these trends are putting teachers on the defensive. They recognize the growing public pressure for staff reductions, larger classes, and salary increases that fail to match inflation.

Table 1 compares average salaries for teachers in 1969-70 and in 1979-80. During this 10-year period, the average salary of classroom teachers increased by $7,366 -- or 6.3% per year, compounded and based on the 1969-70 average salary of $8,635. But if we estimate an average increase in the consumer price index of 8% per year (also compounded) for this same period, the annual decrease in buying power for teachers is 1.7% per year or 17% for these ten years. In 1969 dollars, this amounts to $7,167 -- a loss of $1,468 in purchasing power.

State and regional differences in average teacher salaries are shown in Table 2. The greatest percentage increase (compounded over 10 years) occurred in Alaska (9.5%), Hawaii (7.7%), Kentucky (7.6%), Mississippi (7.5%), Colorado (7.5%), Rhode Island (7.4%), and Washington (7.3%). Of the 50 states, only Alaska man-

Reprinted from PHI DELTA KAPPAN, 61 (10): 677-79 (June 1980), by permission of author and publisher.

aged to exceed the 8% inflation rate. However, Alaska was the state with the highest inflation rate above the national average. Meanwhile, Kentucky, Mississippi, and Colorado started with low base salaries 10 years ago, and, despite higher percentage increases than most other states, teachers in those states today still earn lower salaries than the national average. When state inflation rates and base salaries for 1969-70 are taken into account, teachers in Rhode Island and Washington have made the greatest gains.

Table 1. Average Salary of Public Classroom Teachers, 1969-70 and 1979-80*

	69-70	79-80	% Increase over 69-70	Purchasing Power in 1969 Dollars**
Average salary of classroom teachers	$8,635	$16,001	6.3	$7,167
Elementary	$8,412	$15,661		
Secondary	$8,891	$16,387		

*Differences in salary between elementary and secondary teachers reflect the fact that the latter group has more experience and education.
**Author's estimate.
Source: Adapted from Estimates of School Statistics, 1970-71 (Washington, D.C.: National Education Association, 1970), Table 7, p. 32; Estimates of School Statistics, 1979-80 (Washington, D.C.: National Education Association, 1979), Table 7, p. 32.

There are regional salary differences too. The average teacher salary in the Great Lakes region today ($16, 624) comes closest to the 1979-80 national average ($16,001), just as it did in 1969-70. The Southeast continues to be the lowest-paid region ($13,819), as it was 10 years ago, while the Far West ($18,678) continues to rank at the top.

Table 2. Average Salary of Public Classroom Teachers
by Regions and States, 1969-70 and 1979-80

Regions and States	1969-70	1979-80	%Increase Compounded over 10 Years*
50 States & D.C.	$8,635	$16,001	6.4**
New England	8,694	16,296	6.5
Conn.	9,271	16,344	5.8
Me.	7,572	13,100	5.6
Mass.	8,770	17,500	7.2
N.H.	7,789	12,550	4.9
R.I.	8,776	17,896	7.4
Vt.	7,960	12,430	4.6
Mideast (inc. D.C.)	9,655	17,987	6.4
Del.	9,015	16,157	6.0
Md.	9,383	17,580	6.5
N.J.	9,150	17,075	6.4
N.Y.	10,390	19,200	6.3
Penn.	8,858	16,760	6.6
Southeast	7,319	13,819	6.6
Ala.	6,817	13,520	7.1
Ark.	6,277	12,419	7.1
Fla.	8,410	14,570	5.7
Ga.	7,278	14,027	6.8
Ky.	6,939	14,480	7.6
La.	7,028	13,770	7.0
Miss.	5,798	11,900	7.5
N.C.	7,494	14,355	6.7
S.C.	6,883	13,000	6.6
Tenn.	7,050	13,668	6.9
Va.	8,070	14,025	5.7
W.Va.	7,650	13,642	6.0
Great Lakes	9,137	16,624	6.2
Ill.	9,569	17,399	6.2
Ind.	8,832	15,078	5.5
Mich.	9,823	18,840	6.7
Ohio	8,300	15,187	6.2
Wisc.	9,000	15,930	5.9

Table 2. (Continued)

Plains	$7,947	$14,601	6.3
Iowa	8,398	15,030	6.0
Kans.	7,620	14,016	6.3
Minn.	8,658	16,751	6.8
Mo.	7,844	13,725	5.8
Nebr.	7,354	13,519	6.3
N.D.	6.696	13,148	7.0
S.D.	6,403	12,220	6.8
Southwest	7,401	14,076	6.6
Ariz.	8,715	15,835	6.2
N.M.	7,796	13,915	6.0
Okla.	6,882	13,210	6.7
Tex.	7,277	14,000	6.8
Rocky Mountains	7,632	15,226	7.2
Colo.	7,760	15,950	7.5
Ida.	6,884	13,615	7.1
Mont.	7,606	14,680	6.8
Utah	7,643	14,965	7.0
Wyo.	8,271	16,030	6.8
Far West	10,015	18,678	6.4
Calif.	10,324	19,090	6.3
Nev.	9,248	16,390	5.9
Ore.	8,814	16,245	6.3
Wash.	9,237	18,745	7.3
Alaska	10,560	26,173	9.5
Hawaii	9,440	19,750	7.7

*Author's Estimates Based on Texas Instruments MBA (1969 salary x PV x 1979 Salary x FV x 10 years x N x CPT x %i).
**The NEA uses a 6.3 figure because of nonrounding (see Table 1). The author has rounded 6.36 to 6.4
Source: Same as Table 1.

There are greater differences in salaries among states than among regions, however. Alaskan teachers are the highest paid, at an annual salary of $26,173. Hawaii ($19,750), New York ($19,200), and California

($19,090) follow. These states also ranked at the top
10 years ago, with Hawaii making the greatest dollar
gain. The lowest salaries were reported in Mississippi
($11,900), South Dakota ($12,220), Arkansas ($12,419),
Vermont ($12,430), and New Hampshire ($12,550). The
dollar may go further in the South than elsewhere, but
some New England states have experienced economic re-
cession and high energy costs that have pinched the
funds available for education.

As is often the case, averages conceal a great
deal of variation. These figures do not show, for example, that the average teacher in Oak Park, Illinois,
earns over $8,000 a year more than other teachers in
that state. Niles, Illinois, teachers earn over
$10,000 a year more than other Illinois teachers, and
so on. The range is narrower in Southern states where
the mean salaries are low, but sizable differences
still exist. In Georgia, for example, if you teach in
Cobb County your maximum salary is more than $5,000
lower than if you teach in Atlanta.

Table 3 compares teacher salaries with variations
in the intermediate standard budget. The intermediate
standard budget is set annually by the Department of
Labor as the amount of income required for a family of
four, living in a solidly middle-class but not affluent fashion. As the last column in Table 3 indicates,
the average teacher salary, as a percentage of the
standard intermediate budget, rose substantially from
the end of the 1960s to the early 1970s. Then it began
to decline, leveling off at a little better than 80%
of the amount necessary for a middle-class life-style
-- until 1979, when it dipped below.

Projected average annual salaries of classroom
teachers during the next decade are shown in Table 4.
The calculations are based on a continuation of the
trend from 1969-70 to 1979-80, using $16,001 as the
base and adding 6.3% each year. These projected gains
ignore intervening variables that may affect future
salaries, such as increased inflation or price and
wage controls, and they assume numerous constants,
such as public sentiment toward educational spending
and teacher pressure for salary increases. With a
continuous oversupply of teachers, eroding school budgets, and taxpayer pressure to reduce school spending,
it is doubtful that teachers can expect average annual
salary increases of much more than 6.3% in the foreseeable future.

Table 3. Comparison of an Intermediate Standard of
Living for a Family of Four with Average Salaries
Paid Public Classroom Teachers, 1967-1979

Budget Date	Intermediate Standard Budget (ISB)	Average Salary Paid Teachers	Ratio of Teacher's Salary/ISB
Spr. 1967	$ 9,076	$ 6,830	75.3
Spr. 1969	10,077	8,635	85.7
Spr. 1970	10,666	9,269	86.9
Fall 1971	10,971	9,705	88.5
Fall 1972	11,446	10,176	88.9
Fall 1973	12,626	10,675	84.5
Fall 1974	14,333	11,656	81.3
Fall 1975	15,318	12,600	82.3
Fall 1976	16,236	13,297	81.9
Fall 1977	17,106	14,247	83.3
Fall 1978	18,622	15,040	80.1
Fall 1979	20,856a	16,001b	76.7

Note: a = author's estimates, based on 12% inflation
for 1979. b = See Tables 1, 2.
Source: Price, Budgets, Salaries, and Income, 1979
(Washington, D.C.: National Education Association,
1979), p. 13.

Although the projections are not exact, they correspond with my previous projections of teacher salaries, using both this method and others (1). The data
indicate that in 1985-86 the average teacher salary
will be approximately $23,100; by 1990 it will approx-
imate $31,300. Whether these salaries will correspond
with a middle-class or intermediate standard budget
will depend on the rate of inflation. Using the past
few years as guidelines, and considering our current
and future monetary and fiscal policies, inflation
will probably be in double digits throughout most of
the 1980s. Most likely, then, future teacher salaries
will fall further below the intermediate budget for a
family of four.

Table 5 provides some data about future salaries
in relation to future inflation and the standard of
living. Figuring an annual inflation rate of 10%

Table 4. Average Annual Salaries of Public
Classroom Teachers, 1969-70 to 1979-80

School Year	Average Salary	Percentage Inc.
1969-70	$ 8,635	
1970-71	9,629	7.3
1971-72	9,706	4.7
1972-73	10,164	4.7
1973-74	10,673	5.0
1974-75	11,595	8.6
1975-76	12,448	6.8
1976-77	13,235	6.3
1977-78	14,082	6.4
1978-79	15,057	6.3
1979-80	16,001	6.3
Average annual % increase		6.3

Projected Salary Based on
Average Annual 6.3% Increase

School Year	Projected Average Salary
1980-81....................................	$17,009
1981-82....................................	18,081
1982-83....................................	19,220
1983-84....................................	20,431
1984-85....................................	21,718
1985-86....................................	23,086
1986-87....................................	24,540
1987-88....................................	26,086
1988-89....................................	27,729
1989-90....................................	29,476
1990-91....................................	31,333

(considered modest today) and using a 1979 intermediate standard budget of $20,856, some grim conclusions
can be drawn. By 1985 the average teacher's salary
will amount to less than two-thirds of the family budget needed for an intermediate standard of living, and
by 1990 it will approach a mere half (2).

These data and projections pose a grave threat to
the teaching profession, affecting entry standards,

357

Table 5. Comparison of an Intermediate Standard
of Living for a Family of Four with Average Salaries
Paid Public Classroom Teachers, 1980-1990

Year	Intermed. Standard Budget, Inflation Rate 10%	Average Projected Teacher Salary at 6.3%	Ratio Teacher Salary/ Intermed. Budget
1980	$22,942	$17,709	77.2%
1981	25,236	18,081	71.6
1982	27,760	19,220	69.2
1983	30,536	20,431	66.9
1984	33,590	21,718	64.7
1985	36,949	23,086	62.5
1986	40,644	24,540	60.4
1987	44,708	26,086	58.3
1988	49,179	27,729	56.4
1989	54,097	29,476	54.5
1990	59,507	31,333	52.7

job performance, and teacher morale. The bleak prospect will put tremendous pressure on teachers organizations to resort to strikes for improved salaries. Strikes, in turn, will pit teachers against the public. Departments and colleges of education will not escape unscathed. Fewer students -- especially the academically talented -- will seek careers in teaching. Unless we can convince the public that education is a wise investment, the future looks grim indeed.

Notes

1. Using this method, I projected three years in advance the average teacher salary in 1979-80 to be $16,109. It turned out, of course, to be $16,001. See Allan C. Ornstein, EDUCATION AND SOCIAL INQUIRY (Itasca, Ill.: Peacock, 1978), Tables 6.4 and 6.5, p. 231. Based on a survey of what the future has in store for education, I have also predicted "with better that 50% possibility" that the average teacher will earn slightly more than $30,000 by 1990. See Allan C. Ornstein and Harry L. Miller, LOOKING INTO

TEACHING (Chicago: Rand McNally, 1980), Table 14.2, p. 496.

2. Some readers may raise the point that other occupations will also suffer a salary/inflation gap, but the extent of that gap is beyond the scope of this article. Other readers may assert that a 6.3% salary increase for teachers during the 1980s is too low. That figure is the appropriate choice based on the precedent of the last 10 years (see Table 4). Moreover, it does not vary substantially from the last three years, when inflation was double-digit. In the same vein, a 10% inflation figure could also be considered too low; a higher adjustment for annual salary increases and inflation could lead to a worsening gap between future teacher salaries and inflation, since the latter would most likely vary more than salaries.

TUITION TAX CREDITS

Virginia Sparling

Tax credits for tuition are making headlines
again. Now before Congress -- and some state legislatures -- are proposals to give tax breaks to families
that send their children to private schools. The debates over tuition tax credits will take place in many
capitals, but the one in Washington will be the most
crucial: Any proposal Congress enacts will affect
every classroom in the country.

The Background

Tuition tax credits do their work at income tax
time. In general, the various plans proposed would
allow taxpayers to credit toward their income tax bill
for a given year a designated portion of the tuition
they had paid to certain kinds of educational institutions. Various types and levels of institutions would
be eligible under various plans. The bills that are
currently being introduced are likely to target tuition paid to private elementary and secondary schools
and to private and public postsecondary institutions.

Tuition-tax-credit proposals have been introduced
in Congress since the early 1950s. But the debate
about their merits has intensified recently.

In 1978, a tax credit for tuition paid to private
elementary and secondary schools as well as to postsecondary institutions passed the House of Representatives. The Senate deleted the credit for elementary
and secondary schools, but passed the postsecondary
tax credit. The National Coalition for Public Education, a group of some 40 national organizations (including both NEA and the National PTA), was in the

Reprinted from TODAY'S EDUCATION, 70 (4): 11-14 (Nov.-
Dec. 1981), by permission of author and publisher.

forefront of efforts to defeat the bill. When the House and Senate could not resolve their differences, the legislation died in conference.

During the last Congress, tuition-tax-credit plans were introduced again. Senator Daniel Moynihan, Democrat of New York, wanted to extend to students in private elementary and secondary schools eligibility for Basic Educational Opportunity Grants of up to $750 a year. His effort was defeated.

In the present Congress, Senator Robert Packwood, Republican of Oregon, and Senator Moynihan are the primary sponsors of S.550, a bill that would eventually provide tax credits of up to $500 per student for tuition paid to private elementary and secondary schools and to postsecondary institutions as well.

Senator Moynihan also proposed, during the deliberations by the Senate Finance Committee on the Administration's massive tax cut plan earlier this year, a $250-a-year tax credit for tuition paid to private elementary and secondary schools. The Committee defeated that plan.

Since the 1980 Republican platform favored a tax credit, and since the President is said to support the idea, it seems most unlikely that the 97th Congress has heard the last of tuition tax credits.

The Debate

One observer has outlined the various arguments over tuition tax credits as follows:

"In the late 1960s, the chief proponents of tuition tax credits were nonpublic school representatives. Their primary claim was that parochial schools were under such great fiscal strain that they faced massive tuition increases in order to survive. These increases in turn would, they said, drive away most of their pupils.

"The high point in nonpublic school enrollment in the United States occurred in about 1968, and these schools lost a fourth of their pupils during the next five years. Since 1973, nonpublic enrollments have been remarkably stable, even in the face of annual declines in the U.S. school-age pupulation. So the main early argument for tuition tax credits withered of its own accord.

"New arguments have arisen in place of the old. The foremost is that nonpublic school parents pay for private schooling through tuition and also for public schooling, in which their children do not participate. Shouldn't they, proponents say, be reimbursed for this double payment for schooling?

"A more general argument is the desire to promote competition and quality among all schools by encouraging choice....

"Finally, social issues abound in the debate. Who should control the child's education -- the family or the educational professional? Should the general taxpayers' generosity (in paying higher taxes than they would pay if no one could take tuition tax credits) extend the power to choose to pupils and families who cannot now afford nonpublic options? Where is the boundary between public education and other educational experiences?"(1)

Impact of Public Policy

In our society, public and private schools have, as their levels of selectivity often indicate, quite different tasks. Private schools educate only those children whose families elect to send them to the schools and whom the schools accept. Public schools, on the other hand, do not control the composition of their student bodies by excluding students; they cannot, for example, dismiss children whose behavior disrupts the education of others or who cannot meet some pre-established standard of academic "aptitude."

Public schools meet public needs and carry out public policies. The genius of U.S. public education is in its diversity -- meeting the needs of the disadvantaged, the handicapped, the talented, the gifted, the non-English-speaking, and other special student populations, in 16,000 school districts. Nowhere in the world is access to educational opportunity broader than in the United States. Our system of free public education is a cornerstone of our democratic society.

In contrast, the degree to which nonpublic schools would -- or should -- achieve the public and social purposes of education is not clear. Private and parochial schools are not conceived to serve public purposes; do not have to adhere to federal, state, and local mandates; and are not officially accountable to the public for the use of public dollars. Moreover, many of these schools do not have policies of open admissions. Thus, the provision of tax credits, which would subsidize nonpublic schools, would have far-reaching effects on public policy. A resulting public education policy that condoned the maintenance of two sets of standards, one for the public schools and one for the nonpublic, would be inconsistent with democratic principles and would thwart the public's interest in developing a citizenry with common backgrounds, common educational experiences, and a common sense of civic responsbility.

Who Would Benefit?

Not all families would benefit equally from tuition tax credits. While private schools enroll more than 10 percent of the nation's students, these students do not represent a cross-section of American youth. The following are some of the demographic characteristics of private schools and their students:

-- Of the nation's 19,666 private schools, 9,849 are Catholic, 5,870 have other religious affiliations, and 3,944 have no religious affiliations.

-- According to 1978 data, private school attendance rates are highest in the Northeastern and North Central states and lowest in the South and West.

-- Tuitions vary significantly across the nation, with students in the South and West paying more to attend private schools than their counterparts in the North Central and Northeastern regions. This pattern may reflect the dominance in the latter areas of Catholic schools, which receive relatively large school subsidies and therefore can charge low tuitions.

-- Despite recent increases in nonpublic school enrollment among Blacks and Hispanics, pronounced differences exist among the nonpublic school attendance rates of different racial and ethnic groups. Differences between these rates for Black and for White elementary students are especially large. The rate for White students (12.6 percent) is nearly three times the rate for Black students (4.6 percent).

-- The private school attendance rate for students from families with at least $25,000 income is about five times the rate for students from families with incomes of less than $5,000. Consequently, a policy objection often raised against tax credits is that they would be regressive, since children from the wealthiest families are overrepresented in the private school population.

In general, according to the Congressional Budget Office, lower-income families would benefit less than higher-income ones from a tuition tax credit. This is because in most proposals the credit is nonrefundable, i.e., if the tax credit exceeds the tax liability, the government will not refund the balance to the taxpayer. Thus, families that pay no taxes (most often because they have low incomes) would receive no credit even if they could somehow raise the money to enroll their children in a private school. Furthermore, those who actually can obtain the full credit would find that being reimbursed a year after paying tuition would not do much to provide them with resources to pay tuition expenditures when due.

Budgetary and Tax Implications

Tuition tax credits would cost the taxpayers a lot of money. The Congressional Budget Office has estimated that if the families of all 5 million nonpublic elementary and secondary school pupils were to claim a maximum nonrefundable credit of $500, the cost to the federal government this year would be $1.9 billion. If postsecondary education were included, the total cost would be in excess of $3 billion. (Obviously, the figures will vary with the details of the particular plan and the number of taxpayers who actually claim the credits. These variations make it difficult to project exact costs.)

Like special deductions and exemptions, credits against taxes do not appear in the budget as expenditures or outgo, but as limits on the government's income. Tax credits and deductions have increased dramatically in recent years. The federal government now loses billions of dollars in revenue each year through such programs.

Each one has its own political or ideological constituency that will not permit the "expenditure" to die once it is in place. If Congress passes tuition-tax-credit legislation -- no matter how trivial the original amount of the credit -- one can safely predict that every year the tuition-tax-credit lobby will ensure that a fight takes place over how much _more_ money to give nonpublic schools this time.

Are Credits Constitutional?

Aside from the political questions, tax credits based on tuition paid to private schools pose a constitutional dilemma. The controversy arises from the clauses of the First Amendment to the U.S. Constitution that mandate that there be "no law respecting an establishment of religion, or prohibiting the free exercise thereof." The question is whether these clauses restrict government aid in the form of tuition tax credits on the ground that they are in fact aid to private, church-related schools. Suits questioning the propriety of state and local aid to church schools have proliferated in the past decade in response to the persistence of state legislatures in authorizing such aid.

The leading Supreme Court case involving tax credits or income exclusions for tuition payments is Committee for Public Education and Religious Liberty v. Nyquist, 413 U.S. 756 (1973). In Nyquist, the Court struck down New York state laws that not only provided benefits to tuition-paying parents of private school pupils, but also gave direct grants to certain private schools themselves.

The standards the Court applied in Nyquist came in turn from an earlier case, Lemon v. Kurtzman, 403 U.S. 602 (1971). Lemon is the source of the now famous "three-pronged" test for constitutionality of aid to church-related schools. A statute permitting such aid must (1) have a secular purpose, (2) have a "primary" effect that neither advances nor inhibits religion, and (3) not lead to "excessive entanglement" of church and state.

The argument that tuition tax credits are constitutional is based on the "child benefit" theory, i.e., that children rather than religious institutions benefit from the public expenditures. The argument against their constitutionality holds the opposite, i.e., that it is the religious schools or churches that benefit.

Nyquist and the other decisions that have found various tuition-tax-credit schemes unconstitutional are based on the prong of the Lemon test that warns against a "primary effect of advancing religion." In Nyquist, the court implicitly rejected the child benefit theory when it noted that the beneficiaries of the New York statutes were parents of children in non-public schools and that 85 percent of those schools were church-related. Thus, the Court held, the statutes had the primary effect of advancing and fostering religion at public expense.

Tuition tax credits may also fail to pass the excessive entanglement prong of the Lemon test. It is inconceivable that the federal government could sanction a multibillion dollar tax credit without some mechanism for ensuring that the schools to which tuition is paid meet some agreed-upon definition of "school" and that the tuition payment itself is actually made. But how does the federal government determine the legitimacy of a private school? By having it meet federal guidelines? By requiring state monitoring and reporting systems? If nonpublic schools do not satisfy their patrons, won't the federal government be pressured to scrutinize and ultimately to regulate the quality of private schools? Even if anyone thought it would be desirable public policy, such scrutiny would surely run afoul of the entanglement "prong" and be held unconstitutional.

A Summing Up

The particulars of the tuition tax credit issue are complex. Beneath the complexity, however, is the simple fact that a tuition tax credit is constitutionally questionable, fiscally senseless, and contrary to the fundamental principles of democratic government. As an opponent of tuition tax credits, Senator Ernest Hollings, Democrat of South Carolina, recently put it:

"It's an obligation of the government to support public schools....Our great task today is to rebuild public education."

Tuition-tax-credit plans amount to a renunciation of this obligation and a flight from this task. No

366

time is the right time for such irresponsibility.

Note

1. Catterall, James. "Tuition Tax Credits for Schools: A Federal Priority for the 1980's?" IFG POLICY PERSPECTIVES. Stanford, CA: Institute for Research on Educational Finance and Governance, (n.d.).

INTERPRETATIONS, MISCONCEPTIONS, AND RESPONSIBILITIES RELATING TO PUBLIC LAW 94-142

Natalie C. Barraga

Prior to the 1950's, society and educators were content for children with a variety of impairments to be educated as long as they were placed in separate facilities in the communities or in state residential schools. Early in that decade, special education began to be defined and state legislation passed in some areas. Provision was made for funding of selected programs for groups of handicapped students who attended public schools. In most cases, only those who might fit into the academic classes and progress along with the other children were accepted. Even then, the children were placed in self-contained classrooms, far away from the center of activities in many schools. Later, at the insistence of their teachers, a few were integrated into regular classrooms if they could "keep up" with the other children. Generally, these were children with mild sensory and motor impairments which had little effect on their academic learning.

Obviously, there was little required of the public schools in the way of accommodation or adaptation for these students except for the employment of a special teacher and the acquisition of a few different materials. Many of the students readily lost their identity as handicapped as long as they could do the academic work without requiring too much of the teacher's time or too many requests for exceptions from administrators. Parents of the children formed groups and became advocates for special education and at the same time gave assistance to the schools in purchasing needed materials or equipment.

The whole attitude of society was influenced by

Reprinted from DELTA KAPPA GAMMA BULLETIN, 47 (3): 6-12 (Spring 1981), by permission of author and publisher.

the passage of the Civil Rights Act in the 1960's. Although the tenets of that law applied primarily to black and other ethnic minority groups, there were strong implications that the civil rights of handicapped persons and others were being violated in many ways. Section 504 of the Rehabilitation Act of 1973 addressed the critical issues and focused on environmental accessibility and exclusion of handicapped individuals from participation in equal opportunity for jobs, sharing in community activities, and in educational programs available to the general public. Although the regulations for implementation of Section 504 were delayed until several years later, the Act paved the way for the design and passage of Public Law 94-142 in 1975.

Critical Components of PL 94-142

Specific element of the law are spelled out in great detail in the Congressional Record and elsewhere so only a selected few will be discussed here. Those aspects which seem to be interpreted in a variety of ways are surrounded by misconceptions and controversy, and those which are the basis for court cases will be identified.

Free Appropriate Public Education
for All Handicapped Children

What does this really mean? Legislative intent is that each school district is responsible for identifying and providing free educational services for all handicapped children between the ages of three and 21 years of age unless that age span is contrary to state law. "Free" means that parents may not be charged for any aspect of the identification of the child or the service to be provided. "Special education" for the child is defined as specially designed instruction in the classroom, physical education, and/or home instruction. Related services to be provided are defined as transportation, supportive services (occupational or physical therapy, mobility, etc.). Priorities are given first to all those children presently unserved and, next, to severely handicapped and multihandicapped who are inadequately served because of the small numbers in each district. If the public schools cannot or do not provide the services needed, they are responsible for securing the services and paying for them. The services must meet the standards of the services provided by that district to all children (1).

Because the law says that the education must be provided in the least restrictive environment but does not define that precisely, there is much confusion about the relationship between appropriate and least restrictive environment. Appropriate is meant to focus on the needs of the individual child and what will enable that child to progress socially, emotionally, and mentally to his maximum potential.

To further cloud the issue, the word "mainstreaming" has been equated with least restrictive environment, but that word does not appear anywhere in the law itself. The concept of mainstreaming recognizes that exceptional children have a wide range of special educational needs. There is a recognized continuum of educational settings which may, at a given time, be appropriate for an individual child's needs, and to the maximum extent possible, exceptional children should be educated with children who have no exceptional differences. The law does not require that the child be placed in any one specific setting. It does require, however, that alternative options be available when the child's progress indicates that a different type program will be more appropriate (2).

"Least restrictive environment" does not refer to physical boundaries but to the milieu where students will be least restricted in attaining educational growth compatible with their abilities. As an example, can you imagine anything more restrictive than placing a blind child in a regular classroom without communication and movement skills required to participate in the classroom? The child must have the skills to be a part of the group with whom learning is taking place.

Protection for Handicapped Children and Their Parents

The many facets of this portion make interpretation difficult. The first protection is that of nondiscriminatory testing and evaluation in the child's native language and by a person qualified to do the assessment. The parents may have the information acquired in the evaluation available to them and are to

370

participate in all decisions regarding selection of placement, development of educational plans, and any changes to be made in the plan during the school year.

The inclusion of parents in all decision-making regarding their children is a new concept for many schools, and administrators are often concerned about getting too involved with parents. Unfortunately, a small percentage of parents have seemed to be unreasonable in their expectations. Good faith effort on the part of both parents and administrators can assist in the communication process and prevent the confrontations, threats, and/or court cases headlined in the newspapers. This protection clause in the law has opened the way for many parents of children with special problems to become more concerned and involved with the records kept by the school on their own children (3).

The requirement of assessment in the native language and by qualified personnel has indicated a new approach to the whole process of testing and evaluating children. If the parents are not satisfied with the qualifications of the examiner for a child with a particular type of handicap, they may request that a qualified examiner be secured or that the school pay for the assessment by a person of their choice. Sensory impaired children need to be evaluated on different instruments, through a different process, and by a person familiar with the impact of the impairment on the responses of the child. Instruments standardized on a normal group are seldom appropriate for determination of scores or for comparison of educational progress.

The Individualized Educational Plan (IEP)

This plan is to be designed after the appropriate assessment procedures have been completed and is to be based on the functional and learning needs of the student as revealed by the assessment. Ideally, the plan is developed by the teacher(s) in communication and cooperation with the parents. The individual plan is the heart of the entire educational experience for that child. It must state in writing the following: a) present level of functional and educational performance; b) annual goals and short term objectives stated in behavioral terms; c) the nature of the services to be provided, the materials to be used, the amount of time and the duration of the service; d) who is to give the service and in what setting; and e) the evaluation criteria for determining that the objectives have been achieved. This must be signed by the parents, reviewed each year, and modified or adjusted according to the individual needs of each child.

Management at all levels

Management of this complicated law may be a factor causing some of the greatest concern. There are interlocking responsibilities between the local education agencies, the state education agencies, and the U.S. Commissioner of Education. Funds for implementation are subject to approval of the state plan, and entitlement to the follow-through money from the state to the local district is based on acceptance of the local and state plan. Miscommunication between agencies at the federal, state, or local level may make implementation difficult (4). Parents and teachers do not always understand the possible complicating elements in the management process and may become very impatient with the local district or the state agency.

The fact that there is a manpower development component in the law does not relieve the shortage of qualified personnel immediately. For example, the small number of teacher preparation programs for teachers of the visually handicapped has limited severely the number of people who can be trained in any given year. The shortage was critical before 1975 and has become increasingly so each year since. Some states need as many as several hundred teachers to serve the visually handicapped children already in the schools. Because of the special needs of children with impaired vision and hearing, specially trained teachers are imperative if these children are to have opportunities for learning comparable with their abilities. Attempts have been made to move toward a generic type preparation for special education teachers to help relieve the shortage. This has been less than successful even for the mildly handicapped and a disaster for the severely handicapped and low incidence populations. Special knowledge and skills are needed to provide the services, materials, and related consultative needs of these children (5).

Differences in state laws, philosophies, and service delivery systems, along with the requirement to begin services by last fall (1980), has resulted in a hodgepodge of programming patterns. In many cases, there has not been time nor funds to design the programs appropriate to the needs of the children, and much may have been sacrificed for the sake of expediency. For example, some teachers serving low incidence children on an itinerant basis may drive more than a thousand miles a week in an attempt to give some support and consultative service to regular class teachers who have severely handicapped or low incidence children in their classrooms. Development of cooperative arrangements between small districts so that a special teacher can work with three or four districts helps to eliminate some of the travel time, but more importantly, provides the daily specialized attention required by the majority of the children.

Mention should be made here of the large number of regular class teachers around the country who have accepted the responsibility and challenge of working with handicapped children. They have led the way in suggesting adaptations which can be made easily with little extra time. The attitude of the receptive teachers has been a strong factor in the success of integrating severely vision and hearing impaired children into regular classrooms. One such teacher wrote of her experience and made it sound as if she was thoroughly enjoying having a blind child in her class. She made a few suggestions about physical arrangements, teaching methodologies, and individual needs which she and a consulting specialist had designed. She concluded by saying that the child is helping her to overcome her handicap of thinking that he needed pity, and that "leaves all of us free to enjoy his spirit and personality" (6).

Issues for Responsible Consideration

Some evidence has been acquired through research studies on various aspects of the implementation process. Consideration of the following may enable us to meet the responsibilities more effectively in the next few years:

°Two major factors are the educational and social philosophies of teachers and their understanding of the intent of the legislation. Teachers seem to feel better prepared for accepting exceptional children when they have had academic preparation rather than just inservice preparation (7).

°Teachers are probably the most qualified evaluators of the effects of integrating handicapped students into the regular classrooms (8).

°The type of exceptionality of the child, the teacher's experience, the courses or inservice training, and the service delivery model seem to be critical factors in the time required and the quality of the IEP's developed. If the assessment persons would choose instruments with educational relevance and write their reports to focus on educational needs, they could save teachers much time (9).

°The special education teacher consultant model for service delivery is most appropriate when the regular teacher is assured of ongoing skill development from the special consultant so that new ideas are exchanged, and there is adequate contact time between the two (10).

°Effective integration of visually handicapped children seems to be highly related to chronological age and to a lesser degree, to such variables as visual pathology, reading achievement, race, and intelligence, as one might expect (11).

°Visually handicapped students in regular classrooms tend to interact less than do their nonhandicapped peers. If interaction is a desired outcome of integration, then some specific guidelines may need to be developed in order to foster this interaction (12).

°The most important influences in decision-making in special education are parental pressure, available programs and resources, vested interests of agencies, maturity of students, teacher and administrator influence, and academic and school behavior of the students (13).

°The critical things that regular class teachers need to know are: the facts of legislation, appropriate procedures for identifying and assessing academic skills of handicapped children, a variety of instructional methods and techniques and how to use them, and skills in management and evaluation of students.

Conclusions

Despite the fact that the implementation of PL 94-142 has been frustrating for some, complicated for others, and resisted by a few, there is evidence that great strides have been made in educational services to handicapped students in their local districts. As indicated, the misconceptions surrounding interpretations of the law have been rampant. A lot of "nervous energy" has been generated that needs to be harnessed into positive benefits. Through inter- and intra-disciplinary communication, we may be able to realize our hope that we are not pursuing an impossible dream. There is much yet to be done, and more information is needed to enable persons at all levels to be more efficient and effective in service delivery. The strengths of the law far outweigh the weaknesses and these are important to identify:

°The public schools have had no alternative but to provide services to all children in their district as they should.

°Parents of all children are becoming more involved and, in turn, are contributing more to the educational progress of their children than ever before.

°There is responsibility for accountability in special education and there will be documentary evidence of children's characteristics and their progress over time.

°At last, the primary focus in education is on the children and their needs. No longer are they expected to make the adaptations and accommodations necessary to fit the school's mold.

°The individualized approach may help to improve education for thousands of nonhandicapped children who need individual attention.

°In combination with Section 504, PL 94-142 puts the national spotlight on the positive issues relating to the handicapped.

°This year of 1981 has been declared the International Year of Disabled Persons throughout the world because of the strong leadership of the United States in attending to the needs of handicapped children and adults. We are all worthwhile human beings.

References

1. Harvey J. "Legislative Intent and Progress." EXCEPTIONAL CHILDREN, 1978, 44.

2. Champion, R. "Mainstreaming -- Least Restrictive Environment," JOURNAL OF VISUAL IMPAIRMENT AND BLINDNESS, 1979.

3. Abeson, A., N. Bolick and J. Haas. A PRIMER ON DUE PROCESS -- EDUCATION DECISIONS FOR HANDICAPPED CHILDREN. Reston, Virginia: The Council for Exceptional Children, 1976.

4. Ballard, J. and J. J. Zettel. "The Managerial Aspects of PL 94-142," EXCEPTIONAL CHILDREN, 1978, 44.

5. Spungin, S.J. "Mainstreaming Visually Handicapped Children: Problems and Issues," JOURNAL OF VISUAL IMPAIRMENT AND BLINDNESS, 1978, 72.

6. Whitelaw, N. "Mainstreaming a Blind Child -- One Classroom Teacher's Experience," JOURNAL OF VISUAL IMPAIRMENT AND BLINDNESS, 1978, 72.

7. Ringlaben, R.P. and J.R. Price. "Regular Classroom Teacher's Perception of Mainstreaming Effects," EXCEPTIONAL CHILDREN, 1981, 47.

8. Jones, R.L., J. Gottlieb, S. Guskin, and R.K. Yoshida. "Evaluating Mainstreaming Programs: Models, Caveats, Considerations, and Guidelines," EXCEPTIONAL CHILDREN, 1978, 44.

9. Price, M. and L. Goodman. "Individualized Education Programs: A Cost Study," EXCEPTIONAL CHILDREN, 198_, 46.

10. Miller, T.L. and D.A. Sabatino. "An Evaluation of the Teacher Consultant Model as an Approach to Mainstreaming," EXCEPTIONAL CHILDREN, 1978, 44.

11. Thomas, J.E. "Factors Influencing the Integration of Visually Impaired Children," JOURNAL OF VISUAL IMPAIRMENT AND BLINDNESS, 1979, 73.

12. Hoben, M. and V. Lindstrom. "Evidence of Isolation in the Mainstream," JOURNAL OF VISUAL IMPAIRMENT AND BLINDNESS, 1980, 74.

13. Holland, R.P. "An Analysis of the Decision Making Processes in Special Education," EXCEPTIONAL CHILDREN, 1980, 46.

14. Marmont, W. and D. Zeller. "Training Regular Educators with Exceptional Kids," COUNTERPOINT, 1980, 2.

15. Weiner, B.B. "Common Concerns for a Common Cause," TEACHING EXCEPTIONAL CHILDREN, 1978, 10.